WESTMAR COLLE ☑ P9-CRS-863

Religious Education, Catechesis, and Freedom

Religious Education, Catechesis, and Freedom

KENNETH R. BARKER

Religious Education Press
Birmingham, Alabama

BV
1464
.B374

Copyright © 1981 by Religious Education Press
All rights reserved

Published with ecclesiastical approval.

No part of this publication may be reproduced, stored in a retrieval
system, or transmitted, in any form or by any means, electronic, photo-
copying, recording, or otherwise, without the prior written permission
of the publisher.

Library of Congress Cataloging in Publication Data

Barker, Kenneth R. (Kenneth Robert), 1948–
  Religious education, catechesis, and
freedom.

  Includes bibliographical references and
index.
  1. Christian education—Philosophy—History
—20th century.   2. Freedom (Theology)—
History of doctrines—20th century.   I. Title.
BV1464.B374   207   81-13962
ISBN 0-89135-028-4   AACR2

Religious Education Press, Inc.
1531 Wellington Road
Birmingham, Alabama 35209
10 9 8 7 6 5 4 3 2

Religious Education Press publishes books exclusively in religious education and in areas closely related to religious education. It is committed
to enhancing and professionalizing religious education through the publication of serious, significant, and scholarly works.

100050

PUBLISHER TO THE PROFESSION

Contents

Abbreviations

Documents of Vatican Council II and Recent Catechetical
Documents

GS   *Pastoral Constitution on the Church in the Modern World
(Gaudium et Spes)*

DH   *Declaration on Religious Freedom (Dignitatis Humanae)*

GCD   *The General Catechetical Directory*

SLF   *Sharing the Light of Faith: The National Catechetical Directory for Catholics of the United States*

MPG   *Message to the People of God*

CT   *Catechesi Trandendae*

Books by Lewis Joseph Sherrill

SS   *The Struggle of the Soul*

GP   *The Gift of Power*

GR   *Guilt and Redemption*

Books by Josef Goldbrunner

CMCS   *Cure of Mind and Cure of Soul*

Realization   *Realization: Anthropology of Pastoral Care*

Books by Gabriel Moran

DR   *Design for Religion: Toward Ecumenical Education*

PR   *The Present Revelation: The Search for Religious Foundations*

RB   *Religious Body: Design for a New Reformation*

Books by C. Ellis Nelson and John H. Westerhoff, III

WFB   *Where Faith Begins*

WOC   *Will Our Children Have Faith?*

Foreword

"My brothers, remember that you have been called to live in freedom. . ." (Gal. 5:13).
"Always speak and act as men destined for judgment under the law of freedom" (James 2:12).

Christian theologians from St. Paul in the first century to the exponents of liberation theology in the twentieth have been preoccupied with the interaction of divine grace and human freedom. St. Paul links freedom to the presence of the Spirit: "Where the spirit of the Lord is, there is freedom" (2 Cor. 3:17). "The law of the spirit," he says, "the spirit of life in Christ Jesus, has freed you from the law of sin and death" (Rom.8:2). The early Church Fathers, reflecting on the opening chapter of Genesis, say that it is because of their spiritual nature that humans are said to resemble God. Vatican II picks up a theme found in Cyril of Alexandria, Tertullian, and others, stating that "authentic freedom is an exceptional sign of the divine image within man" (*Gaudium et Spes*, 17).

St. Augustine's preoccupation with the themes of sin, grace, and free will situates him squarely in the Pauline tradition. The autobiographical *Confessions* chronicles the way he experienced grace as a force in the shifting succession of successes and failures, of absurdity and sense, of slavery to passion and freedom to love.

Martin Luther had his roots in the Pauline-Augustinian tradition. One of the paradoxes of the great reformer's thought is that while attributing everything to grace and denying free will, he

1

authored "The Liberty of a Christian Man." Luther, however, does not deny what most people nowadays understand by free will. Although humans through sin have forfeited the dominion that God gave them over all creation, they nonetheless can exercise a genuine freedom in respect to what Luther calls "things below." It is in relationship to God that humans have lost their freedom.

Nicolas Berdyaev in his *Freedom and the Spirit* compares Luther favorably to the Jesuits of the time. (Berdyaev says that the Jesuits, while championing free will, "knew nothing of the pattern of spiritual freedom and rejected liberty of conscience.") It is the sixteenth-century Jesuit Luis Molina who is credited with formulating the traditional scholastic definition of freedom: an individual is free if, when everything is ready and in order for action, he can act or not act, choose one alternative or the other, without any determination from within or compulsion from without. Although Molina's definition continues to be quoted, modern thinkers fault it for not saying enough. Contemporary theologians describe human freedom under grace as infinitely more than the independence and power of the will to do as one pleases.

A free act is not just an exercise of the will; it is the act of a responsible person. The exercise of freedom snowballs. A person is the sum total of all his choices. He is what he has made himself to be by opting for this lifestyle, this pattern of behavior, this plan of action. While closing off some options, each decision opens up new opportunities. Each successive choice is influenced by previous decisions, made perhaps years before. Consciously or unconsciously one acts in accord with his own self-image, his own sense of identity. Persons, not actions, are properly said to be free. It is the person who loves. It is the person who sins. Persons, not actions, are the objects of redemption.

Liberation theology is quick to point out, however, that persons do not exist in a vacuum. They live in a particular cultural and historical milieu. To a great extent the person is the product of familial, social, economic, educational, and religious influences. One's freedom is conditioned by the concrete circumstances of life. Even God's grace is mediated by history, by the community in which one lives, by the "significant others" (or absence thereof) in one's life. Salvation is in final analysis the liberation of persons from the conditions that impede their freedom and stand in the way of their becoming fully human.

It is the preoccupation with questions of human freedom that forms the backdrop for this study by Kenneth Barker. For Christian educators, freedom is more than a speculative theological issue. Religious education and moral catechesis must deal with the formation of conscience, values clarification, decision making, and responsible behavior. Their audience runs the gambit from small children who are getting their first lessons in the meaning of "don't," to adolescents who are struggling with problems of personal identity vis-à-vis family and society, to self-directed, mature adults who are being called upon to choose among various shades of grey.

In the practical arena of religious education and catechesis, educators cannot avoid coming face to face with the psychological factors and socio-economic conditions that influence decisions and conduct. *Religious Education, Catechesis, and Freedom*, however, asks whether enough attention is being given on the theoretical level to education in freedom. What are the assumptions taken for granted by Christian educators as they set goals and objectives for their ministry? Do they expect small children and teenagers to behave like mature adults? Do they truly respect (or merely tolerate) the individual's right to dissent? Are they sensitive to societal and peer pressures that restrict options, distort judgment, and impede responsible action? It is Kenneth Barker's point in this study that every approach to religious education and catechesis has many presuppositions that need to be understood if the freedom of Christians is to be safeguarded and fostered.

Each approach builds on certain presuppositions about the structure of the person, the value of human experience, and the nature of moral development. Each makes assumptions about the aims and objectives, bolstering its position perhaps with the findings of the social sciences or perhaps not. Moreover, the understanding of freedom differs from approach to approach. Christian educators generally agree that they are called to liberate individuals from a meaningless existence by expounding the Good News of salvation. Some are more concerned, however, with freeing their fellow Christians from the drives of their inner compulsions than with alleviating the determinism of external forces and social pressures.

To define freedom in terms of responsible action rather than personal responsibility has far-reaching ramifications in one's approach to religious education and catechesis. Even a cursory investigation of catechetical programs and religious education texts reveals a focus which is almost exclusively on "morality of actions"; freedom is presented in terms of virtue and sin, of obedience to laws and conformity to an extrinsic moral code. Such programs present a detailed taxonomy of sins, serious and not so serious. By way of contrast, texts that define freedom primarily in terms of personal responsibility stress moral development and growth and a self-image of oneself as a Christian. The emphasis is on virtue, a sense of integrity, and the fostering of a healthy self-image. These latter contain strategies whereby the learner is led to clarify values and internalize moral norms.

Most of what Kenneth Barker has to say about religious education, catechesis, and freedom speaks across denominational lines. Even the Roman Catholic dilemma of reconciling personal freedom with the official positions taken by the church is experienced in some ways by all Christians. All are called to stand humbly before God and to heed the voice of the Spirit speaking in the scriptures, in prayer and in the Christian community. Children and adolescents (and a fortiori, adults) have a right to examine moral choices, to weigh their personal values against the conventional wisdom of the community, and to act accordingly. In these terms the freedom of the individual is not a denominational issue.

Religious Education, Catechesis, and Freedom is a subtle reminder that long before Lawrence Kohlberg found a name for it Christians were preoccupied with post conventional morality. It is a summons back to our roots. In effect, Kenneth Barker says with Paul, "Remember that you have been called to freedom." It is only in freedom that we become fully human and truly ourselves. Like the liberation theologians he cites, Barker says in effect that Christians must be free because God does not prize the service of slaves.

BERARD L. MARTHALER

Acknowledgements

In the course of a project such as this there are many people who lend a helping hand. I am indebted to the scholarly community of the Religion and Religious Education Department at the Catholic University of America. The many interactions with faculty and students over the past few years provided the learning experience that has yielded this work. While it is difficult to single out any individuals, I find it appropriate to express my gratitude especially to Berard Marthaler, who believed in my ability to complete the project more than I did myself. He offered valuable assistance in the clarification of methodology and suggested many improvements to the text. In a work devoted to freedom, I was privileged to have him as a mentor who facilitated my own free inquiry. He helped me explore the full implications of my own intuitions and encouraged me to come to my own conclusions. While my conclusions mainly support his "socialization" approach to catechesis, I present them as a stimulus for him to develop his theory further. Mary Charles Bryce diligently perused the entire work. She helped me especially to refine parts of the historical section. It was also a privilege for me to have Gabriel Moran, C. Ellis Nelson, and John H. Westerhoff read and comment on the sections of the manuscript which deal with their respective theories. I am also thankful to Paul Philibert for his insightful comments and constant encouragement.

My gratitude goes as well to the Archdiocese of Canberra, Australia, which has released me from pastoral responsibilities

6

to undertake this study. The work is dedicated to my mother and family who have patiently waited these last four years for my return. Finally, but by no means least, I am especially thankful for the support of those close friends who literally kept me alive during the difficult periods of composition.

Introduction

In recent years issues of freedom have occupied center stage in the Catholic church's intellectual life. At Vatican II there was a manifest concern for freedom. *Gaudium et Spes*[1] stressed that all human beings have a right to be free because they have the personal dignity of being created in the image and likeness of God.

> But that which is truly freedom is an exceptional sign of the image of God in man. . . . Man's dignity therefore requires him to act out of conscious and free choice, as moved and drawn in a personal way from within, and not by blind impulses in himself or by mere external constraint. (GS, 17)

The Council was aware of the human slavery caused by ignorance, poor working conditions, extreme destitution, and overindulgence in the good things of life (GS, 60, 67, 31). Human beings are often treated as "mere tools for profit rather than free and responsible persons . . ." (GS, 27). With the rise of technology there have been increased opportunities for human growth; yet scientific advances have unleashed "new forms of slavery in living and thinking" (GS 4; also 9). While a few individuals enjoy an almost unlimited opportunity to choose for themselves, "the vast majority have no chance whatever of exercising personal initiative and responsibility . . ." (GS, 63). These evils of our present day impede full human development for many, reducing human freedom almost to a vanishing point.

The *Declaration of Religious Freedom* also grounds the right to freedom in the very nature of the human person.[2] It is a dignity that every person possesses simply by being a person. It is not dependent on whether one behaves rightly or wrongly in the moral field. In view of the inescapable responsibility of persons to decide their own eternal destiny, they have the right to be immune from coercion in religious matters (*DH*, 2).

In addition to the Council documents, liberation theology has taken up the cry of freedom from the point of view of the economically and politically oppressed.[3] The scriptural symbols of freedom are being reinterpreted from the standpoint of those deprived of their dignity as human beings and reduced to mere slaves in the international structures of injustice. There is a new awareness that religious institutions can function to legitimize these structures of oppression. Liberation theology is an attempt to restore transformative power to the Christian tradition, so that the church will not be wedded to the status quo, but will exercise a critical prophetic function, being transformed within itself, and serving to transform the culture within which it is embedded.

Liberation theology affirms that human persons are not just molded by culture; they are also shapers of culture. Human beings are active agents of change. Rather than be fatalistically at the mercy of external forces, they are called to be shapers of history, to become masters of their own destiny.

In the documents of Vatican II, and in liberation theology, two important characteristics of human freedom are being emphasized. First, since human beings are created in the image and likeness of God, the more fully human they become the more fully they resemble God. Therefore, as they grow in authentic humanness they are growing into deeper participation in the freedom of God. Here is a basic assumption in this book—that human freedom is the outcome of authentic human development, which is itself a quest that is only satisfied in God.

Second, liberation theology especially emphasizes that human freedom is not an abstraction. It grows or diminishes within the historical existence of human beings. Admittedly, we all have "essential freedom," a free will that is constitutive of human existence. However, this radical ability to choose the direction of one's life is only exercised in concrete historical circumstances. "Effective freedom" is always subject to external conditions and internal subjective factors which limit the range of options available for persons to make decisions.[4]

Freedom has always been an underlying issue in religious education theory, but in recent years it has begun to occupy center stage. Religious education theorists have become more aware that education does not occur in a social and cultural vacuum. It is conducted in a context of interlocking influences upon individuals and groups. These influences can either enhance the possibility of freedom or they can seriously impair the realization of this human capacity. For example, in a technological age we are becoming more aware of new forces of mass manipulation that can render persons docile and cripple their power for self-determination. Religious educationalists cannot ignore this threat by pretending to operate in hermetically sealed compartments. There is a whole range of interpersonal social and cultural influences that condition the exercise of human freedom. Programs in religious education need to be able to deal with these factors to enhance the possibility of growth to freedom.

The issue of freedom has become especially crucial in the specific form of religious education called catechesis. As a form of the Catholic church's ministry of the word, catechesis aims to foster growth in faith. But faith is a free response to the grace of the revealing God (DH, 10). Catechesis, therefore, must be careful to preserve freedom and to establish the best conditions for its exercise.

The *General Catechetical Directory* (GCD) alerts us to the problem of freedom in catechesis. While on the one hand the GCD points out that ". . . adherence on the part of those to be taught is a fruit of grace and freedom" (GCD, 71), on the other hand it insists that "Christian freedom still needs to be ruled and directed in the concrete circumstances of human life" (GCD, 63). Human freedom is not an absolute, but is situated within conditioning circumstances. Not the least of these limiting circumstances for the Catholic Christian are the received beliefs and values of the tradition. Since catechesis aims to impart those beliefs and values in such a way that persons accept them as their own, it is possible that the enterprise could degenerate into a form of crass indoctrination. The problem of freedom, therefore, is inherent in the imperative to transmit the tradition from one generation to the next.

The National Catechetical Directory for the United States, *Sharing the Light of Faith* (SLF), notes the importance for catechetical theorists to deal with this problem:

> Psychological difficulties or external conditions can diminish the exercise of freedom slightly, considerably or almost to the vanishing point. Therefore, conditions favorable to the exercise of genuine human freedom must be promoted, not only for the sake of our temporal welfare but also for the sake of considerations bearing upon grace and eternal salvation. (SLF, 101)

To come to terms with this issue of freedom, the documents of the church call for theorists to collaborate with the human sciences. The GCD draws attention to "the researches and modern progress in the anthropological sciences concerning the use and limits of human freedom" (*GCD*, 61). Elsewhere the *GCD* states that ". . . the catechetical movement will in no way advance without scientific study . . ." (*GCD*, 131). It goes on to single out the relationship between catechesis and anthropology as one of the areas of research that has "universal importance." By studying human development under various aspects, the human sciences "help us to understand how people grow in their capacity for responding in faith to God's grace" (*NCD*, 175).

In light of the Catholic church's growing openness to the human sciences, a major aim of this volume is to show how some religious educational theorists use the human sciences and thus make certain assumptions in relation to human freedom. After this has been done, we will be in a better position to consider the goals of the catechetical enterprise in the Catholic church and to assess whether they support human freedom.

While contemporary religious education theorists are concerned with the problem of freedom, they do not reflect a uniform understanding of what human freedom is or how it should be fostered. Therefore this book aims to disclose the various ways theorists propose freedom as a goal of religious education, to examine the reasons for their differences, and to ascertain if these differences are irreconcilable. This examination of the theorists provides a framework within which the recent official statements of the Catholic church on catechesis can be analyzed. In this way the problem of freedom in catechesis can be brought to light more clearly.

A COMMON PROBLEM

The issue of freedom has been, and still is, a common problem for both Protestant and Catholic religious education theorists. Part One begins with an historical investigation into the evolution of religious education theory within this century. The Protestant and Catholic traditions are explored separately up until the mid-sixties. At that time they began to converge. Theorists from the two traditions were engaging in more open dialogue with one another, and were beginning to manifest common concerns. Official Catholic catechetical statements began to stress the notions of "initiation" and "nurture" within the Christian community. This broadened concept of catechesis was highly acceptable to most mainline Protestant churches in the U.S. which already had a long tradition of Christian nurture. In the meeting of the two traditions there was a mutual learning experience, without fusion of identity.

In view of the common concerns that now exist between Catholics and Protestants in the U.S., Part Three assumes that the official documents of the Catholic community are of interest to all Christian educators—Protestants as well as Catholics. Since these texts are to a greater or lesser extent consensus documents, they represent the predominant Catholic viewpoint. They are the rich distillate of a highly effervescent period of catechetical ferment. In this final section, recent documents of the Catholic church are examined from the point of view of freedom. The concept of catechesis which they promote is evaluated from this perspective and suggestions are made for further theoretical research.

Many writers from both traditions are manifesting a growing concern to ground the theory of religious education in an understanding of what it means to be and become human in today's world. They seem to share the conviction, often unstated, that the human sciences can contribute greatly to this endeavor. Theorists from both traditions share a renewed interest in finding a place for the human sciences in religious education. This appeal to the human sciences provides a larger context for the issue of freedom as such. Therefore, Part Two selects certain religious education theorists to illustrate some distinctive approaches to the problem of freedom.

These theorists were not selected for denominational reasons, but because their theories illustrate the various approaches that are being taken to an education for freedom. Their theories are examined from the point of view of education and the human sciences. Theological assertions are bracketed out. Even though chapter 4 deals with Gabriel Moran, a theorist from the Catholic tradition, there is no hint of denominational bias in this selection. Moran repudiates any crass denominationalism, and his writings have had considerable impact in Protestant circles. And even though chapter 5 deals only with Protestants, John Westerhoff III and C. Ellis Nelson, the approach described in that chapter is not restricted to Protestant theorists alone. These two were chosen simply because they are the most articulate spokespersons of that approach.

A TYPOLOGICAL EXPOSITION

This study assumes that freedom is an outcome of human development.[5] Theorists do not always make explicit their assumptions about human development and how education should promote it. However, these assumptions can be dug out of the literature and laid open for critical appraisal. When they are brought to the light of day, they can be shown to rest on certain preferences in regard to the human sciences. Human development, and therefore freedom, as a goal of education takes on different forms depending on whether humanistic psychology, behavioral psychology, or cultural anthropology undergird the theory.

The research for this part was guided by the hypothesis that there are at least three typical approaches to an education for freedom taken explicitly or implicitly by contemporary religious education theorists. This hypothesis was expanded from an initial insight that dawned on the author after plowing through mountains of material that seemed to be full on inconsistencies and contradictions. When the "penny dropped," it became clear that most contemporary religious education theorists assume one of three more-or-less distinct approaches to human freedom, each having its own anthropological base:

1. The *psychological approach,* taken by those who staunchly defend human freedom, but who tend to understand it in an individualistic-existential way. Human freedom is promoted in terms of growth to "authentic selfhood." The freedom is *from* coercion, and *for* personal wholeness.

2. The *political* approach, taken by those critical of a privatized arena of human freedom, who stress the socio-political dimension of this freedom. The freedom is *from* cultural oppression and *for* the power to work together to change existing conditions and participate in building the kingdom of justice and peace.

3. The *cultural* approach, taken by those who stress the cultural transmission of beliefs and values to the new generation. The freedom is *from* alienation, loneliness, and fragmentation and *for* the opportunity of full life within the community of nurture.

PROCEDURE

Having formulated the hypothesis, the task at hand was to validate the existence of the three types in the literature. To do this, a search was made for one or two theorists who would represent each type and best illustrate the features of this type. For the psychological approach Lewis Joseph Sherrill and Josef Goldbrunner were chosen. These authors were relatively early pathfinders in the use of neo-Freudian and Jungian psychology in religious education. For the political approach, Gabriel Moran was chosen since he represents a recent revival of the ideal of education as an instrument for social transformation, reminiscent of the early liberal religious education movement. For the cultural approach, C. Ellis Nelson and John H. Westerhoff were chosen because they represent a new reliance upon cultural anthropology in explaining the process of faith communication. The technique of centering attention on one or two authors in each type allows these authors, as it were, to speak for themselves. Every temptation to force theorists into categories in which they would find themselves uncomfortable has been studiously avoided.

To spin out the distinctiveness of each type, four categories were chosen which would aid the exposition. The categories are of such a nature that they are like threads normally woven together in the tapestry of any one approach. The four strands appear in each tapestry, but they appear in different colors. When the tapestry of any one type is viewed as a whole, the colors of the four strands blend with one another. However, the strands of any one tapestry can be unraveled to reveal more clearly the distinctive color combination in the weaving. As the image indicates, the four categories were not invented arbitrarily; they are integral to each approach.

The base strand in each type, which is sometimes mainly hidden and can only be occasionally glimpsed by the casual observer, is a distinctive *educational anthropology*. [6] Unraveling this strand reveals how religious education theorists view human development within the educational enterprise.

The second strand demonstrates how the selected theorists *rely on the human sciences* [7] to acquire such a vision of human growth. It has a different color in the tapestry of each approach.

The third strand shows how theorists envisage *the goal of education and the means to attain it.*

The fourth strand interweaves with all the others and can only be fully seen when the others have been unraveled. It is the *way freedom is posed as a goal of education.* In this category the traditional distinction between *negative* and *positive* freedom, that is, between freedom *from* and freedom *for,* is employed. They are really two threads of the one strand which have different shadings depending on how one looks at it.

THE SOURCES

Throughout the book, primary sources were consulted. Secondary sources were used to provide background and depth for the primary material. In the historical part, the researcher was faced with an enormous amount of material that almost defies generalizations. To the present, there are no comprehensive accounts of the history of Christian education theory and of the development of theory within the Catholic catechetical movement. The two historical chapters, therefore, are in their own right a pioneering effort to bring some order into a jungle of collected data.

The chapters in Part Two which expose three different approaches in recent theory emerged also from a survey of primary sources. After reading widely in the field, the focus could be narrowed to the particular theorists chosen, and then to the most significant works that these theorists have produced. The works of each theorist selected for concentrated attention were judged to be the most pertinent because they reveal how each individual understands freedom as a goal of education.

In the final part, the major sources are four recent catechetical documents of the Catholic church. While there have been overviews and general commentaries on these documents published, there has been no attempt until now to show their interdependence, and the approach to catechesis that they have in common.

CONTRIBUTION TO A DISCIPLINE

This work is theoretical and even though there are numerous references to other disciplines, it belongs properly within the field of religious education as such. In many ways religious education is still a "discipline in quest of an identity."[8] The current literature indicates a staggering amount of disagreement and confusion among theorists about terminology.[9] This terminological debate in itself is a sign of an identity problem. However, the problem is deeper than words alone. Practitioners in religious education work close to the daily "blood, sweat, and tears" of the church's continual regeneration of itself. They are often so preoccupied with fulfilling immediate pastoral demands that they rarely have the leisure time for reflection upon their practice. Consequently, the foundational principles underlying their programs go unquestioned. Compared to the thousands of practitioners in the field, often using resources uncritically, there are few theoreticians who have the time and competence to ask questions about the foundations of religious education.

The theoretical foundations of religious education are becoming firmer as researchers probe carefully into the theory and practice of earlier years. The historical part of this study offers further assistance in this quest for an understanding of the past roots to present problems.

As a discipline, religious education also needs theoretical and conceptual clarity about the various philosophical options available in a highly volatile marketplace for ideas. This clarity can only be achieved through a painstaking examination of the underlying principles propounded by writers in the field. The present study offers such an examination. It exposes foundational principles governing various assertions by theorists. It reveals varying anthropological assumptions that theorists make when they advocate human freedom as an outcome of education. It also exposes assumptions underlying the official catechetical stance of the Catholic church, assumptions that are crucial for the issue of freedom. This expository and comparative exercise offers a unique contribution to an emerging discipline, a contribution which is not only important for theorists, but which ultimately has significance for the future of religious education as an authentic enterprise.

NOTES FOR INTRODUCTION

1. The text of *Gaudium et Spes* (hereinafter referred to as GS) can be found in *Vatican Council II: The Conciliar and Post Conciliar Documents*, general editor Austin Flannery, O.P. (New York: Costello Publishing Company, 1975), pp. 903–1001.

2. The text of the *Declaration on Religious Freedom*, or *Dignitatis Humanae* (hereinafter referred to as *DH*), can be found in *Vatican Council II: The Conciliar and Post Conciliar Documents*, general editor Austin Flannery, O.P. (New York: Costello Publishing Company, 1975), pp. 799–812.

3. The literature is extensive. As an introduction to the Latin American contribution, see Gustavo Gutiérrez, *A Theology of Liberation: History, Politics and Salvation*, trans. and ed. Caridad Inda and John Eagleson (Maryknoll, N.Y.: Orbis Books, 1973); Ruben A. Alves, *A Theology of Hope* (Washington, D.C.: Corpus Books, 1969); idem, *Tomorrow's Child: Imagination, Creativity and the Rebirth of Culture* (London: SCM Press Ltd., 1972). An example of black theology in North America can be found in James H. Cone, *A Black Theology of Liberation* (Philadelphia: J. B. Lippincott Company, 1970), and idem, *God of the Oppressed* (New York: The Seabury Press, 1975). Some helpful summary articles of the Latin American challenge are Gustavo Gutiérrez, "Notes for a Theology of Liberation," *Theological Studies* 31 (June 1970): 243–61; Philip E. Berryman, "Latin American Liberation Theology," *Theological Studies* 34 (September 1973): 357–95; T. Howland Sanks, S.J. and Brian H.

Smith, S.J. "Liberation Ecclesiology: Praxis, Theory, Praxis," *Theological Studies* 38 (March 1977): 3–38; Alfred T. Hennelly, S.J., "The Challenge of Juan Luis Segundo," *Theological Studies* 38 (March 1977): 123–35; Jacques Van Nieuwenhove, "The Theological Project of Gustavo Gutiérrez: Reflections on His 'Theology of Liberation,'" *Lumen Vitae* 28 (September 1973): 398–432.

4. The distinction between "essential freedom" and "effective freedom" is made by Bernard Lonergan. See Bernard Lonergan, *Insight: a Study of Human Understanding* (New York: Longmans, Green and Co., 1958), pp.607–33.

5. That freedom is the outcome of authentic human development does not mean that there is a cause-effect relationship between human development and freedom, nor does it mean that freedom only follows upon human development. The philosophical option exercised here is that human beings possess an inner dynamic directed toward an indeterminate end, and that development is a linked sequence of dynamic higher integrations and greater differentiations. Total human development occurs within organic, psychic, intellectual, and spiritual dimensions of the human person. The potentialities of the human being are in process of development towards a full, effective freedom. Effective freedom can be frustrated by blockages or regressions at the psychic level (e.g. undue anxiety or obsessions); it can be impeded by obtuseness at the levels of understanding (the narrowing or fixing of horizons); it can be set back by loss of willingness (e.g., holding no hope for change, fatalism). All of these levels of human development or regression are inhibited or aided by external circumstances. So external social, economic, and political conditions either create the conditions for possibility of development, and hence freedom, or they eliminate the possibility of exercising freedom. Growth in freedom and human development occur hand in hand. See Bernard J. F. Lonergan, *Insight: A Study of Human Understanding*, pp. 451–458, 616–626.

6. The word "anthropology" is being used here in a special sense. Anthropology, here, refers to the distinctive perspective on human being and becoming that is characteristic of a given educational approach. It is a way of viewing the human quest, a way of imaging the essential characteristics that make us human, a way of articulating what human nature is and how it develops. Some of the questions anthropology asks are: What are the basic needs of the human being? What are the fundamental internal and external conflicts that inhibit human development? What is the destiny of the human being? What influences, both internal and external, are necessary for the fulfillment of that destiny? This usage of the term "anthropology" has to be distinguished from the ordinary American usage which refers to an empirical science. The adjective "educational" specifies one enterprise, namely education, in which practitioners and theorists maintain varying images of what it means to be and become human. For initial reading in philosophical anthropology, see William L. Kelly and Andrew Tallon, *Readings in the Philosophy of Man* (New York:

McGraw-Hill Book Company, 1967), Perry Le Ferre, *Understandings of Man,* (Philadelphia: The Westminister Press, 1966), Edmund F. Byrne and Edward A. Maziarz, *Human Being and Being Human : Man's Philosophies of Man* (New York: Appleton-Century-Crofts, 1969). For an interesting study of models of being and becoming human which are implicit in the human sciences, see James J. Dagenais, *Models of Man: A Phenomenological Critique of some Paradigms in the Human Sciences* (The Hague: Martinus Nijhoff, 1972).

7. The human sciences are concerned with that which is specifically human. They do not include physiology and anatomy or any of the physical sciences. The human sciences study concrete human beings, both as individuals and as collectivities. They use empirical methods of investigation to establish their results. The conglomerate of human sciences includes history, comparative religion, cultural anthropology, political science, psychology, and sociology. Theology is not one of the human sciences, but this is due to methodological differences. The term "human sciences" is not intended to carry with it an outdated notion that the so-called sacred sciences have a superior claim in the pursuit of knowledge. See Stephen Strasser, *Phenomenology and the Human Sciences: A Contribution to a New Scientific Ideal* (Pittsburgh: Duquesne University Press, 1963), pp. 3-9.

8. See Berard Marthaler, "A Discipline in Quest of an Identity: Religious Education," *Horizons* 3, No. 2 (1976): 203-15.

9. This terminological debate can be seen from taking a few prominent theorists and asking them to define the enterprise. James Michael Lee claims that "religious instruction" is the proper term. He considers the word "catechesis" to be archaic and confusing: ". . . I strongly urge that the terms 'catechesis' and 'catechetics', when intended to denote contemporary religious education or religious instruction, be completely abandoned." James Michael Lee, "Key Issues in the Development of a Workable Foundation for Religious Instruction," in *Foundations of Religious Education,* ed. Padraic O'Hare (New York: Paulist Press, 1978), p. 43. On the other hand, Berard Marthaler upholds the term "catechesis," emphasizing that it need not be understood as an enterprise bound exclusively to Catholic theology. See Berard Marthaler, "Socialization as a Model for Catechetics," in *Foundations of Religious Education.* ed. Padraic O'Hare (New York; Paulist Press, 1978), p. 65. Gabriel Moran argues that the terms "Catechetics" or "Christian education" have the operative meaning of producing church members through indoctrination. He prefers "religious education," which he claims is the intersection of good religion and good education. See Gabriel Moran "Where Now, What Next," in *Foundations of Religious Education,* ed. Padraic O'Hare (New York: Paulist Press, 1978), pp. 98-101. See also idem, "Catechetics R.I.P.," *Commonweal,* 18 December 1970, pp. 299-302. In reaction to this article, Mary Charles Bryce appealed to the *General Catechetical Directory* which emphasizes that catechesis is a pastoral

activity of the church occurring whenever people are sharing their faith with one another. It has a history that predates our modern school systems and the educational theory attached to them. See Mary Charles Bryce, "The Identity Crisis of 'Catechetics,'" *National Catholic Reporter*, 27 April 1973, p. 11. See also Martin A. Lang, "Catechetics, Theology and Religious Education," *America* 24 July 1971, pp. 39–41. In this book "religious education" refers to the more general and ecumenical enterprise that embraces both Protestant and Catholic traditions. The term "catechesis" denotes a particular manifestation of religious education within the Catholic tradition.

PART ONE

Chapter 1
Historical Background

Before making an analysis of several catechetical theorists under the aspect of human freedom it is necessary to situate these theories, and the persons who have proposed them, within their historical context. Consequently, this chapter first gives an overview of the development of Christian education theory within the American Protestant tradition of this century. Second, it provides an historical survey of the development of theory within the modern Catholic catechetical movement. These developments are traced up to the early sixties when new trends began to emerge in both traditions that brought them more closely into dialogue. These trends will become the subject of the following chapter.

The separate treatment of the two traditions before the period of the early sixties is necessary for two reasons. First, the principal developments of theory within the contemporary Catholic catechetical movement in the first half of this century occurred outside the United States. The Catholic catechetical movement in North America was, in its initial stages, a European import. Therefore, to discover the background of recent trends in theory within this country, one must go to the roots of the catechetical movement in the broad family of the international Catholic church. On the other hand, the Protestant Christian nurture theory within the United States has grown mainly out of the experience of communicating the faith in this country alone. The Christian education movement in American Protestantism has been mainly beholden unto itself, and for this reason it is more distinctively American in its flavor, and can therefore be studied in isolation.

The second reason for making the distinction between the Catholic and Protestant traditions is ecumenical in character. The separate treatment is in accord with the ecumenical principle that authentic dialogue between communions is only possible if the distinctiveness of each tradition is fully recognized, and if the participants in the dialogue become conversant with their own unique identity. Thus, it is hoped that both Protestants and Catholics will benefit from these overviews, which should serve to promote mutual understanding between different ecclesial communities.

CHRISTIAN NURTURE IN AMERICAN PROTESTANTISM

The concept of Christian "nurture" in American Protestantism has its roots in the writings of Horace Bushnell. Bushnell has been acclaimed as the father of the Christian education movement in America.[1] As a pastor in Hartford, Connecticut, in the mid-nineteenth century, Bushnell reacted against the popular revivalist conception that children had no redemptive significance. According to the revivalist notion, it was only in adolescence, once one had been convinced of personal sinfulness, that conversion was possible, and hence entry into the community of faith. Bushnell found this doctrine repulsive. In his book *Christian Nurture* he set out an alternative way for people to enter the Christian community. It is summarized in his famous dictum: "The child is to grow up a Christian and never know himself to be otherwise."[2]

During the nineteenth century the Sunday school movement became the major institution of religious instruction in Protestantism. At first the curriculum centered around the classical Reformation catechisms, but as the century progressed the bible became the central text. Children were expected to memorize texts from the bible; possessing the divinely inspired truth contained in the scriptural texts was considered sufficient to ensure growth in Christian faith.[3]

Around the turn of the century a major challenge to the Sunday-school evangelism came from the confluence of liberal theology, the "social gospel," and the progressive educational movement. These three streams flowed into one movement, which became known as the religious education movement. This movement was symbolized and given concrete shape in the Religious Education Association formed in 1903, with William Rainey Harper as its foremost convener.[4] The threefold purpose of the Religious Education Association was formulated as follows:

> To inspire the educational forces of our country with the religious ideal; to inspire the religious forces of our country with the educational ideal; and to keep before the public mind the idea of Religious Education and the sense of its need and value.[5]

Liberal religious thought was the first of the underlying foundations of this movement. American religious liberalism at this time reflected a popular credo that was pervasive in its effect upon religious education. Some of the features of this credo that were particularly influential upon religious education were as follows:[6]

a) The principle of divine immanence—that God is an indwelling reality of one organic and developing process.

b) The idea that religion in the individual is a gradual, developing experience, coming mainly from within and unfolding outwards.

c) The idea that human nature is basically good, contrary to any doctrine of human depravity. Within humanity there are the seeds of divinity, so humans may grow God-like by the gradual unfolding of their own inner nature.

d) The confidence that historical criticism could disclose the man Jesus in all the details of his personal biography. With this came a tendency to see Jesus as a great teacher of a new way of life, and to present him primarily as an example to be followed.

e) A view of the bible less as a divine revelation than as a record of human religious experience.

f) An optimism in the application of the scientific method in religious matters. As one devotee of the religious education movement stated:

> . . . Instead of, in the realm of religion, standing with helpless hands waiting for desirable events to happen, we can plan, with the certainty of the scientist, our processes and be sure of their effects. We have become a part of the universe of orderly dependable processes.[7]

The optimism of liberalism joined with the ethical enthusiasm of the "social gospel." The "social gospel" arose out of a response to the new industrial society and as a corrective to the current individualism of the churches.[8] Some prominent names associated with the movement were George D. Herran, Walter Rauschenbusch, and Shailer Matthews. They also proposed the immanence of God—the indwelling God who works out his purposes within the solidarity of men and women. The two basic tenets were the fatherhood of God and the brotherhood of men. The kingdom of God was not a distant future event; it was being progressively realized here and now in the democracy that people build through their social relations. Charles Hopkins interprets the general characteristics of the movement as follows:[9]

a) The emphasis on the ethical ideal of the kingdom which is coming about now on earth.

b) The appeal to social reconstruction as the only way to create the conditions within which individuals can realize their potential.

c) The idea of progressive social redemption which defined sin in social terms, but tended to neglect the more pessimistic aspects of sin.

d) The belief in inevitable progress. God's method of bringing about the kingdom is by gradual growth. There is no discontinuity between this world and the next.

e) The prophetic denunciation of the existing social order without offering much in the way of a practical program of reform.

Liberalism and the "social gospel" joined league with the other great protagonist of the modern spirit, progressive education. The titan associated with the birth of progressive education was John Dewey. However, a distinction must be made between Dewey's philosophy of education as such, which can be found well-formulated in *Democracy and Education* (1916), and the progressive education movement. [10] The latter was a revolt against formalism in schools; it was more a pattern and practice in education than a philosophy. Some of the main features of this new educational practice listed by J. Donald Butler were as follows: [11] a) greater freedom for the individual, b) stress on interest rather than discipline as motivation for the learner, c) flexible ordering of timetable, d) encouragement for each child to work at his/her own pace, e) learning through doing, f) reaction against teaching as the transmission of information, g) a greater dependence on the natural maturation process of the child, and h) a tendency to open the school out to the community. Both the philosophy of John Dewey and the more pervasive attitudes and experimental practices of progressive education had a profound impact on the growing religious education movement. [12]

Some of the major theorists who came out of this background, and were the architects of the religious education movement, were George Albert Coe, William Clayton Bower, and Ernest Chave.[13] An indication of the mind-set of the movement is found in Paul Vieth's *Objectives in Religious Education* (1930), where he included a fairly moderate statement of liberal objectives, which he himself had formulated, and which were consequently adopted by the International Council of Religious Education.[14] The emphasis was on "growing persons" within a society undergoing progressive reconstruction. The presumption was that growth is inevitable; it remained for the educator to steer it in the right direction. There was a tendency to downplay the role of the church in mediating its tradition and initiating new members. Likewise, the role of the bible was minimized.[15] With these theorists, it was experience, interpreted by scientific methodology, that had become normative for religious education.

The Turn to Neo-orthodoxy

The religious education movement rode on the crest of a wave during the 1920s, but with the Depression in the thirties and the experience of the two great wars, the surging optimism about the possibilities of the human being began to fade. In addition, there was an influx of so-called neo-orthodox theology from Europeans such as Karl Barth and Emil Brunner that began to challenge the roots of liberal religious education.[16] A significant turning point came in 1940, when Harrison S. Elliott published a book entitled *Can Religious Education be Christian?*[17] In this book, Elliott attempted to confront the challenge neo-orthodox theology presented to the liberal assumptions of the current religious educationists. The conflict, according to Elliott, was between "theological" interpreters, who considered religious education to be theocentric (and hence in service of an a priori theology of revelation), and the religious education theorists, such as Coe, who argued for an anthropocentric starting point, relying first upon psychology and sociology to establish educational foundations.[18] He could see no possibility of rapprochement with neo-orthodoxy and opted for the standard approach of the religious educationists until that time.

Elliott accused neo-orthodoxy of being a new type of authoritarianism. He saw it as an attempt to make children Christians, rather than to educate them so they can make a free choice in regard to Christian beliefs and practices.[19] He said:

> The issues in regard to religious education center in the source of authority. Those with an authoritarian approach seek to find authority for their interpretations outside of human responsibility in some direct revelation of God. Those with an educational approach recognize that while God has not left himself without witness, man has not been given any direct revelation of the meaning of these manifestations.[20]

Elliott argued that a true educational process is denied if it becomes a servant of dogmatism, as neo-orthodoxy suggests. He strongly endorsed the liberal educational ideal that individuals and groups be able to seek their own interpretation of life and destiny without having the search predetermined from the beginning by dogmatic assumptions.

This strong reaction of Elliott against neo-orthodoxy echoed one of the basic beliefs in the credo of liberal religious education—that there should be no coercion or restraint of the freely unfolding personality. George Albert Coe has espoused this fundamental belief, pointing out its origin in Kantian philosophy and the philosophers of the American revolutions.[21] However, he was quick to warn against any privatism contained in the idea. For Coe, authentic religious freedom was not found in a private world free from coercion and restraint, but in the joint positive struggle for emancipation of all from the oppressive social structures of his day, with a view to building the "democracy of God."[22] Coe applauded the liberal spirit of intelligent inquiry as opposed to dogmatism, but pointed out that this can become a privatistic intellectualism which is opposed to vital religion.[23] He also applauded the relativizing of ecclesiastical structures, but insisted on the necessity of the church, which should be in the service of the "democracy of God."[24]

Elliott's reaction to neo-orthodoxy arose out of the fear that this new theology was simply a veiled attempt at introducing a transmissive theory of church education, where the primary aim would be to induct people into the status quo without respecting their freedom to choose and without fostering their potential to build a new society. The weighty injunctions of the authority of the revealing God to legitimize the process would make the transmission system even more restrictive, and would eliminate any possibility of its being challenged.

Only one year later, a book was authored by H. Shelton Smith, called *Faith and Nurture,* which addressed the same crisis that Elliott had exposed.[25] However, Smith's conclusion was diametrically opposed to Elliott's. The issue, said Smith, was "Shall Protestant nurture realign its theological foundations with the newer currents of Christian thought, or shall it resist those currents and merely reaffirm its faith in traditional liberalism?"[26] Elliott had opted for the latter alternative; now Smith emphatically opted for the former alternative.

Some of the more significant prongs of Smith's attack on liberal religious education were as follows:

1. Religious education had begun unquestioningly to take the social sciences as normative for an understanding of the human being and his relations with others. Said Smith:

... Twentieth century religious education has concerned itself so completely with man in his empirical manifestation that it has tended to obscure, and in some instances to deny, the ultimate ground of human existence.[27]

2. The over-reliance on psychology and sociology had led to a fading consciousness of man's sinful predicament. The theocentric side of sin had been lost because of the emphasis on interhuman relations. Smith argued that Christianity does not find the ultimate source of sin in social systems, but in the private order of the human self.[28]

3. The emphasis on the "social gospel," which had been a healthy reaction against an other-worldly and individualistic idea of the kingdom of God had led to the extreme of collapsing the tension between the world in process and the kingdom of God. The kingdom of God was equated with the "democracy of God." There was not a denial of the divine dimension, but an obscuring of it, since the emphasis was on a growing "society of persons."[29]

4. With the growth in social consciousness, laudable as it may have been, the meaning of individual selfhood had been lost. The unique character of the individual, who is the object of God's personal concern, and who is ultimately dependent on and responsible to God alone, had been depreciated.[30]

5. Religious educators had concerned themselves with "educational" activities over against "church" activities. The theories of education had such an influence that there was no interest in the church as a distinctive community of nurture.[31] The interest was in the "school," not in the "church." The institutional aspects of the church had been considered more as a hindrance than as an asset in religious education.[32]

6. When the church *had* been considered, it had been studied empirically as a reality of history within the wider social matrix.

Smith agreed that this approach had the advantage of preserving Christian nurture from dogmatism and obscurantism, but it had tended to ignore that the ultimate source of Christian fellowship is found in God. For Smith, the uniting bond between Christians is the Holy Spirit.[33]

The New Christian Nurture Theory

Shelton Smith's *Faith and Nurture* was a watershed in religious education theory. It signaled the beginning of a new era. A new school of theorists appeared, preferring the title "Christian" education to "religious" education. They sought to ground Christian education in a neo-orthodox theology of revelation. They sought to bring the bible back into the center of the curriculum, and struggled to attain a new understanding of how the church transmits its life and message from generation to generation. They made use of existential philosophy, education theory, and psychology, but they kept these disciplines in a position subordinate to theology.

The following presentation outlines the general characteristics of the new movement and its chief protagonists. These general characteristics were, to a greater or lesser degree, common to them all. The theorists have been included under a particular heading, not becuase this describes their total contribution, but because this author has judged that their distinctive contribution to the movement has been in that area. It will become clear that there is much overlap, but even this overlap is a clue to the emphasis that the movement put on each of these various aspects.

Theology as the Clue.   Randolph Crump Miller was one of the first writers to take up the challenge of constructing a new basis for Christian education. In 1950 he acknowledged that Shelton

Smith provided "the chief stimulus to my thought."[34] With Smith's criticism of the earlier school in mind, Miller proposed "the clue to Christian education." The clue, he said, was

> a relevant theology which will bridge the gap between content and methods, providing the background and perspective of Christian truth by which the best methods and content will be used as tools to bring the learners into the right relationship with the living God who is revealed to us in Jesus Christ, using the guidance of parents and the fellowship of life in the church as the environment in which Christian nurture will take place.[35]

Now the continuum between religion and secular education, which the religious education movement had sought to foster, was broken. Instead of a primary concern for participation in the broad cultural life of the society, there was a concern to make a sharp break between the distinctive nurturing process within the church and any other educational activity. Miller made this even clearer in his later book, *Christian Nurture and the Church*. Individuals were to be brought out of the environment that formed them with many characteristics common to others and brought into the *koinonia* of the Christian community, where they would be able to search for the meaning of existence. The individual, said Miller, enters into the history of God's people and discovers the gift of new being from faith in Jesus Christ. This new perspective, which one gains from the redemptive community, and the heritage it preserves, then enables one to be a Christian citizen in the metropolis.[36]

In *Education for Christian Living* (1956), Miller again stressed that Christian theology is the foundation for Christian educational theory and practice. Theology, he said, provides the fundamental truths about all of life; these are the truths that Christians know from their interpretation of the events in history by which God establishes a relationship with man. He agreed that the insights of modern science and educational theory are useful in Christian education, but he said "we begin with the truth that is ours as Christians"; the observations, experiments and insights of non-Christians may be used, but always "within the framework of Christian truth."[37]

The Gospel as the Foundation.   In *The Task of Christian Education,* written in 1955, D. Campbell Wyckoff joined the growing body of theorists who espoused a neo-orthodox, biblically based understanding of Christian education. Like Miller, the aim of Christian education for Wyckoff was "to nurture the Christian life."[38] This involves instruction in faith and doctrine, developing Christian personality, and finally the ongoing reconstruction of the Christian community so that the processes of this community do not hinder the Christian growth of individuals within it. The desired outcomes of church education are "intelligent belief, Christian commitment, Christian character, Churchmanship, and a participation in the redemption of the community."[39]

Wyckoff's major interest was in curriculum design. He did not attempt to elaborate a broad theory of Christian nurture. Rather, his focus was upon the propagation of the "gospel," and especially upon the bible, the "indispensable book" in any curriculum because it is the "revelation of God to men, and as such is the record of the history of man's grasp of the truth that is revealed."[40]

In *The Gospel and Christian Education* (1959), Wyckoff emphasized the centrality of the gospel when he said:

> The most promising clue to orienting Christian education theory so that it will be both worthy and communicable is to be found in recognizing and using the gospel of God's redeeming activity in Jesus Christ as its guiding principle.[41]

The gospel is the reason for the church's existence; it brings the church into existence, sustains it, directs it, and corrects it. For Wyckoff, the gospel is also the clue to the meaning of history and to the meaning of personal existence. When the church teaches, it communicates the gospel. Individuals may remain trapped in the bondage of their human predicament or they may become free persons through response to the gospel.[42] They may remain enclosed in egocentrism, with an entirely warped attitude to life, or they may surrender to the powerful message of the Good News, accepting a new life in Christ.[43]

The Church as the Context.   One of the early contributors to the new theological foundations for a nurture theory was James D. Smart. In his book *The Teaching Ministry of the Church* (1954), he grounds his ecclesiology in the Word which is spoken in Jesus Christ and incarnate in him.[44] The Word incarnate, said Smart, calls the new people of God into being. The church exists to serve the Word.[45] As in the ministry of Jesus, in the church there is a twofold ministry of the word—that of preaching and teaching. The content of preaching and teaching are the same (viz., Jesus Christ). Smart saw preaching as the "proclamation of the Word of God to man in his unbelief," both inside and outside the church. On the other hand, teaching, he said, is directed to "the situation of children of believers who through the influence of their parents have in them a measure of faith, even though they also have a large measure of unfaith."[46] The two functions cannot be separated. Without preaching, teaching lapses into moralism. Without teaching, preaching becomes remote and aloof from people's continued growth in faith.

Smart attacked any attempt to make "character building" the goal of the church's teaching ministry.[47] This, he said, is a form of moralism aimed at producing "ordinary Christians." A person only becomes a Christian through being confronted with the risen Lord and entering into a new relationship with him. In this way one gains a new perspective on life and is able to lay open one's being as an instrument of God's redemptive purpose in the world. Smart insisted that it is not sufficient to aim toward forming Christians with the credentials of a "good character." The aim of the church's education is to serve the Word by nurturing people into acquiring a missionary evangelizing outlook. Children, said Smart, should be educated by "being led step by step into an ever fuller realization of what it means to be church." The call, he continued, is "to respond to faith in Jesus Christ, and this necessarily involves growing within the church, the call to be church."[48]

The parable that Smart found most apt to describe the teaching ministry of the church is that of the growing grain. The preacher and teacher sow the seed faithfully, then they wait for the growth that takes place in God's time. Between the planting of the seed and the ripening of the grain the sower must be patient and not try to force the process of conversion. Conversion is a gift of God alone; the transformation that takes place cannot be scheduled. However, the sower is also the harvester. The harvester must sense the time of ripening and be ready to move the individual into an increased fruitfulness of faith at that time. There may be many harvest times in the development of the individual—it is for the preacher and teacher to be alert to these times.[49]

The parable also indicates, for Smart, that the process of growth in faith cannot be manipulated. The teacher cannot produce Christians. The freedom and integrity of the human person was respected infinitely by God's choice to come into the world as Word incarnate. Each person must be allowed to choose freely, so that one's faith and obedience are one's own. Smart repudiated any attempt at establishing conformity to Christian standards of faith and conduct as the primary goal of Christian education. Rather, he claimed that the primary concern should be that persons "find their way to an immediate personal knowledge of God in his Word and Spirit."[50]

Smart was also aware that, not only do individuals have to undergo transformation, but also the church itself. He looked to scripture to supply the critical principle within the community. Scriptural education is imperative because the scriptures stand over in judgment upon the church. "Insofar as the existing church fails to be that church of Jesus Christ, our education in scriptures makes us rebels within it, working for its reform, that it may be reshaped into its true likeness."[51]

Relationships as the Medium.   One of the most influential commitments of this new approach to Christian nurture was made to so-called "relationship theology."[52] Randolph Crump Miller, for example, had spoken of the church as a "new structure of personal relationships," since God never enters into personal relationship with individuals apart from other human persons. Miller was convinced that it is only within the person-person interaction with the nurturing community that the integration of the total person becomes possible.[53]

Many Christian educators turned to Martin Buber's thought to understand the dynamics of personal relationships.[54] In his *I and Thou,* Buber had presented life itself as a meeting. The meaning of an individual's existence is found in the relations he has with God and with others. Says Buber: "If I face a human being as my Thou, and say the primary I-Thou to him, he is not a thing among things.... When Thou is spoken the speaker stands in relation...."[55]

Reuel Howe is one Christian educator who acknowledged his indebtedness to Buber, especially to the essay on "Education" in *Between Man and Man.*[56] Howe built upon Buber's notion that education is a "dialogical relation," and that the genuine educator is the one who is "experiencing the other side."[57] For Howe, Christian education takes place in personal encounter, and is only secondarily transmissive.[58] It takes place in the "language of relationship," that is, in the mutual address and response, in the trust that begets trust, in the affirmation that begets the affirming person.[59]

Relying also on Paul Tillich, Howe pointed to the existential loneliness of concrete human existence; the state of separation and estrangement from self, others, and God.[60] All our life is an effort to overcome separation. The fundamental human need is the need for at-one-ness. Answering this need, God's reconciliation in Christ is mediated within the church, which is a structure of persons in a new relationship with one another and with God.[61] Christian education then, according to Howe, involves the person-to-person meeting in which there is a flow of meaning between persons in spite of all the obstacles that would normally block that flow.[62] Howe follows Buber's dictum that "it is not the educational intention but it is the meeting which is educationally fruitful."[63] Only through being accepted unconditionally can a person be released from the bondage of loneliness and empowered to be other-centered.

Howe did not place the full burden of this love and acceptance upon the educator, since God's power of acceptance is at work in and through every accepting human relationship. Whenever two persons enter into genuine dialogue their own limited efforts are transcended by the love of God who brings about results beyond what they are capable of doing.[64]

Another proponent of education through relationships was David Hunter. He introduced the term "engagement" to Christian education. Hunter agreed with Miller's stance that the principles and methodology of Christian education derive from the "theological imperative,"[65] and he agreed with Wyckoff that

Christian education is "nothing less than the communication of the gospel."[66] But he sought a methodology that would facilitate confrontation with God now. He concluded that for successful methodology "engagement must be the immediate and the ultimate criterion."[67]

By "engagement" Hunter meant "meeting, knowing (not knowing about), responding to or ignoring, loving, hating." In Christian experience, he said, "engagement" is our "changing and unchanging encounter with God, our response to His action."[68] In order to orient people for Christian nurture, Hunter suggested, among other methods, the use of group dynamics as a way to sensitize people to the barriers that exist between one another and between them and God. He endorsed the use of findings from the social sciences in these "laboratories" in Christian living, where the sharing between persons involves an ongoing conversion experience.[69]

The nurture that persons receive within the church, said Hunter, enables them to find a place in the community of the Spirit, and also is the first step in training them for a ministry of reconciliation in the world.[70] The mission to the world was also presented by Hunter in terms of "engagement." He regarded it as an attempt to relate oneself to an action of God in life; it is to respond to the mission of Christ already present in the world and to draw out others to a similar response.[71]

Psychology as Descriptive of Growth.   Psychological insights have been used by Christian education theorists to describe the process of self-integration within the nurturing community. One prominent example was Lewis Joseph Sherrill. In 1955 he wrote *The Gift of Power.* Influenced by Erik Erikson, Otto Rank, Karen Horney, Harry Stack Sullivan, and Carl Jung. Sherrill rejected behavioral psychology, since he saw it as a means of manipulating people, and favored psychotherapy because it is concerned with the whole person, especially the relational dimension of a person's life.[72]

Sherrill developed a theory of the self coming to authenticity within relationships. The focus is on the unique individual who "can be relatively free to become the self which he truly is thus fulfilling his own inward destiny."[73] This "coming to be" of the self is attainment of wholeness, or integrity. However, there are many hindrances to the process of becoming oneself. These hindrances include anxiety, which divides the self, and impersonal institutions that threaten the self from without.[74] Therefore, the divine self enters into relationship with human selves with a redemptive purpose. This redemptive activity is continued within the nurturing community which is the context and means of Christian education.[75]

The insights of developmental psychology have also been used by the nurture theorists. Wayne Rood is one example. In his book *On Nurturing Christians,* Rood subscribed to the principle of "mutuality" as the essence of the teaching-learning process that characterizes Christian education. By mutuality Rood means a double movement—first, there is the initiative of the teacher who reaches out in an act of love; second, there is a movement of response on the part of the learner, and this is an act of faith. This giving and receiving, said Rood, is a continuous process in the experience of the Christian community; the nurturing effort raises this process to intentionality and conducts it with sensitivity.[76]

The effective nurturer, said Rood, is especially sensitive to the developmental phases of human growth. Nurture involves introducing persons to the bible, which is the story of the privileged experience of God's people; but this must be done according to the capacity of the learner. There is a different style of biblical presentation for each age group.[77] In a similar way, the mode of initiation into the *koinonia* itself ought respect the age and maturation level of the child or adult.[78] Rood suggested that a person's religious stance toward life differs according to age and mental capacity. Therefore, it is important not to introduce abstract and linear concepts too early.[79]

Rood has attempted to fit these now familiar developmental principles into his nurture theory in such a way that it is not so much a matter of adapting a message to make it intelligible to a particular age group, but rather it is a matter of the Christian community itself being both the medium and the message for every age level.

SUMMARY

The Christian nurture approach arose out of a reaction to the "liberal" notion that salvation can be attained through good education. It retreated from liberal optimism about the possibilities of the human enterprise into the enclave of the "redemptive community" which finds its ultimate authority in scripture rather than human experience. While some of its adherents, such as Sherrill and Rood, used the findings of the human sciences in the construction of their theories, there was an inherent suspicion of the contemporary human endeavor. The aim of Christian education, they claimed, is to serve the word of God which has broken into history in a series of redemptive events that found their fulfillment in Jesus. The privileged locus of the continuing redemptive activity of God is in the church. Therefore, for them, all salvific education is church education.

In the international Catholic community a similar reawakening of neo-orthodox theology was taking place. In catechetical theory it was manifest in the so-called "kerygmatic" approach. However, unlike American Protestantism the modern catechetical movement at the beginning of the century had not been laboring under the tenets of liberalism but had been bound into scholastic theology which was transmitted in simplified form within catechism texts. The "kerygmatic" approach came as a reaction to this. It is to this development of Catholic catechetical theory that we must now turn our attention.

THEORETICAL DEVELOPMENT WITHIN THE CATHOLIC CATECHETICAL MOVEMENT

The modern catechetical movement arrived in the United States as a European import. In the 1950s there was an influx of bearers of the "good news," such as Johannes Hofinger and Marcel Van Caster, who were international figures promoting the new enthusiasm of the movement wherever they landed. The new movement was not without some preparatory foundations in this country. There had already been pioneering work done by educational innovators such as Thomas Shields, Edmund Aloysius Pace, Edwin Vincent O'Hara, and Virgil Michel.[80] However, the Catholic catechetical movement, as such, cannot attribute its origins or its initial inspiration and zeal to North Americans. As important as the home-grown contributions were in the early part of this century, they were the work of isolated individuals. Admittedly, these individuals exercised considerable influence, and to some degree reflected the concerns of the broader international venture, but they remained largely out of contact with the international dialogue. The catechetical movement, and especially the theoretical development within it, until the early 1960s can legitimately be considered as largely independent of American thought. Even Gerard Sloyan, who, it will be shown, did so much to promote the new movement, functioned primarily as a mediator between the Europeans and the hungry American audience. The distinctively American contribution began to appear with the turn to experiential catechetics in the late sixties, and is associated with names such as Gabriel Moran and Berard Marthaler.

This section deals with the development of theory within the catechetical movement in this century as theorists grappled first with problems of pedagogical technique, then centered upon the problem of the renewal of content, and finally groped towards some way of overcoming the content-method duality. Like the preceding section, this one also serves as historical background for the emergence of the issue of freedom. The kerygmatic approach of the second phase of development had largely overlooked the issue. As Moran claimed, the kerygmatic phase actually contributed towards the diminishment of human freedom, because it supplanted the extrinsic doctrinal structure of scholastic theology with an equally extrinsic historical, biblical, and liturgical structure. The movement from catechism to kerygma was ultimately another form of slavery, since it still involved an imposition upon the individual from outside the realm of personal experience. The attempts to find a truly anthropological catechetics in the most recent era of the movement are attempts to make room in catechetics for human freedom.

Teaching the Catechism

At the beginning of this century, Catholic religious education meant teaching the catechism in school classrooms. The catechisms were compendiums of doctrinal teachings organized in question and answer format. The aim was to ensure orthodoxy of belief and uniformity of lifestyle. The choice of content for catechisms was governed by post-Reformation apologetical concerns; this content was little more than a simplified version of systematic scholastic theology.[81]

The method used to teach the catechism involved the memory, almost to the exclusion of the reason and feelings. The text was sometimes explained; the questions and answers would be recited or read by the teacher, and then analyzed and expressed in different words, with perhaps a few illustrations to try to make it more intelligible. After the exegesis, the students were expected to memorize the text and to be able to parrot it back in review sessions. This method demanded little brain-work and much rote-learning. In general, little accommodation was made for the capacity of the learner. Pedagogical efforts were geared toward the transmission of a set of "truths" from the catechism to the minds of children, even if, at this stage in life, they were unable to comprehend the meaning of the words which they were learning to speak. The emphasis was on accuracy of content, and that this content should be faithfully passed on to the next generation without any loss of its integrity.

Early in the present century, especially in Vienna and Munich, religion teachers became disenchanted with the old method. In 1912, a small group of catechists gathered in Vienna on the occasion of an International Eucharistic Congress. Influenced by advances in pedagogical technique in secular subjects, these catechists sought new methods of instruction that would respect the psychological make-up of the child.[82] Later, at a congress in Munich in 1928, the incipient catechetical movement gained impetus from the adoption of a method of teaching catechism which attempted in three steps to make the catechism text more related to the life of the student.[83] The fundamental inspiration for this new technique, called the "Munich method," came from Johann Friedrich Herbart (1776–1841), an educationalist and philosopher, who formulated a theory of teaching according to steps. Advances in psychology at the time had stressed that the child learns by first perceiving an object through the senses, then by understanding what is perceived, and finally by an act of the will leading to action. The Herbartian step-by-step movement in teaching was intended to correspond to this psychological learning pattern.[84]

Rather than start by explaining the text, the teacher using the "Munich method" began by presenting a visual aid or dramatic story to fire the imagination and memory of the student. Then certain notions would be singled out of the preliminary presentation; these would be the doctrinal or moral points from the catechism that the teacher wished to convey to the understanding of the children. Finally, a practical application would be made of these doctrinal or moral principles so the students could comprehend the connection with everyday life and be moved to action. Rather than use the "text-explanatory" method, teachers now used what came to be called the "text-developing" method. At this stage in the century, catechetical theorists retained their concern for purity of content, but they showed an increased interest in finding the right pedagogical technique to get the message across.

Kerygmatic Catechesis

Josef A. Jungmann (1889-1975).   A turning point came with Josef Jungmann's book *The Good News and Our Proclamation of the Faith* (1936).[85] Jungmann, an Austrian Jesuit, whose major contribution to scholarly research was in pastoral and liturgical studies, held a chair in pastoral theology at the University of Innsbruck for many years. His book was at first greeted with suspicion from the establishment, and was unfortunately withdrawn from circulation by the General of the Jesuits to placate the opposition. Despite the official disapproval, this book, with the other catechetical writings of Jungmann, became the basis for the kerygmatic movement in modern catechetics. Jungmann brought an end to the mentality that catechesis can be made successful simply by finding the right techniques to communicate the catechism. The problem, he said, was with the *content*. What was needed was a better understanding and more relevant presentation of the core of the Christian message.[86]

Jungmann's analysis arose out of his appreciation of the historical situation of the church in his time. He was convinced that the church in Europe was experiencing a movement from conventional Christianity to a Christianity based on personal commitment. He welcomed this transition as a sign that a new form of catechesis was necessary. Religious instruction based on the catechism had been sufficient in earlier times because Christianity had been imbibed as part of the culture into which one was initiated. This was the legacy of the Middle Ages, in which hardly any religious instruction was given to children; they grew up under the all-encompassing formative influence of the manners, customs, piety, and images of their environment. Now, said Jungmann, the church is entering an era in which it is again put on a missionary footing. The environment is no longer conducive to religious formation, and so there is a greater urgency to recapture the spirit of the early church in its proclamation of the central core of the Christian message, the saving love of God in the paschal mystery of Jesus Christ. Christians, Jungmann maintained, can no longer rely on conventional supports to nourish them and give them security; they must be given the opportunity of welcoming the love of God in Jesus in a wholehearted manner, so that they can live joyfully and confidently in the present age.[87]

Jungmann attacked "dry bones" scholastic intellectualism and called for a vital understanding of the core of the message. He made a sharp distinction between scholastic theology, which he understood as a logical, abstract, and deductive enterprise, and the proclamation of the faith, which he understood as oriented to life and engaging of the entire person. The catechisms existing at the time were compendiums of watered-down scholastic theology and did not order their material around the central core of the Christian message. The task of catechesis, said Jungmann, is to proclaim the joyful tidings of the Good News, stirring up faith, hope, and love in the hearts of the listeners. The catechisms, he said, had to be rewritten so that the doctrines are organized around the burning center of the good news.[88]

Jungmann's call to centering in the mystery of Christ involved not only the systematic exposition of the catechism. He regarded the liturgy as an integral part of catechesis, because it is a celebration of the mystery of Christ. He also regarded the scriptures as vitally important in catechesis, because they contain the story of salvation history which culminates in Christ. Telling this story is to introduce the listener into the saving history of God's people. Celebrating the liturgy is to become involved in the paschal mystery throughout the church year.[89] For this reason the biblical and liturgical revival, which was gaining impetus in Europe at the time, was a powerful stimulus to Jungmann's catechetical approach.

For teaching, Jungmann retained the "Munich method," adding two further pedagogical principles—"learning by doing," which came from Progressivism, and "personal experience," which stressed the engagement of the whole person, intellect, will, imagination, etc.[90]

Johannes Hofinger.   Johannes Hofinger, also an Austrian Jesuit, and one-time student of Jungmann, has probably done more than any other person to make his master's insights known throughout the world. From 1949 until recently, Hofinger was a member of the East Asian Pastoral Institute in Manila. He served as the director of the institute from 1957 to 1965. Hofinger has lectured extensively around the globe, and has consistently championed the kerygmatic cause. An indefatigable preacher, teacher, and organizer, Hofinger worked tirelessly at promoting the modern catechetical movement. He was the initiator of the six International Study Weeks on catechetics held in different locations around the world between 1959 and 1968. These study weeks brought together leading catechetical practitioners and theorists from many nations in order to share experiences of what had already happened and to formulate principles that would shape the future course of the movement.[91]

Hofinger strongly supported the shift from method to content. He stated that this shift involved three elements:

1. Concentrating all our teaching on the fundamental core of Christian doctrine which is Christ, who is *the* way to God our Father.
2. Presenting the whole Christian message as an organic unit in the light of this central theme.
3. Putting into relief the distinctive feature of Christian teaching, namely, that it heralds Good Tidings.[92]

In both *The Art of Teaching Christian Doctrine* (1957), written before the Second Vatican Council and in one of his later books, *Our Message is Christ* (1974), Hofinger showed an unswerving interest in the proclamation of the message.[93] In the later book, he endeavored to incorporate the spirit of the conciliar documents, and quoted liberally from the *General Catechetical Directory* (1971), but he still had the same principal concern as in the former book. In each of these works, Hofinger set out a way of presenting the fundamental doctrines of the faith in the light of the mystery of Christ. The greater part of both books was devoted to a summary of Christian doctrine arranged for teaching purposes. Each doctrine was elaborated in terms of its relation to the central mystery of God's love revealed for us in Christ. He insisted that ordering of the material must be according to theological criteria, rather than pedagogical or psychological criteria; and the value of any subject matter must be judged according to its relation to the core of the message itself.[94] Hofinger's preoccupation with the content of the message is undoubtedly his most valuable legacy to the catechetical movement.

Hofinger viewed the catechist as a messenger of Christ, called to communicate Christ's life, to lead people into a participation in his mystery. Teaching Christian doctrine, he said, is not an arid intellectual exercise, but involves heralding the Good News of Jesus Christ. The catechist's presentation should be designed to show that God has graciously invited his people to respond to his love throughout salvation history, and that this revelation finds its fulfillment in Jesus Christ.[95]

While Hofinger's concern for doctrine was paramount, he never intended it to be isolated from liturgical expression, biblical catechesis, or the testimony of Christian life. He subscribed to one of the principles enunciated by the Eichstätt study week, and reaffirmed at Bangkok, that there is a fourfold presentation of the Good News in catechesis—through liturgy, bible, doctrine, and Christian witness.[96] These four "signs," or "languages," of catechesis have their roots in Jungmann's works, and were popularized by the Lumen Vitae school, especially in its international journal carrying the same title.[97] The four "signs" were considered necessary for catechesis for the following reasons. The bible relates the wonderful works of God in salvation history; therefore, catechesis must involve a narration of biblical events. The liturgy celebrates the redemptive events in the history of God's people, especially the paschal mystery; therefore, catechesis must involve participation in the liturgy. The church's doctrine embodies the message of salvation; therefore, catechesis must involve systematic presentation of this message. The life of the church is the continuation of the redeeming work of God in Jesus; therefore, catechesis must involve the testimony of the Christian life of believers.

In Germany, the kerygmatic approach found embodiment in the "green catechism" (1955), which was translated into thirty languages.[98] In the same year that the "green catechism" became mandatory in Germany, Johannes Hofinger made his first lecture tour in the U.S.[99] In the following years a plethora of manuals and textbooks appeared based on the kerygmatic approach.[100]

Gerard S. Sloyan.   An important figure in this kerygmatic renewal in the U.S. was Gerard Sloyan. Sloyan's efforts were directed towards promoting the biblical and liturgical revival, as well as raising the standard of priestly homilies. During the decade of kerygmatic ascendancy in the U.S., Sloyan was head of the Department of Religious Education at the Catholic University of America, a post he relinquished in 1967. His commitment to liturgical renewal was expressed in his presidency of the Liturgical Conference (1962–64). Sloyan was also highly regarded by the theological community, being for two years president of the College Theology Society (1966–68).

Sloyan served as a mediator between the burgeoning catechetical movement in the U.S. and its European counterpart. In 1958 he edited a collection of articles entitled *Shaping the Christian Message,* containing the work of numerous European scholars.[101] Some of these scholars, such as Jungmann, Hofinger, and Francis Drinkwater, were already beginning to be known in the U.S., but others, such as Joseph Colomb, François Coudreau, Georges Delcuve, and Pierre Ranwez, were newcomers to the American scene. Sloyan later edited another similar volume in 1962, called *Modern Catechetics,* but in this volume it was noticeable that American writers figured more prominently, an indication of the growing number of catechists in the U.S.

receiving specialized training.[102] It was no coincidence that the subtitle to this second volume was "Message and Method in Religious Formation," since catechetical theorists at the time were still thinking in terms of the duality of content and method.

Sloyan also served as an eloquent opponent of the "Baltimore Catechism," which had been revised as late as 1941, and was still widely in use even after the Second Vatican Council.[103] He argued that the 1941 revision was theologically, biblically, and pedagogically inadequate. It was theologically inadequate, said Sloyan, because it viewed revelation as a set of propositions handed down from the original deposit. And it viewed faith simply as an intellectual adherence to these propositions. It was biblically inadequate, he said, because it was still a *summa theologica*, untouched by the "return to the sources" already afoot by 1941. It was pedagogically inadequate because it gave the answers before the questions were asked, overlooking the fact that the questions have to be the students' questions arising out of their existential situation.[104]

Antecedents to an Anthropological Approach

The turn toward catechesis as the interpretation of human experience, which took place in the sixties, had historical antecedents in the concept of "pre-evangelization" and in the principle of *catéchisme progressif*. It was the French school in particular that had a tradition of taking seriously the person's psychological and sociological situation. Alfonso Nebreda, himself heavily influenced by the French school, relates that at Eichstätt there was much argument between the German kerygmatists, who emphasized the approach taken in the German catechism, and the French and Belgian contingent, who wanted more stress upon the uniqueness of personal development.[105] French catechesis had never been fully converted to the purely historical, biblical,

and liturgical approach favored by the Germans. They had bene-
fited from empirical psychological research and, as a result, had
stressed a catechesis according to age levels. They were not im-
pressed with a catechetical approach that simply presented a
lesson on biblical history. The unique situation of the persons
catechized had to be taken into account, evaluated, and expressed in catechesis.

Pre-evangelization.   In the late forties and early fifties, French
pastoral theologians and catechists became increasingly aware of
the "de-Christianization" of their country under the pressures of
a new technological era. They began to realize that the church in
France must become again a "missionary" church, and they
looked to Catholic Action to be the vanguard of this new evangelical thrust.[106] In this context, Pierre Liégé used the word
"pre-evangelization." It was obvious that the proclamation of the
Good News in itself was falling on deaf ears, so Liégé set about
analyzing the obstacles that prevented people responding
wholeheartedly in faith to the gospel. The first type of obstacle,
he said, was bad dispositions of the heart, such as prejudice or
boredom. A second barrier preventing people from joyfully receiving the good news, according to Liégé, was caused by inhuman social and cultural conditions. Pre-evangelization, said
Liégé, must address itself to overcoming both those obstacles
by creating favorable internal dispositions and attempting to
change inhuman social, cultural, and economic conditions.
Liégé considered that the Catholic Action movement was well
equipped to accomplish both tasks because it involved lay people
working in the secular world, witnessing to Christian values, and
acting as leaven in the midst to humanize social structures.[107]

This anthropocentric approach of Liégé had been overlooked
during the Eichstätt conference in 1960, when concentration
upon the kerygma, as the content of the message, had clouded
any consideration of the persons who were to receive the mes-

sage. The reaction to the purely kerygmatic approach came swiftly, especially in missionary countries. The high-minded German "kerygma" had to face "adaptation to the present human situation." For this task, French catechesis had been better prepared. Only two years after Eichstätt, the East Asian Study Week on Mission Catechetics was held in Bangkok, Thailand (1962). There the word and the concept "pre-evangelization" came into its own. Missionary catechesis was described as no longer a concern for some churches in so-called "mission lands" and not for others. All churches are missionary, and should engage in missionary catechesis. The principles of Eichstätt were reaffirmed, but the process of catechesis was described in three stages: pre-evangelization, evangelization, and catechesis proper. The first stage was addressed to unbelievers and aimed to prepare the ground by removing prejudice and arousing interest. The method was to be dialogical and anthropocentric. The second stage involved challenging prepared unbelievers with the gospel message; this is proclamation of the Good News and is Christocentric in nature. The third stage involved instruction, formation and initiation into the Christian life by a detailed elaboration of Christian doctrine, always oriented to the core of the message.[108]

If Johannes Hofinger was the "apostle of the kerygma" in the United States, Alfonso Nebreda was the apostle of "pre-evangelization." Nebreda had studied under Liégé at the Paris Institute for Pastoral Catechetics and had written a doctoral thesis on the topic of pre-evangelization at the Gregorian University in Rome. In 1965, he wrote a book with the dramatic title *Kerygma in Crisis?* In this book, he asked whether the kerygmatic approach is sufficient. He called for a nuancing of the kerygmatic approach by a "kind of threshold apologetics," a phrase equivalent to "pre-evangelization for the sake of the kerygma."[109] Good apologetics, said Nebreda, does not appeal to abstract, formal reasoning, but takes into consideration the person to whom one speaks. It takes the human person where he/she is. The first goal, he said, is to establish a real human dialogue by approaching men and women "shut in by culture prejudices, sociological ties, and psychological patterns."[110] The dialogue should have respect for the freedom of the other; it is a type of inviting, appealing, knocking at the door, hoping to loosen the earth so the seed may be planted and take root at a later date. In pre-evangelization, argued Nebreda, psychology has priority over logic; but pre-evangelization is never an end in itself, it is always geared toward preparing the way for the kerygma. Nebreda has always insisted that pre-evangelization, evangelization, and catechesis are not necessarily in strict chronological sequence; catechists in a secularized situation can find themselves performing at different times these three tasks with the same group.[111]

Nebreda's approach to catechesis became the predominant accent of the East Asian Pastoral Institute after 1965, when he inherited its directorship from Johannes Hofinger. The institute had been founded in Manila by Hofinger in 1953, and had been a strong influence in the dissemination of the central principles of kerygmatic catechesis.[112] Under Nebreda, the institute formulated goals consonant with its director's interests. The new aim became "to render missionaries, laity, and religious capable of setting up an intelligent dialogue with the Asiatic community today."[113] There was concern to equip a missionary with a knowledge of the traditions, customs, folklore, religious practices, and social-political conditions of the people with whom they would be working as catechists.

Joseph Colomb: Catéchisme Progressif. French catechesis had also prepared the way for the turn toward the human dimension in catechesis by studies in developmental psychology. One of the most prominent French catechists, Joseph Colomb, had, in the late forties and early fifties, popularized the principle of adaptation to human needs and psychological states, a principle that catechists in the United States, rebounding in the late sixties from the exaltation of the kerygmatic approach, rediscovered with delight. As early as 1950, Joseph Colomb had written a three-volume catechism, with accompanying teacher's manuals, which he entitled *Catéchisme progressif.* [114] The distinguishing feature of this catechism was that it presented a progressive program according to the age level of the child. The content was ordered, not according to a theological system, but according to the chronological development of the child and the religious needs of each respective age. [115] This series and other publications of Colomb were widely read and used. Colomb absorbed the main lines of the turn to liturgical and biblical content, and was intent upon promoting living doctrine, within the context of the church's witness—the concerns of the kerygmatic movement. [116] However, his attention to the psychological development of the human person made him somewhat of a pathfinder for anthropological catechesis. He also shared with his fellow Frenchmen a concern for the freedom of the child. It was not just a matter of preserving and transmitting the formulas of the past and encouraging loyalty to these; rather, it was a matter of developing free persons who can make a genuine faith response. [117]

The *catéchisme progressif* came up against stiff opposition from the French Episcopal Commission on Religious Teaching in 1957, which announced certain "corrections" that had to be made. The commission, an arm of the French episcopacy, denounced as fallacious any attempt, on psychological or pedagogical grounds alone, to omit doctrines such as original sin and the divinity of Christ from the catechisms for small children. The commission went on to say:

> Very small children will be taught, in a global way at least, the fundamental truths. When they reach the age of reason, these truths will be presented more and more explicitly and be explained more and more widely. In this way teaching will be complete from the

beginning and progress will bear only on the explanation of religious truths and the manner of presenting them.[118]

To avoid what it considered to be ambiguous, the commission called for the suppression of the term *catéchisme progressif.*

In his most important and mature work, *Le service de l'Evangile,* written after the controversy, Colomb does not retract his position but makes a distinction between *le programme concentrique* and *le programme progressif.*[119] The first type of program seems close to what the bishops proposed. The same materials are developed each time with greater explication. It can be represented to the imagination as a series of concentric circles. The inner circle contains the essential data and essential formulas and these are elaborated more explicitly as the years go by. Colomb could see some value in this approach, but he claimed it fails because it does not respect the psychological progression of the person. It does not incorporate the principle of adaptation to the mental and emotional state of the person at different age levels. As Colomb said: "The progression is not required by the intrinsic difficulty of the mysteries to be taught but by human feebleness."[120] By this he meant that the governing criterion for progression has nothing to do with the content; rather, the governing criterion is the development that is occurring in the mental state of the person. Colomb agreed that the entire message should be proclaimed at each step, but he insisted that the presentation and organization of the material must be consonant with the particular psychological level of the child.

Efforts to Bridge the Gap Between the Divine Word and Human Existence

Kerygmatic theorists, who also wanted to stress the value of human experience in itself, were caught in a dilemma. On the one hand, they felt bound in fidelity to the "word of God" which is proclaimed in the great events of salvation history, and is revealed in scriptures and re-presented in liturgy. On the other hand, they were beginning to see that the age, disposition, and concrete situation of the person were factors that cannot be overlooked in catechesis. While giving primacy to the divine word, they were, to some degree, growing in awareness that this word must meet a human person according to the person's mode of present existence. A type of dualism arose in their thinking, between allegiance to God or allegiance to man. Two representatives of this dualistic thinking, who ultimately, each in his own way, opted more for the kerygma than for the human person, are Josef Goldbrunner and Marcel Van Caster.

Josef Goldbrunner, a German pastoral psychologist and catechetical theorist, had a strong background in Jungian psychology; three of his early works testify to this: *Holiness is Wholeness* (1955), *Individuation* (1956), and *Cure of Mind and Cure of Soul* (1958).[121] His anthropology was a combination of depth psychology and existentialist philosophy.[122] Both existential philosophy and depth psychology, said Goldbrunner, attempt to show how existence can be taken hold of, how a person is actuated and becomes authentic.[123] Individuals, he said, realize themselves within close personal relationships; hence, the focus of the pastoral effort of the church should be upon the individual way of redemption. There is a need for creating a personal atmosphere of fellowship within the church so individuals have room to grow.[124]

However, for Goldbrunner, the efforts to facilitate personal development are simply a way of creating the preconditions for the favorable entry of the kerygma. Goldbrunner was adamant that "revelation cannot be discovered; it can only be proclaimed, that is, authoritatively proclaimed and listened to."[125] Efforts at psychological formation are in the service of the proclamation of the word. At Eichstätt, Goldbrunner presented a paper entitled

"Cathechetical Method as Handmaid of Kerygma." The method, said Goldbrunner, "aims at the encounter of human reality with the reality of the divine message."[126] Despite Goldbrunner's sophisticated anthropology, he maintained a method whereby one attempts to open the situation, ready the human heart, and then inject the words of Christ.[127] Elsewhere, Goldbrunner spoke of the interior realization of the subject matter presented in the proclamation as an "incarnation." "The task of Christian pastoral care and religious education," he said, "is to encourage the incarnation of the divine life in man.... To condition human existence to be receptive to divine life ...."[128]

Throughout his works, Goldbrunner labored with an extrinsic theology of relevation,[129] while trying at the same time to establish a partnership between this theology and his anthropology. The closest he came to any reconciliation between the two was in his elaboration of the future dimension of catechesis. The message of the kingdom of God, said Goldbrunner, offers liberation from the past and opens the person to fuller self-realization. The future kingdom revealed in the gospels corresponds to the ultimate striving of the human psyche. Catechesis stimulates a person's desire for self-realization and opens the way for the gospel proclamation. Thus, it serves the realization of the kingdom.[130]

Marcel Van Caster, the second representative of this dualistic trend, is a professor at the International Center for Studies in Religious Education in Brussels, Belgium. Over the years he has been a prolific contributor to *Lumen Vitae*, of which he is one of the editors. Like Goldbrunner, he was one of the early pathfinders in the application of personalist philosophy and encounter theology to kerygmatic catechetics. Throughout his writings he struggled with the problem: What is the primary aim of the catechist—to proclaim the kerygma for today's world, or to invite the human person to discover the presence of God in daily life? Does one have to make a choice between fidelity to the kerygma and fidelity to human experience? Like Goldbrunner, he turned toward the anthropological perspective, but still maintained a supernaturalist kerygmatic theology. He was never able to fully throw off the world-view that he inherited as an early kerygmatist.

As Van Caster tussled with the tension between the revelation, already given in the "signs," and his conviction that catechesis may well begin in authentic human experience, there was a development in his thought. In his earlier writings, he would not allow for the secular to be a manifestation of God's revealing presence, except as a shadowy pointer, or "summons."[131] Revelation remained extrinsic to human experience. In his later writings, Van Caster was able to give greater credibility to human experience by stating: "Revelation is not purely extrinsic to man's life and thought; but is both intrinsic to human experience and transcendental to this experience."[132] Now he was more confident that God acts in the ordinary events of life.

Van Caster pointed to the one-sidedness of an anthropology that views the human person as a passive recipient of the Good News. The human person, he said, is also creative in faith response. He could see that a purely kerygmatic approach could lead to a catechesis for conformity. It needs to be complemented by the "life-situation" or "experience centered" approach which stresses the importance of the self-transcendence of the person and the possibility of personal creativity in response to the good news. Both approaches are needed. Van Caster summarized his attempted synthesis by stating: "Christian meaning of life (as content of faith) is partly 'already given' by God and partly 'still to be given' by man, who brings into play the creativity entrusted to him by God."[134]

CONCLUSION

As long as theorists maintained a supernaturalist kerygmatic world view, they found it impossible to successfully incorporate human experience. Human experience was employed as a "starting point" for the journey back to the word of God proclaimed in the wonderful works of God recorded in scripture, or as a "springboard" launching the catechized upwards toward contact with the descending word of God. Often the human situation was expounded colorfully and attractively, only to have the leaden "word" parachuted in at the last moment to "save the day." Or, on the other hand, sometimes a human event or value was dealt with extensively, but the connection with scriptural revelation was never made. Theorists were challenged to shed their extrincist view of revelation and to devise a new unity of the "divine word" and "human experience," of "content" and "method."

NOTES FOR CHAPTER 1

1. Wayne R. Rood, *Understanding Christian Education* (Nashville: Abingdon Press, 1970), p. 11. This title has become ambiguous. Bushnell has been claimed as the predecessor of the early religious education movement, with its "liberal" presuppositions. On the other hand, "nurture" theorists such as Rood tend to downplay any "liberalism" that can be found in Bushnell, and point to his emphasis on scripture, family, and church as the primary elements of Christian education. For an example of the first opinion, see A. J. Wm. Myers, *Horace Bushnell and Religious Education* (Boston: Manthorne and Burrack, 1937), p. 144. For an example of the latter position, see Garland Knott, "Bushnell Re-visited." *Religious Education* 64 (July–August 1969): 294. Whatever conclusion one draws about Bushnell's inherent liberalism, it is undoubtedly true that his work has inadvertently had a profound influence on the consequent shape of Protestant Christian nurture.

2. Horace Bushnell, *Christian Nurture* (New Haven: Yale University Press, 1967), p. 4. The first edition of this book was published as *Views of Christian Nurture and Subjects Adjacent Thereto* (Hartford: Edwin Hunt, 1847).

3. Marvin J. Taylor, "A Historical Introduction to Religious Education," in *Religious Education: A Comprehensive Survey*, ed. Marvin J. Taylor (New York: Abingdon Press, 1960), p. 18.

4. See the *Proceedings of the First Convention of the Religious Education Association* (Chicago, 1903). The movement of religious education found an organizational body in the association, but it would be incorrect to identify the association with the movement, which was a broader phenomenon.

5. *The Aims of Religious Education*. The Proceedings of the Third Annual Convention of the Religious Education Association, Boston (Chicago: Religious Education Association, 1905), p. 474.

6. This list does not claim to be exhaustive. It is composed mainly from the characteristics listed by H. Shelton Smith, *Faith and Nurture* (New York: Charles Scribner's Sons, 1950), pp. 5–26, and the features given by Knott, "Bushnell Re-visited," pp. 291–96.

7. H. F. Cope, "Twenty Years' Progress in Religious Education," *Religious Education* 18 (1923): 307–16.

8. *The New Catholic Encyclopedia* 1967 ed. s.v. "Social Gospel," by E. Duff.

9. Charles Howard Hopkins, *The Rise of the Social Gospel in American Protestantism 1865–1915* (New Haven: Yale University Press, 1940), pp. 320–22.

10. John Dewey, *Democracy and Education* (New York: The Free Press, 1966). Dewey defined education as "that reconstruction and reorganization of experience which adds to the meaning of experience, and which increases ability to direct the course of subsequent experience" (p. 76). The educator's part in the enterprise was "to furnish the environment which stimulates responses and directs the learner's course (p. 180). This theory of education flows out of his philosophy of thinking within experiencing.

11. J. Donald Butler, *Religious Education: The Foundations and Practice of Nurture* (New York: Harper and Row, 1962), pp. 107–108.

12. Dewey had a love-hate relationship with progressivism. While he contributed more than anyone else to its powerful thrust, he dissociated himself from it as a movement, and he was especially critical of its excesses. See *Dewey on Education: Selections*, ed. Martin S. Dworkin (New York: Bureau of Publications, 1959), p. 10. Dewey's relationship with the Religious Education Association was also ambivalent. He gave a major address at its opening meeting, but gradually drifted out of the movement, since his primary interest was the improvement of secular education. See John Dewey, "Religious Education as Conditioned by Modern Psychology," in *The Proceedings of the First Convention of the Religious Association* (Chicago, 1903), pp. 60–66.

13. An overview of the works and orientations of these three theorists can be found in Harold William Burgess, *An Invitation to Religious Education* (Birmingham, Al.: Religious Education Press, 1975), pp. 59–87. Burgess classifies them as representative of the "socio-cultural" approach to religious education.

14. Paul H. Vieth, *Objectives in Religious Education* (New York: Harper and Brothers, 1930), pp. 80–88.

15. The last two major objectives (VI and VII) deal with the church and the bible, respectively. Vieth comments that these are on a "lower plane of importance than the remaining five." See *Objectives in Religious Education*, p.89.

16. Kendig Brubaker Cully, *The Search for a Christian Education Since 1940* (Philadelphia: The Westminster Press, 1965), p. 14, and J. Donald Butler, *Religious Education*, p. 117. Cully's thesis has been especially influential in shaping the perspective taken in the following account of this transition.

17. Harrison S. Elliott, *Can Religious Education be Christian?* (New York: The Macmillan Company, 1940).

18. Ibid., pp. 1–11.

19. Ibid., p. 315.

20. Ibid., p. 319.

21. George Albert Coe, *A Social Theory of Religious Education* (New York: Charles Scribner's Sons, 1927), pp. 25–26. Harold Burgess says of Coe that he "may well have been the most widely read and followed Protestant religious educational thinker during the first half of the twentieth century." See *Invitation to Religious Education*, p. 64. For this reason, Coe's understanding of freedom can be considered representative of the religious education movement.

22. Ibid., p. 338. The term "democracy of God" was used by Coe to refer to the divine-human society whose dynamic was divine love. For Coe, the creation of this kingdom was the object of social endeavor, and the ultimate purpose of religious education.

23. Ibid., p. 339.

24. Ibid., p. 342.

25. H. Shelton Smith, *Faith and Nurture* (New York: Charles Scribner's Sons, 1950).

26. Ibid., p. vii.

27. Ibid., p. 69.

28. Ibid., p. 97.

29. Ibid., pp. 34–38.

30. Ibid., p. 84.

31. Ibid., p. 137.

32. Ibid., p. 139.

33. Ibid., pp. 145–46.

34. Randolph Crump Miller, *The Clue to Christian Education* (New York: Charles Scribner's Sons, 1950), p. vii.

35. Ibid., p. 15.

36. Randolph Crump Miller, *Christian Nurture and the Church* (New York: Charles Scribner's Sons, 1961), pp. 59–60.

37. Idem, *Education for Christian Living,* 2d ed. (Englewood Cliffs, N.J.: Prentice-Hall, Inc., 1963), p. 7.

38. D. Campbell Wyckoff, *The Task of Christian Education* (Philadelphia: The Westminster Press, 1955), p. 23.

39. Ibid., p. 24.

40. Ibid., pp. 61.-62.

41. D. Campbell Wyckoff, *The Gospel and Christian Education: A Theory of Christian Education for Our Times* (Philadelphia: The Westminster Press, 1959), p. 98.

42. Ibid., p. 109.

43. Ibid., p. 106.

44. James D. Smart, *The Teaching Ministry of the Church: An Examination of the Basic Principle of Christian Education* (Philadelphia: Westminster Press, 1954).

45. Ibid., pp. 26-27.

46. Ibid., p. 19.

47. Ibid., p. 101; see also p. 91.

48. Ibid., p. 112.

49. Ibid., pp. 165-66.

50. Ibid., p. 167.

51. Ibid., p. 117.

52. William Bedford Williamson, *Language and Concepts in Christian Education* (Philadelphia: The Westminster Press, 1970), pp. 77 ff.

53. Miller, *Education for Christian Living*, pp. 70-72.

54. Haim Gordon, "Martin Buber's Impact on Religious Education: Reflections on the Centennial of His Birth," *Religious Education* 72 (November-December 1977): 586. Gordon gives the characteristics of "dialogical education" as the meeting of personalities, the quest for simplicity, and rejecting the superficial. For a critical perspective on Buber's impact, see Eugene B. Borowitz. "Education is not I-Thou," *Religious Education* 66 (September-October 1971); 326-31. The author claims many Christian educators have trivialized Buber by equating the "encounter" in education with the I-Thou relationship. Buber, he says, stressed the "role" of the teacher; the teacher-student relationship, according to Buber, is not one of friendship per se.

55. Martin Buber, *I and Thou*, 2d ed., with postscript by author added, trans. Ronald Gregor Smith (New York: Charles Scribner's Sons, 1958), pp. 8-9.

56. Martin Buber, "Education," in *Between Man and Man* (New York: The Macmillan Company, 1965); and Reuel Howe, *The Miracle of Dialogue* (New York: The Seabury Press, 1963), p. vii.

57. Buber, *Between Man and Man*, pp. 96-97.

58. Reuel Howe, *Man's Need and God's Action* (New York: The Seabury Press, 1953), p. 114.

59. Ibid., p. 73.

60. Ibid., p. 10.

61. Ibid., p. 21.

62. Howe, *The Miracle of Dialogue*, p. 37.

63. Martin Buber, "Education of Character," in *Between Man and Man* (New York: The Macmillan Company, 1965), p. 107.

64. Howe, *Man's Need and God's Action*, p. 119.

65. David Hunter, *Christian Education as Engagement* (New York: The Seabury Press, 1963), p. 31.

66. Ibid., p. 27.

67. Ibid., p. 28.

68. Ibid., p. 7.

69. Ibid., pp. 62–63.

70. Ibid., p. 73.

71. Ibid., p. 76.

72. For my understanding of Sherrill, I am indebted to a dissertation by Maureen Murphy, *The Contribution of the Psychological Approach of Lewis Joseph Sherrill to the Twentieth Century American Religious Educational Scene* (Ann Arbor, Mich.: University Microfilms, 1973). Since a later chapter will deal with Sherrill more extensively, he is given only brief treatment here.

73. Lewis Joseph Sherrill, *The Gift of Power* (New York: The Macmillan Company, 1955), p. 21.

74. Ibid., pp. 28–30.

75. Ibid., p. 45.

76. Wayne R. Rood, *On Nurturing Christians: Perhaps a Manifesto for Education* (Nashville: Abingdon Press, 1968), pp. 27–37. Rood's emphasis on dialogue could easily have placed him in the section on relationships.

77. Rood, *On Nurturing Christians*, pp. 69–94.

78. Ibid., pp. 95–118.

79. Ibid., pp. 119–44.

80. See Mary Charles Bryce, "Four Decades of Roman Catholic Innovators," *Religious Education* 73, Special Edition (September–October 1978): s36–s56.

81. The Reformation was a watershed in the history of catechetics. With the introduction of the first printing press by John Gutenberg in 1438, and the increased literacy of the general population, the time was ripe for a transition from communication of the faith by an oral tradition to handing on doctrines in the literary genre of the *catechism*. Martin Luther was a key figure in precipitating the catechism movement. His popular catechism, noted for its conciseness and lucidity, and its question and answer style, was imitated by other Reformation figures. The proliferation of such "erroneous" catechisms provoked a rebuttal from Counter-Reformation forces. Three of the most influential Counter-Reformation catechisms have been Peter Canisius' *Catechismus Minor seu Parvus Catholicorum* (1589), Trent's *Catechismus Romanus* (1566), and Robert Bellarmine's *De Dottrina Christiana* (1597). Bellarmine's catechism, in particular, gained rapid and widespread popularity, becoming the most commonly used catechism in mission areas.

In the United States, the most famous catechism in existence at the turn of the present century was the "Baltimore Catechism," a compendium prepared and enjoined by the Third Plenary Council of Baltimore (1885). It exhibited the classic features of the catechism genre. Mary Charles Bryce has pointed out that the catechism genre failed to impart the wholeness of the church's teaching, first, because of the effort to be precise and economize on words, and, second, because of the defensive emphasis on doctrines under attack by the Reformers, thus often missing other doctrines of greater importance. See Mary Charles Bryce, *The Influence of the Catechism of the Third Plenary Council of Baltimore on Widely Used Elementary Religious Text Books from Its Composition in 1885 to Its 1941 Revision* (Ann Arbor, Mich.: University Microfilms, 1972).

82. The new opportunities that advances in psychology and pedagogy offered to religious instruction prompted the Vienna conference to plan for a follow-up congress to be held in Munich. See A. M. Fuerst, *The Systematic Teaching of Religion* (New York: Benziger Brothers, 1939), p. 96. Gerard Sloyan alludes to these congresses in an illuminating survey of the modern catechetical movement. See Gerard Sloyan, "Developments in Religious Education Since 1800," *The Living Light* 2 (Winter 1965–66): 83.

83. At the Munich congress, the participants represented different nations, but the speeches were almost all in German, given by German catechetical experts. See *Katechetische Blätter* 54 (September–October 1928): 369–84.

84. Josef Jungmann gives a good presentation of the origin and function of the "Munich method" in his discussion on general catechetical method. See Josef Jungmann, *Handing on the Faith: A Manual of Catechetics* (New York: Herder and Herder, 1959), pp. 180–93. Jungmann describes how Otto Willman (d. 1920), a pupil of Ziller, modified the Herbartian steps, and this modified form was adopted by the Munich congress.

85. The original German title was *Die Frohbotschaft und Unsere Glaubensverkundigung* (1936). The English version was translated, abridged, and edited by William A. Huesman, under the initiative and general editorship of Johannes Hofinger. See Josef Andreas Jungmann, *The Good News Yesterday and Today* (New York: W. H. Sadlier, Inc., 1962).

86. Johannes Hofinger has included in the English version of *The Good News* an account of the reception of the original book and its impact on the catechetical movement. See Johannes Hofinger, "J. A. Jungmann (1889–1975): In Memoriam." *The Living Light* 13 (Fall 1976): 350–59. For an authoritative account of the use of salvation history in catechetics see Mary C. Boys *Biblical Interpretation in Religious Education* (Birmingham, Alabama: Religious Education Press, 1980).

87. Jungmann, *The Good News: Yesterday and Today*, pp. 3–8 Jungmann's study of catechesis in the Middle Ages also illustrates this point. See Josef A. Jungmann, "Religious Education in Late Mediaeval Times," in *Shaping the Christian Message: Essays in Religious Education*, ed. Gerard S. Sloyan (New York: The Macmillan Company, 1958), pp. 38–62.

88. Ibid., p. 33.

89. Ibid., pp. 114–31.

90. Jungmann, *Handing on the Faith*, pp. 193–216.

91. These study weeks were held at Nijmegen (1959), Eichstätt (1960), Bangkok (1962), Katigondo (1964), Manila (1967), and Medellin (1968). Luis Erdozain has given a helpful overview of the evolution of thought within these sessions. See Luis Erdozain, "The Evolution of Catechetics," *Lumen Vitae* 25 (1970): 7–31.

92. Johannes Hofinger (in collaboration with William J. Reedy), *The ABC's of Modern Catechetics* (New York: William H. Sadlier, Inc., 1962), p. 9.

93. Johannes Hofinger, *The Art of Teaching Christian Doctrine: The Good News and Its Proclamation* (Notre Dame, Indiana.: University of Notre Dame Press, 1957); and *Our Message is Christ: The More Outstanding Elements of the Christian Message* (Notre Dame, Indiana: Fides Publishers, 1974).

94. For example, *Our Message is Christ*, p. 17; *The Art of Teaching Christian Doctrine*, p. 55.

95. For example, *The Art of Teaching Christian Doctrine*, p.7. In the later book, he uses the language of "herald," but stresses the need for "laying the foundations" first. See *Our Message is Christ*, p. 13.

96. The Eichstätt study week was the high point of kerygmatic catechesis. For the proceedings of Eichstätt, see *Teaching All Nations: A Symposium on Modern Catechetics*, ed. Johannes Hofinger (New York: Herder and Herder, 1961), pp. 394–400. These basic kerygmatic principles were reaffirmed at Bangkok. See Alfonso Nebreda, "East Asian Study Week on Mission Catechetics: Bangkok (Oct. 31–Nov. 3, 1962)," *Lumen Vitae* 17 (December 1962): 717–30. It would be an oversimplification to claim that the four "signs" represent the kerygmatic movement *in toto*. The inclusion of the four signs in the final conclusions of Eichstätt was a compromise measure that did not receive the approval of all. See Alfonso Nebreda, "Some Reflections on Father Gleeson's Paper on History and Present Scene in Religious Education," *Teaching All Nations*, 11, no. 2 (1974); 85.

97. "Lumen Vitae" is the popular title of the International Center for Studies in Religious Education in Brussels, Belgium. Originally it was a center of research and study, set up by the Jesuit Faculty of Theology at Louvain in 1935, under the title of "Catechetical Documentary Center." The most famous product of the early center was a descriptive international bibliography published in 1937 as *Où en est l'enseignement religieux?* In 1946, the center left Louvain for Brussels, and launched the international review, *Lumen Vitae*. The center, under the leadership of Georges Delcuve and Pierre Ranwez, promoted national and international gatherings of catechists. The many international contacts have led to establishment of associated centers in many countries throughout the world. See Jean Pelissier, "The International Centre: 'Lumen Vitae'." *Lumen Vitae* 15 (June 1960): 217–30. For an indication of how the Lumen Vitae center popularized the four "signs," see *Lumen Vitae* 10 (January–March

1955) on the bible as narrative of salvation history; 10 (April–September 1955) on the liturgy as representation of salvation history; and 10 (October–December 1955) on doctrine as the message of salvation. For an indication of the change in tone of the journal in recent years, see Jean Bouvy, "Editorial: On Re-reading the Review 'Lumen Vitae' from 1965 to 1975," *Lumen Vitae* 30, nos. 3–4 (1975): 303–22.

98. The English translation was entitled *The Catholic Catechism*, trans. Clifford Howell (New York: Herder and Herder, 1957). See Josef Jungmann, "The New German Catechism: A Manual Presentation of the Message of Salvation," *Lumen Vitae* 10 (October–December 1955): 573–86. Also, Johannes Hofinger, "The Catechism Yesterday and Today," *Lumen Vitae* 11 (July–September 1956): 479–86.

99. Hofinger was invited to The University of Notre Dame to participate in their summer liturgy program. It was at the initiative of the liturgy program that the University of Notre Dame Press published the *Art of Teaching Christian Doctrine* in 1957. See Johannes Hofinger, "The Place of the Good News in Modern Catechetics," in *The Good News*, p. 181.

100. Among them was a manual by a Canadian catechist, Emmett Carter, who had been present at Eichstätt. At the time, Hofinger called it "surely the most remarkable we have at present in North America." See Gerald Emmett Carter, *The Modern Challenge to Religious Education* (New York: Sadlier, 1961), and Johannes Hofinger, "America's First Kerygmatic Manual of Catechetics," *Lumen Vitae* 16 (March 1961): 536–40. One of the most influential textbook series to emerge at the time was written under Hofinger's guidance. It was published first in three grades with accompanying teacher's guides. See Sister Maria de la Cruz and Sister Mary Richard, *On Our Way Series, Grade One: With Christ to the Father; Grade Two: Christ's Life in Us; Grade Three: Christ Our Savior* (New York: W. H. Sadlier, 1957–59).

101. *Shaping the Christian Message: Essays in Religious Education*, ed. Gerard S. Sloyan (New York: The Macmillan Company, 1958).

102. *Modern Catechetics: Message and Method in Religious Formation*, ed. Gerard S. Sloyan (New York: The Macmillan Company, 1960).

103. The revision of the Baltimore catechism involved a departure from the sequential treatment of content in the original edition. The original edition had followed the order set by Trent (creed, sacraments, commandments), which had the theological advantage of placing the sacraments at the heart of the Christian mystery. The revised order placed the commandments before the sacraments (creed, commandments, sacraments). The sacraments were therefore treated as merely supernatural aids for doing good works. The significance of this change should not be overplayed, since the users of the original Baltimore catechism were probably not aware of the theological implications of the centrality of the sacraments in the text. Even in that text, the sacraments were described as sources of grace and not as redemptive events of salvation. See

Bryce, *The Influence of the Catechism of the Third Plenary Council*, pp. 201, 231–32.

104. Gerard S. Sloyan, "Religious Education as a Correlate of 'Religious Knowledge': Some Problem Areas," in *Speaking of Religious Education* (New York: Herder and Herder, 1968), pp. 15–26. This article first appeared in *Religious Education* 61 (July–August 1966): 286–91, 298.

105. See Nebreda, "Some Reflections on Father Gleeson's Paper," p. 85.

106. For example, Emmanuel Cardinal Suhard, *Growth or Decline? The Church Today*, trans. James J. Corbett (Chicago: Fides Publishers, 1948), pp. 56–57, 60–61, 86–87. See also Henri Godin and Y. Daniel, *La France Pays de Mission?* (Paris: Les Editions du Cerf, 1950).

Catholic Action refers to a mode of organization and mobilization of Catholic laity for apostolic works. Under Pope Pius XI, and later with Pius XII, Catholic Action gained a charter, and a spirit of apocalyptic urgency. It referred primarily to action or work of the laity which was organized, apostolic, and done as an extension of the apostolate of the hierarchy. In Italy, Catholic Action aimed at establishing better relations between church and government, as well as reviving Catholic practice among the negligent. In Belgium, Jocism aimed to Christianize economic and social institutions through Joseph Cardijn's formula of "see, judge, and act". In France, the situation was complicated by the existence of *Action Francaise*, a political movement associated with the brilliant writer Charles Maurras. He preached a return to monarchy in France and attracted many Catholic followers. While Pius X showed initial sympathy for the *Action Francaise*, in 1926 Pius XI forbad Catholic participation. The condemnation of *Action Francaise* cleared the way for Catholic Action of a missionary nature to take root in France. Contemporary theology of the laity questions the necessity of a hierarchical mandate for genuine lay participation in the mission of the church. See D. J. Geaney, "Catholic Action," in *New Catholic Encyclopedia* Vol. III, (New York: McGraw-Hill Book Company, 1967), pp. 262–263.

107. P. A. Liégé, "Evangélisation," in *Catholicisme*, 7 vols., ed. J. Jacquement (Paris: Letouzey et Ané, 1956), vol. 4. See also A. Liégé, "La Foi," in *Initiation théologique* 111 (Paris: Les Editions du Cerf, 1952), pp. 485–86.

108. Alfonso Nebreda, "East Asian Study Week on Mission Catechetics," *Lumen Vitae* 17 (December 1962): 723. See also Theodore G. Stone, "The Bangkok Study Week," *Worship* 37 (February 1963): 184–90.

109. Alfonso Nebreda, *Kerygma in Crisis?* (Chicago: Loyola University Press, 1965), p. 52.

110. Ibid., p. 104.

111. Ibid., pp. 105–6.

112. The EAPI was founded to "stimulate spiritual renewal, awaken theological reflection, and promote pastoral effectiveness," Its organ has been the

journal *Teaching All Nations,* which was first issued in 1964 under the editorship of Hofinger. See "Editorial," *Teaching All Nations* 11 (1974): 2.

113. Quoted from the East Asian Pastoral Institute, Announcement of Programs for Missionaries in South and S.E. Asia 1968, in "Philippines," *Lumen Vitae* 24 (September 1969): 505-14.

114. Joseph Colomb, *Catéchisme progressif,* vol. 1: *Parlez Seigneur!;* vol. 2: *Dieu parmi nous;* vol. 3: *Avec le Christ Jésus* (Lyons: Emmanuel Vitte, 1950), together with teacher's manual: *Guide du catéchiste,* 3 vols. (Lyons: Emmanuel Vitte, 1950).

115. *Guide du catéchiste,* 1:6.

116. Joseph Colomb, *Pour un catéchisme efficace* (Lyons: Emmanuel Vitte, 1948); *Place ouverte: Au flanc de l'Eglise* (Lyons: Emmanuel Vitte, 1954); *Aux sources du catéchisme Histoire sainte et liturgie,* 3 vols. (Paris: Desclée, 1949); *Doctrine de vie au catechisme,* 3 vols. (Paris: Desclée et Cie, 1955); *Au souffle de l'Esprit,* 2 vols. (Paris: Desclée et Cie, 1959).

117. Georges Delcuve, "The Catechetical Movement: The Recent Statement of the Episcopal Commission of Religious Teaching," *Lumen Vitae* 12 (October–December 1957): 671-702.

118. This passage is part of the larger statement, which was inserted into the publications that had been put under suspicion. The statement can also be found translated in Delcuve, "The Catechetical Movement in France," p. 674.

119. Joseph Colomb, *Le service de l'Evangile: Manual Catéchétique,* Vol. 1 (Paris: Desclée et Cie, 1968), pp. 302-19.

120. Ibid., p. 313.

121. Josef Goldbrunner, *Holiness is Wholeness,* trans. Stanley Godman (New York: Pantheon, 1955); *Individuation: A Study of the Depth Psychology of Carl Gustav Jung* (New York: Pantheon, 1956); *Cure of Mind and Cure of Soul,* trans. Stanley Godman (New York: Pantheon, 1958).

122. Idem, *Cure of Mind and Cure of Soul,* p. 30.

123. Ibid., p. 13.

124. Ibid., p. 110.

125. Joseph Goldbrunner, "Catechesis and Encounter," in *New Catechetical Methods,* ed. Josef Goldbrunner, trans. Sister M. Veronica Riedl, O.S.F. (Notre Dame, Ind.: University of Notre Dame Press, 1965), p. 20.

126. Josef Goldbrunner, "Catechetical Method as Handmaid of Kerygma," *Teaching All Nations,* p. 116.

127. Idem, "The Corporal Works of Mercy: Presentation of a Lesson," in *New Catechetical Methods,* p. 112. In this article Goldbrunner employs the Herbartian steps: aim, preparation, presentation, explanation, application. This sequence provides the structure of the lessons outlined in his popular series intended to provide a method for teaching the Catholic catechism. See Josef Goldbrunner, *Teaching the Catholic Catechism,* 3 vols. (New York: Herder and

Herder, 1959). For the same method, see also idem, *Teaching the Sacraments: Penance, Eucharist, Confirmation* (New York: Herder and Herder, 1961).

128. Idem, *Realization: Anthropology of Pastoral Care*, trans. Paul C. Bailey and Elizabeth Reineche (Notre Dame, Ind.: University of Notre Dame Press, 1966), p. 19.

129. An extrinsic notion of revelation explains God's revealing activity as taking place on a different plane to ordinary human experience. The problem then is to try to forge bridges between the definitive revelation (given either in a body of divine truths or in a series of supernatural events) and every day human experience. A more immanentist perspective understands God's self-communication occurring within and through the historical experience of human being and becoming. In this perspective the dichotomy between "revelation" and "experience" no longer exists. For one attempt to develop an understanding of revelation as intrinsic to human life, see Gregory Baum, *Man Becoming : God in Secular Experience*, (New York: Herder and Herder, 1971).

130. Ibid., p. 86; see also, p. 47.

131. Marcel Van Caster, *God's Word Today* (New York: Benziger, 1966), p. 16. See also Marcel Van Caster, *The Structure of Catechetics* (New York: Herder and Herder, 1965), pp. 22, 24, 196. This latter book was the first in a trilogy which was entitled, in the French original, *Dieu nous parle.* The follow-up books were *Themes of Catechesis* (New York: Newman Press, 1966) and *Value Catechetics* (New York: Newman Press, 1970).

132. Marcel Van Caster, "Human Experience and Divine Revelation," *Lumen Vitae* 22 (December 1967): 666. See also "Towards a Christian Understanding of Experience," *Lumen Vitae* 25 (December 1970): 604–5.

133. Idem, "Consent and Creativity in Faith", *Lumen Vitae* 29 (June 1974): 231. See also idem, "Our Faith in Jesus Christ," *Lumen Vitae* 25 (June 1970): 265–78.

134. This two-way approach is found in a book co-authored with Jean Le Du. See Jean Le Du and Marcel Van Caster, *Experiential Catechetics* (New York: Newman Press, 1969).

Chapter 2
Recent Trends

In the sixties the Catholic catechetical movement in the U.S. gained in impetus and began to produce its own theorists. The concerns of these theorists had a striking coincidence with the emerging concerns among the Protestant Christian education theorists. The new concerns of the theorists were unified in a general trend toward "human experience," the so-called "anthropological turn." The neo-orthodox nurture theory had not taken the contemporary human experience seriously enough; and similarly, the kerygmatic approach had tended to ignore the tenets of modernity. Except for early pathfinders, such as Sherrill and Goldbrunner, both approaches had shied away from the human sciences, ignoring the contribution that modern cultural achievements can make to religious education.

The turn to human experience in religious education in the United States took shape in different ways. The first way was that of the personalist-existentialist approach taken by J. Gordon Chamberlin and Gabriel Moran. They entered the arena with a resounding cry of freedom, claiming that the neo-orthodox nurture theory and the kerygmatic approach were transmissive systems that denied the individual's capacity for growth to freedom. Included in this critique was the newfound developmental psychology which stressed the individual's readiness for religion.

Following the psychological-existentialist critique there came four other trends which likewise centered upon human experience, and also found the kerygmatic approach inadequate. The first of these four trends was the emergence of a new awareness of the sociopolitical arena, and its implications for religious education. Religious education for social change emerged. The second trend was the social science approach taken by James Michael Lee. Lee began to talk of religious education as a mode of social science and offset what he called "theological imperialism." The third trend was the linguistic approach, stimulated by Van Buren, in search of a way of communicating faith *post mortem Dei.* The fourth trend was the socialization approach, which dovetailed with the new official Catholic emphasis on the ecclesial task of catechesis. This chapter first shows the initial reaction to the neo-orthodox nurture theory and the kerygmatic movement, and then expands on these four trends discernible in recent Catholic literature.

CRIES FOR FREEDOM OF THE INDIVIDUAL

One of the mutual concerns of theorists in both the Protestant and Catholic traditions in the sixties was the cry for freedom of the individual. In religious education, it arose out of a reaction to a common problem which they shared in their traditions. Both the Protestant Christian nurture theory and the Catholic kerygmatic theory were indebted to the German theology of *Heilsgeschichte.* [1]

The Protestants had emphasized the importance of biblical history and of the ecclesial community which is the continuation of this special line of salvation. To become a Christian meant entering into the unique redemptive community which is always under the judgment of the gospel. The Catholic kerygmatists had likewise stressed the importance of bringing "salvation history" to bear upon the individual. The biblical stories were transmitted in their entirety, with confidence that they would nurture faith, and liturgical celebrations were thrust upon youngsters because of the inherent wealth of the content. From both traditions came a cry for freedom.

J. Gordon Chamberlin.   In the Protestant tradition, the challenge came from J. Gordon Chamberlin in his book *Freedom and Faith* (1965).[2] Influenced by existential philosophy, Chamberlin championed the cause of the individual. His challenge came from the standpoint of personal freedom. He pinpointed what he called an inherent inclination toward indoctrination in the nurture theory.[3] Acknowledging that Miller and Smart had warned against the possibility of manipulation,[4] Chamberlin still raised the question whether the "pattern of covenant relationship, nurture, and induction" might simply be a formula for group conformity with no allowance for the individual's critical powers to be exercised or for the community to undergo reconstruction.[5] Chamberlin championed the cause of the individual.

> The end of Christian education is the educated person who has engaged in a self-conscious re-examination of his own views of the meaning of existence, who has been confronted by a competent interpretation of the Christian faith, and who accepts his responsibility for the many decisions of his life in the light of his education.[6]

Chamberlin accused the transmissive and nurturing activities of the church, which are intent upon inducting children into the faith, of creating the illusion that adolescents make a decision for Christ when, in fact, the conditions for them being able to make responsible decisions are denied adolescents. He likened the uncritical "nurture" approach to an "inoculation."[7] It immunizes children from significant thinking about the meaning of the faith for their lives or about the validity and claims of the church upon them. Only the capacity for critical reflection, claimed Chamberlin, can bring responsible freedom.

Chamberlin argued that the creative reconstruction of the

community, in a way that it does not simply perpetuate institutional loyalties, can only be done by the "educated Christian." By this he meant the person who has been "enabled to reflect upon the meaning of his own existence in the context of the total world of his experience, including confrontation by the whole stream of Christian life and witness . . ."; this person alone is equipped to exercise critical judgment upon the visible church. For Chamberlin, "the educated person becomes the church's own instrument of self-evaluation and renewal."[8] Thus, according to Chamberlin, the re-education of the adults in the church becomes the key for effective education among children.

For Chamberlin, "education is the intentional social activity by which a person is enabled to exercise his responsible freedom."[9] Christian education is a distinctive approach to the basic function of education in general. Thus Christian education is the process of nurturing which has built into it the possibility of each individual accepting or rejecting the Christian heritage. Christianity, he said, does not deserve our loyalty if it can only be spread by promoting institutional loyalty, and protecting its adherents from knowing the truth about other centers of loyalty that integrate the lives of people in this age. "The special task of education," he said, "is to help people understand the real differences among the appealing faiths of our time, and to develop their capacity to make a responsible choice of faith."[10] If a person reared in a Christian tradition later chooses to reject it, this fact alone is not a sufficient criterion to judge that Christian education has failed. If the decision is for Christianity then, said Chamberlin, this is not a once-in-a-lifetime decision, but one that must be renewed over and over again as one confronts the challenges of daily living.

Gabriel Moran.   In the Catholic tradition, the call for freedom came from Gabriel Moran.[11] Moran charged that the "salvation history" approach had simply replaced the scholastic system, which it had rightly rejected, with biblical, liturgical, and historical systems. In Moran's estimation, it was nothing but a "system," a rigid construction of words and ideas imposed upon people from the outside to manipulate their lives."[12] He attacked the optimistic presumption that the "dynamic content" of salvation history was alone guaranteed of success. The so-called "dynamic content" was nothing but a boring story of events that happened centuries ago with little relation to real people and their real experience. The description of past events, said Moran, is nothing more than another scheme of transmitting truths from the past and trying to impose them from outside the realm of contemporary human experience. This is a denial of the freedom of the individual to reflect upon one's own experience and to discover the presence of the revealing God in one's own personal history.[13]

The process of revelation, said Moran, is not the transmission of propositional truths, nor a series of events, but the historical and continuing intersubjective communion between God and his people, in which the human answer is part of the revelation process itself.[14] Jesus is the high point in this inter-subjective communion between God and his people; the fullness of revelation is achieved in the risen glorified Christ. For Moran, in the consciousness of the risen Christ revelation continues to happen.[15] The closing of the deposit of revelation is not an end, but a beginning. Revelation continues within the experience of the life of the church, which is the visible prolongation of the risen Lord, and revelation also continues in the lives of all people, since there is a pre-reflective offer of God's grace to all men and women.[16] Catechesis, said Moran, must take seriously the revealing presence of God in the concrete lives of those being approached. It must start with the personal history of the students and facilitate reflection upon this experience; it aims eventually to help students discover the connection between their own personal history and the cosmic history of God's creative and redeeming activity.[17]

Moran's reaction to the enthusiasm of the kerygmatic movement was in opposition to any approach that sets out to deliver the message at all costs, an approach that would give priority to proclamation of the word over the integrity of the individual who is the recipient of the word.[18] Moran stressed that the most one can do to arouse a faith response in another is to help the person by an indirect kind of communication to discover for oneself the Christian one is called to be. He counseled catechists to have patience, to be prepared to take time, and to be oblique in their approach. The aim, he said, is not to "make" Christians, or to "form" students' freedom, or to "enable" students to encounter Christ.[19] Rather, the aim is to assist people in reflecting freely on the revelation of God in their lives now. The catechist's task is to awaken a person's intelligence and freedom so the person can discover the Holy Spirit in his/her personal life.[20]

Pierre Babin.   Both Chamberlin and Moran critiqued their traditions from a personalist-existential point of view. They placed great value on the significance of the unique individual in the process of ongoing salvation history. Another writer who shared this concern was Pierre Babin. Babin came out of the French catechetical tradition, but the English translations of his works have been published in the United States.[21] He had a background in empirical research into religious development, especially the transition from childhood to adulthood.[22] His writings have a more immediately practical bent than the more speculative approach of Moran. However, certain guiding principles in Babin's approach can be gleaned from them.

Babin endorsed the kerygmatic thrust insofar as he stressed that the task of catechesis for adolescents must be "in this area of making our message come alive as an exciting promise of life, as the good news that Jesus gave."[23] However, Babin's view of humanity, and his early interest in empirical psychology, safeguarded him from making a sharp dichotomy between the kerygma and human experience. He employed the principle of the incarnation; therefore, his understanding of God's involvement in the world was more intrinsic than the German kerygmatic catechists. He stressed that catechesis is not a matter of parachuting divine truths from outside the human situation, but a matter of helping adolescents to discover the area in their lives where, without being formerly aware of it, they live within the dimension of revelation.[24]

Babin, like Moran, resisted any attempt to present an extrinsic message. Dealing mainly with adolescents, Babin stressed their own personal struggle. Adolescence is a stage of inquiry, searching, and personal expansion. Through the will to question what has already been given at this stage of life, adolescents can enter a new maturity of faith. They should be given room for their own responsible decisions and encouraged to grapple with the meaning of their own experience, in which they will ultimately discover God.[25]

Developmental Psychology

The perspective of developmental psychology, which Babin possessed, became part of the new resistance to unqualified kerygmatic fervor. In the United States, the writings of English researcher Ronald Goldman challenged the prevailing assumption that biblical stories can be passed on to youngsters regardless of their level of cognitive maturity.[26] Taking a Piagetian approach, Goldman empirically studied the ideas that children have about the biblical stories they are told. He concluded that the cognitive content of many of these stories is not suitable for small children before a certain developmental age. He argued that too early an introduction of some biblical stories can lead to a fixation in the person's ability to interpret these stories. Childish literalistic, animistic, magical, and anthropomorphic modes of interpretation become fixed in the person. There is a danger of arrested development, the accretion in the child's mind of misconceptions, verbalisms, and focusing on trivialities in the stories. When children reach adolescence and begin to think critically they are liable to jettison the whole package loaded upon them in childhood, since their new cognitive capacity cannot square with the distorted, childish interpretation of the bible which they still carry with them. Goldman claimed there is a time of readiness for religion, and it should not be pre-empted by overly kerygmatic enthusiasm.

FOUR FURTHER TRENDS

The personalist-existentialist approach gained rapid and widespread popularity in the sixties and still is very prominent in popular literature. However, four new trends in theoretical reflection in the last two decades have tended to further modify the "turn to human experience," so that not only the kerygamatic approach is shown to be inadequate, but also the personalist-existentialist approach is claimed to lack the categories for a fully-blown experiential catechetics. These four approaches negate the kerygmatic approach, while at the same time attempting to expand the existentialist approach beyond its own confining parameters.

New Social Awareness.   In 1965, Randolph Crump Miller had wistfully remarked that the churches in America were slowly becoming aware of the inequality in race relations.[27] A special issue in 1964 of *Religious Education* devoted to the topic had sold out rapidly, indicating the mounting interest in the problem.[28] This new concern for racial equality was a reflection of the ferment in the wider society at the time, a revolutionary unrest which reached its peak in the late sixties. The fight for racial justice was a stimulus for a new social consciousness among Christian educators. This was reflected in a popular journal *Colloquy*, which ran a considerable number of articles in the early seventies on the need for an education towards justice and social liberation.[29] In addition, a new black theology was emerging, which emphasized that God's revelation means emancipation from political and economic oppression.[30] The implications of this black theology for Christian education were explored.[31]

In addition to the black theology, the sporadic efforts to shape the Christian educational enterprise toward liberation were given impetus by the writings of Paulo Freire.[32] His concept of "conscientization" and problem-solving education became popular, and appeared often in the literature.[33] Freire became a consultant with the World Council of Churches in 1973, and the publications of this body have also added to the new sociopolitical awareness in some Christian educational theory. One of the aims of religious education began to be formulated in terms of liberation from racial, class, sexual, and cultural oppression.[34]

In the Protestant community we find Iris V. Cully in *Change, Conflict, and Self-Determination* (1972) reflecting some of the changes taking place in the consciousness of Christian thinkers.[35] Throughout her writings, Cully has had a strong ecclesial emphasis, but her focus on freedom has changed over the course of the years. In 1958, she was interested primarily in the individual's freedom vis-à-vis God's personal revelation, and used existential philosophy to expand it.[36] In 1972, in the above-mentioned book, she was interested in the self-determination of people who in the conflict of their common situation can find

ways to exert political action to be freed from oppressive structures.[37]

In the Catholic community, both Moran and Babin showed an
increased social awareness. In 1968, Pierre Babin wrote an article
with the challenging title "J'abandonne la catéchèse."[38] The
article has to be understood in the context of the May riots in the
Sorbonne and the student protest against the Vietnamese war in
the U.S. Students were rebelling violently against traditional
structures of government and schooling. The cry of the young
was for political justice and freedom. In catechetics it prompted a
radicalizing of the turn to human experience. Now, not only the
psychological implications for the human person's quest for authenticity were important, but also the sociological and cultural
conditions that determine this quest. Babin's article was, in part,
a reaction against the "life-situation" catechesis that he himself
had championed for twenty years. He opposed the approach
which uses life-experiences as merely a way towards the desired
end, namely, the adherence to the gospel message. Catechetical
courses which explore ways of finding an excuse to bring in the
name of God or to inject the gospel message at the opportune
time, unexpected by the student but carefully planned by the
teacher, Babin condemned as "pseudo-courses in religious instruction."[39]

Babin proposed a new orientation for catechesis by introducing the concept *l'animation culturelle.*[40] At first, he kept this
orientation separate from the more explicit quest for faith in
group catechesis. But later he began to fuse these two orientations into one, under the rubric of "catechesis for human development."[41] Babin acknowledged his indebtedness to Paulo
Freire's concept of "conscientization" which, he said, "develops
the ideas of Carl Rogers in more sociological and historical dimensions." Catechesis, he continued, is to aid the person to

become "an active subject of history rather than merely its passive object."[42]

In recent years, Babin's major interest has been the use of audiovisual culture. He shares with so many others in the United States the vision that was first promoted by Marshall McLuhan.[43] The modern person cannot be understood outside of the powerful influence of the technological instruments of communication. The "modern man," says Babin, extends himself into the environment in a variety of new ways (radio, TV, etc.), and these extensions bring about a radical change in his personality. A "new man" comes into being.[44] Underlying the interest in audiovisual techniques, so prevalent in catechesis today, is an alertness to the powerful effect of social and cultural forces of our time in shaping the human person and determining who he or she may become.

A similar, but far more sophisticated, shift occurred in the writings of Gabriel Moran. Moran took human experience, understood as the interaction between the organism and the total environment, as his central organizing category. Whenever divisions are brought into human experience, he said, there is oppression. The divisions between "clergy" and "laity," he charged, are at the root of the structural oppression in the church.[45] The division between Christians and non-Christians breeds an imperialistic attitude within theology, and an intramural narcissistic type of catechesis.[46] The division between male and female and between black and white, perpetuates sociopolitical oppression. The division between humans and the nonhuman environment leads to ecological barbarity. He was in search of an all-embracing metaphor that could comprehend the main antagonisms in human experience enabling unity, and hence justice and freedom, within diversity. He argued that the word "revelation" was such a metaphor.[47]

Like Babin, Moran had to come to the conviction that it is not possible for persons to find authenticity without reformation of social structures. Other religious education theorists have begun to espouse similar principles.[48] Many have been influenced by developments in Latin America. A watershed in catechetical theory in the broad Catholic community came with the International Catechetics Week held at Medellín in August 1968.[49] While the study week focused upon the Latin American experience, its conclusions have been widely published in North America. At Medellín there was a radicalizing of anthropology. Now the human being was viewed as a person inextricably bound with others within the historical process. As it was stated in the conclusion of the conference, "the first place to look when seeking God's design for contemporary man is the area of history and authentically human aspirations. These are indispensable parts of catechetics' contents." To do this, catechists are expected to "live fully with men of our time," that is, especially to live in solidarity with the oppressed in their actual historical situation.[50]

This solidarity within the historical process was seen as the way to collapse the previous dualism between content and method, and was based on an approach to revelation in history summed up in the following passage:

> In every situation, catechetics has a fundamental message, which consists of a unifying principle between two poles of total reality. This unifying principle is complex, differentiated, and dynamic. It excludes dichotomy, separation, and dualism, as well as monism, confusion, and simplistic identification. This unifying principle exists: between human values and relations with God; between man's planning and God's salvific plan as manifested in Christ; between the human community and the church; between human history and the history of salvation; between human experience and God's revelation; between the progressive growth of Christianity in our time, and its eschatalogical consummation.[51]

The Social Science Approach

A new theory of religious education burst onto the American scene with James Michael Lee. In 1967, Lee pioneered a new program in the graduate school at Notre Dame University, which he himself heralded as "unique," and as offering a "new direction in the teaching of religion."[52] This "new direction" employed a social science approach to religious instruction, an approach which Lee himself was beginning to build into a full-blown theory. The Notre Dame graduate program in religious education terminated in 1976, but Lee still exerts considerable influence in the United States religious education circles as founder and publisher of the Religious Education Press.

The foundations of Lee's theory were announced in three articles in *Today's Catholic Teacher* (1969) and in the third chapter of *Toward a Future for Religious Education* (1970).[53] Since then he has been engaged in writing a trilogy, in which he set out to give a comprehensive theory of religious education. The first two volumes have been published as *The Shape of Religious Instruction* (1971) and *The Flow of Religious Instruction* (1973). The third volume, *The Content of Religious Instruction*, is still in preparation. Each volume is appropriately subtitled "A Social Science Approach."[54]

Lee argued that the prevailing "macrotheory" that has guided religious education in the past has been the "theological approach," which claims that religious education is a branch of theology. He claimed that it is absolutely imperative for religious education to adopt a social science approach or "macrotheory" and to drop the outdated theological approach.[55] Religious instruction, said Lee, has become a "messenger boy" to theology. This was especially the case in the kerygmatic approach where religious instruction was simply the "handmaid of the message," but Lee insisted it was also the case in what we have called more "experience-oriented" approaches. Catechetical theorists, said

Lee, regard theology as normative to establish the principles, goals, and methods of religious education; theology is called upon to dictate the goals and the shape of the processes devised to attain them.[56] Lee attributed this domination of theology over the "instructional process" to a type of "theological imperialism," that is, "the proclivity to try to bring totally within its jurisdiction and control all those areas of reality which in one way or another are related to theology."[57]

So, for Lee, it is fallacious to think that theology has the task to establish the norms which serve as the basis of religious instruction and also to verify the extent to which religious instruction is successful. Only social science can achieve this task adequately because it has a distinctive methodology suited to the task. Unlike theology, social science, claimed Lee, is an empirical science which has tools that enable explanation, prediction and verification of desired behavioral outcomes.[58] Yet Lee was quick to point out that this does not exclude theology as irrelevant or unimportant to religious instruction. A "congenial, nondominative relationship" between theology and social science is possible within religious instruction.[59] The relationship between theology and social science, he said, is analogous to the relationship between Christianity and human nature:

> As human nature represents the broad framework, the thrust, the starting point, and the ongoing activity within which Christianity congenially and congruently works, so too social science forms the framework, the thrust, the starting point and the on-going activity within which theological science operates within the enterprise of religious instruction.[60]

Lee's approach focused mainly on the act of religious instruction. He reacted against the "transmission-theory" of religious instruction which he observed is a "preaching model," and replaced it with a "structuring theory," which he called a "teaching model."[61] So, for Lee, religious instruction was defined as the deliberate "structuring of the learning situation to most effectively facilitate the modification of behavior along religious lines."[62]

By focusing on the religious instruction act itself, Lee argued he had resolved the content/method duality evident in the history of religious education theory in this century. He called it a false dilemma. The duality only existed in the minds of the theologically oriented theorists whose speculative outlook had considered pedagogical method to be in the service of product content. In fact, he concluded, within the concrete, actual, dynamic teaching-learning process, there is a fusion of method and content. There is only a notional distinction between them, not a real one.[63]

The Use of Language

Religious educators in the sixties became more sensitive to the problem of theological language. One way the problem of theological language arose was through the impact of the "death of God" theology and, specifically, through Paul Van Buren's linguistic analysis of radical secularism. The mushrooming of "a-theistic" theologians at that time was in reaction to the God of neo-orthodoxy. This God, they claimed, is alienating to the contemporary human being. The Christian commitment to liberation demands a negation of this God. Religious educators were challenged to justify their "God-talk."

Van Buren suggested that formal religious instruction *post mortem Dei* consists of teaching about faith by going to the great stories of the tradition that tell about a faith response.[64] In religious instruction, the story itself is not told; that is left to preaching and liturgy. There were numerous negative responses to

Van Buren's approach, but one serious reply to Van Buren's challenge came from Ian T. Ramsey.[65] Ramsey, who as early as 1962 had been considering the implications of linguistic philosophy for religious education, had caught the attention of Randolph Crump Miller.[66] Miller was to make Ramsey's theory a pivotal feature for his next book.[67] For Ramsey, religious language is distinct from theological language. Religious language is not descriptive, systematic, or literally accurate. Religious language is more akin to poetry than prose. It is logically "odd." When we talk about God, it is always obliquely. This odd, peculiar, and unusual language only functions as it should in situations where "disclosure" occurs, i.e., situations which "come alive," in which the "penny drops," the "ice breaks." Therefore, Christian education seeks to evoke disclosures rather than intellectual assent. The primary task of Christian education is "to teach insight, to evoke disclosures in which we come to ourselves when and as we discern a world which has 'come alive' in some particular situation."[68] The disclosure situations are likely to be followed by renewed or new commitments.

Miller pointed out that within the nurture theory, given Ramsey's conclusions, telling the Christian story does not involve transmission of information or reading from a dead text. It involves using the common language of the faith community articulated in bible, doctrine, and worship, within a context of close personal relationships, so that the maximum opportunity for disclosure may be created.[69] Echoing Ramsey, Miller argued that Christian education can prepare persons to receive such a disclosure, but it cannot manipulate the response. In the last analysis, the disclosure is a gift of God's grace.[70]

The concern for language arose in a different way in the writings of Gabriel Moran. Moran's insight into language was connected with the new sociopolitical awareness which he shared with an increasing number of theorists. To work for social change meant also to work for changing the patterns of language which reinforce structures of oppression. Moran began to see how language either enslaves or liberates. For this reason, the old terms must be injected with new meaning.

In *Present Revelation*, he studied the image, ideal, and word "revelation." This metaphor, he said, is a helpful word that can span differences between religions. The difficulty, he charged, is that the Christian church, and its intramural theologians, try to control the language of revelation, and hence maintain a self-satisfied, imperialistic stance toward the rest of human experience outside their own tradition.[71]

In *Religious Body*, he tried to give new meaning to the words "community," "religion," and "education," attempting to free them from domestication to bureaucratic control and hence open their possibilities for liberating people. Religious education became a matter of "honing out" a new language that would be adequate to the total experience of human beings.[72]

Socialization Theory

The nurture theory of American Protestant Christian education took a quantum leap when some of its adherents turned to sociology and anthropology. One of the first to do so was C. Ellis Nelson in his book *Where Faith Begins* (1967).[73] Nelson asked the fundamental question: how is the Christian faith communicated from one generation to the next? Religious people, he said, have provided various answers to the question. However, it is in the social scientists that he claimed to find the "clue" for developing a model of faith-communication. Social scientists, he said, give a description of how culture at its deepest level is transmitted from generation to generation. This, continued Nelson, "is the closest thing we have to an analysis of how faith is communicated."[74]

From the social sciences Nelson gleaned that a culture endures only if it is deliberate in transmitting itself to the rising generation; even though the little everyday exchanges may seem casual, they are, in fact, a powerful formative influence upon us and especially upon the young.[75] Within the faith community, said Nelson, parents and adults are busy transmitting the beliefs and values of the community to the new generation.

Now the nurture theory, which had previously relied upon "relationship theology," was seeking corroboration from the social sciences in a new and daring way. Nelson presumed that faith in the biblical God is the basic reality that Christians desire to share, and that this faith is communicated according to the mode of natural cultural transmission within the community of believers.[76]

Another theorist to turn to the social sciences was John H. Westerhoff, III. In *Generation to Generation* he developed a model of Christian education which he called "religious socialization." By this he meant "a process consisting of life-long formal and informal mechanisms, through which persons sustain and transmit their faith (world view, value system) and life-style."[77] Westerhoff entered into dialogue with Gwen Kennedy Neville, a cultural anthropologist, who assisted him in attempting to bring the analysis of cultural systems into the realm of Christian education.[78]

In appealing to the social sciences, Westerhoff did not see himself returning to the naive optimism of the early liberalism, with its romantic assumption that worthwhile beliefs and values emerge naturally within the course of development. His theory was a refinement of the neo-orthodox nurture theory, having the same urgency to transmit Christian beliefs and values from one generation to the next, but at the same time trying to insist that "nurture" is not enough, since it leads to a catechesis for conformity. Westerhoff acknowledged being influenced by what he called "neo-liberal-liberation-hope theology."[79] In *Will Our Children Have Faith*, he argued that a theological perspective, akin to the "liberation theology" developing in Latin America, provides the catechetical theorist with a way of taking the best from the "liberal" and "neo-orthodox" approaches while eliminating their inadequacies.[80]

In the Catholic community, the socialization approach has received impetus from recent official documents. There has been in these documents a recentering of ministry, including the catechetical ministry, within the ministry of the entire ecclesial community. This trend was present in the documents of the Second Vatican Council. The catechetical application came in the *General Catechetical Directory* and the *Message to the People of God* from the recent Synod of Bishops, both of which stressed that catechesis is a form of the ministry of the word within the context of the whole ecclesial community.[81]

One of the influential figures at the Synod of Bishops was Jacques Audinet.[82] A Frenchman who has a background in sociology as well as theology, Audinet has defined catechesis as a pastoral task of the church, which reconstructs the church within a given culture. Audinet spent some time studying sociology at the University of Chicago, and admits being influenced by John Dewey. For Audinet, catechesis arises out of the contemporary profession of the faith which, in turn, serves to constitute the church on deeper and deeper levels. In the articulation of faith, new language patterns are created to express a changing faith experience. For Audinet, it is the living tradition of the church which is the process of catechesis. Catechesis of the church is not a matter of teaching *about* the church, but a matter of realizing that the *church itself* is the very medium of catechesis. In this sense, he has referred to catechesis as the "transmission of the documents of the faith." However, he has not made a duality between the bible or creed, and today's human situation. The bible and creed themselves are the articulation of human experience in a living tradition; and today's faith experience in the church, in a given culture, is itself the release of the message in a new language. "Message" and "experience" are inextricably united in the fabric of the ongoing life of the church.

Coupled with this reemphasis on catechesis as a pastoral task of the church was a new official effort to restore the adult catechumenate. The restoration work on the catechumenate had been in operation since the 1940s in France and also in many missionary countries.[83] However, in 1972 the Congregation for Divine Worship published the *Rite of Christian Initiation of Adults.* This document was a watershed because it provided a vision of catechesis as an ecclesial process intricately interwoven with the community's celebration, and serving the purpose of ongoing conversion of both the catechumens and the whole community.

Informed by the vision provided by the official church documents, Berard Marthaler has proposed a theory which, like Nelson's and Westerhoff's, appeals to sociology and cultural anthropology for a way of describing the church's mode of catechesis. Marthaler is head of the Department of Religion and Religious Education at the Catholic University of America and also the executive editor of *Living Light,* a professional catechetical journal, which is an official publication of the Department of Education of the United States Catholic Conference. He was also appointed as special advisor to the team preparing the *National Catechetical Directory.* Because of the influential positions he holds, Marthaler's theory of catechesis has probably become more widely accepted in the United States than can be accounted for simply by the impact of his relatively few publications on the topic.[84]

Marthaler's theory of catechesis has an ecclesial orientation, but instead of relying entirely upon liturgical studies of the ancient initiation process or upon strictly theological inquiry into the nature of the Christian community, he has used the idiom of social science to describe the process of catechesis. As he has stated: "Insofar as it was an intentional process, socialization was traditionally called catechesis."[85]

The socialization model, which he has championed, "brackets out aetiological, theological, and epistemological considerations. It takes the present realities of everyday life as its starting point," and examines them from the point of view of the social scientist.[86]

The Christian community, according to Marthaler, has in its lived tradition a fund of shared meanings and values which are externalized in a common symbol system. For the community to perpetuate itself, it must preserve and transmit the symbols of this faith to the new generation. The Christian neophyte finds him/herself initiated into the meanings and values of the community by the socialization process. Marthaler, drawing upon Peter Berger and Thomas Luckmann, has described this process of socialization as a form of interaction between the socializee and the socializing agents (parents, teachers, community, etc.). It is not just a passive absorption of data from the social environment.[87]

Marthaler's socialization model offers a view of catechesis within the empirical church in its process of becoming itself from one generation to the next. He is attempting to empirically ground the liturgical and theological vision of catechesis considered in the last section and joins hands with the Protestants Nelson and Westerhoff, who have tried to do the same for the Protestant Christian nurture theory.

SUMMARY

The four current trends which have been discussed above, while distinguishable for the purposes of identification, are, in fact, aspects of a common search in contemporary religious education theory. Each of the scholars cited has been, in his/her way, in quest of a theory of human development which takes into account the whole range of relationships that form the human person.

The theorists representing these four current trends have a common conviction that education must come to terms with the external familial, social, and cultural conditions impinging upon the individual. Given the powerful influence of the formative milieu upon a person, the question of individual freedom becomes more pressing. The fundamental issue of freedom that lies beneath the surface of current theory is nothing less and nothing more than the tension between the inner thrust toward self-determination and the outer determining influences of the environment. Religious education has the task of facilitating growth toward human maturity. This growth does not occur within a relational, social, or cultural vacuum. Now that theorists have become more aware of the sociocultural context of learning, the issue of freedom becomes more poignant than ever before.

The trend toward greater political awareness has made theorists more aware of the way social institutions, legitimized by political ideologies, can be a form of alienation, creating "false-consciousness" in a people and maintaining them in a position of subservient docility. The trend toward recognizing the importance of language in education has meant that theorists have become more aware of the way language structures consciousness, being either a form of enslavement or liberation. The trend toward behavioral engineering has made theorists more aware of the controlling forces in the environment that affect human behavior; these forces can be beneficial or inimical. The trend toward socialization theory has made theorists aware of the way persons are shaped by their cultural tradition, raising the question of whether they simply adapt and conform to the given social realities, or whether they are also creative in reshaping the culture.

The theorists representing each of these trends are searching for an educational anthropology that fully recognizes the structuring influences of the social and cultural environment upon the individual, while, at the same time, also recognizing that the individual has a creative power of self-determination. If religious education is to promote freedom, then it has a need for such an anthropology. Some theorists, it was shown, have turned to the human sciences to ascertain the dynamics of the creative or destructive external forces upon the individual. For these theorists, the human sciences provide data about the nature of these forces, how they operate, and how to make the most of them in order to facilitate human growth toward freedom.

NOTES FOR CHAPTER 2

1. The "savation history" approach recognizes God's action in the world in a series of specific events. These saving events are independent of our faith. They serve as a "given," which exists prior to our faith. By stressing the objectivity of God's action in the world, it attempts to guarantee against any false notion of self-redemption. *Heilsgeschichte* rejects as a "liberal" distortion any understanding of Jesus that stresses his role as initiator and model of faith. See Gerald O'Collins, S.J., *Foundations of Theology* (Chicago: Loyola University Press, 1970), pp. 93–94.

2. J. Gordon Chamberlin, *Freedom and Faith* (Philadelphia: Westminster, 1965).

3. Ibid., p. 63. By "indoctrination" Chamberlin means imparting beliefs as the "truth" in a way that precludes any questioning on the part of the individual.

4. Miller, *Christian Nurture and the Church*, p. 46.

5. Chamberlin, *Freedom and Faith*, p. 128.

6. Ibid., p. 126.

7. Ibid., p. 129. It is interesting to note that Peter Berger uses the same metaphor in *The Noise of Solemn Assemblies: Christian Commitment and the*

Religious Establishment of America (New York: Doubleday and Company, Inc., 1961), p. 116. Berger speaks of the "small doses of Christianoid concepts and terminology injected into the consciousness." While there is a similarity, Berger stresses the need of an "authentic encounter with the Christian message," and a "conversion," which will break through the taken-for-granted "o.k. world" of community nurture. Berger's context is also different, since he is concerned primarily with the church's confrontation with the beliefs and values of contemporary society.

8. Ibid., p. 133.

9. Ibid., p. 106.

10. Ibid., p. 155.

11. Moran received his Ph.D. from The Catholic University of America in 1965, presenting a dissertation entitled "Contemporary Theology of Revelation and Its Effect Upon Catechetical Theory." This thesis gave him the substantial content for his two early works: *Theology of Revelation (New York: Herder and Herder, 1966) and Catechesis of Revelation* (New York: Herder and Herder, 1966).

12. Moran, *Catechesis of Revelation*, p. 37.

13. Ibid., p. 122.

14. Moran, *Theology of Revelation*, p. 29.

15. Ibid., p. 75.

16. Ibid., p. 167.

17. Moran, *Catechesis of Revelation*, p. 46.

18. Ibid., pp. 38–39.

19. Ibid., p. 71.

20. Ibid., pp. 72–73.

21. For example, Pierre Babin, *Crisis of Faith*, trans. and adapted by Eva Fleischner (New York: Herder and Herder, 1963); *Methods*, trans. and adapted by John Murphy (New York: Herder and Herder, 1969); *Adolescents in Search of a New Church*, trans. and adapted by Nancy Hennessy and Carol White (New York: Herder and Herder, 1969); *Options*, trans. and adapted by John Murphy (New York: Herder and Herder, 1967). The English translations of these works were presented as having been originally written entirely by Babin himself, but this was probably not the case. Babin was accustomed to composing books in collaboration with team workers, writers, and editors. In fact, it is impossible to ascertain what section, if any, of those writings came originally from Babin's own pen. Sections of the books attributed to his authorship, and possibly entire works, were in fact the product of a team effort under his guidance. While it is important to acknowledge this fact, it is still justifiable to analyze these works under the generic authorship of Pierre Babin. For this information, I am indebted to a discussion by Michael Warren, *The Approach of Pierre Babin to Adolescent Catechesis and Its Influence on American Catholic Catechetical Literature, 1963–1972* (Ann Arbor, Mich.: University Microfilms, 1974).

22. See Pierre Babin, *Dieu et l'adolescent* (Lyons: Editions du Chalet, 1963). This work was translated into English as *Faith and the Adolescent*, trans. David Gibson (New York: Herder and Herder, 1965).

23. Babin, *Options*, p. 20.

24. Ibid., p. 70.

25. Ibid., p. 109; see also Babin, *Methods*, p. 36.

26. Ronald Goldman, *Religious Thinking from Childhood to Adolescence* (New York: Seabury Press, 1964), and *Readiness for Religion: A Basis for Developmental Religious Education* (New York: Seabury Press, 1965).

27. Randolph Crump Miller, "From Where I Sit: Some Issues in Christian Education," *Religious Education* 60 (March–April 1965): 103.

28. *Religious Education* 59 (January–February 1964).

29. *Colloquy* 4 (November 1971); Reuben Sheares, "The Search for Justice," *Colloquy* 6 (March 1973): 14–15; *Colloquy* 3 (July–August 1970), an issue devoted to women's rights.

30. For example, James H. Cone, *A Black Theology of Liberation* (New York: Lippincott, 1970); and J. Deontis Roberts, *Liberation and Reconciliation: A Black Theology* (Westminster: Newman Press, 1971).

31. For example, William Jones, "Reconciliation and Liberation in Black Theology: Some implications for Religious Education," *Religious Education* 67 (September–October 1972): 383–89; Olivia Pearl Stokes, "Education in the Black Church: Design for Change," *Religious Education* 69 (July–August 1974): 433–45; and C. D. Coleman, "Agenda for the Black Church," *Religious Education* 64 (November–December 1969): 441–46.

32. The most influential of these were: Paulo Freire, *Pedagogy of the Oppressed* (New York: The Seabury Press, 1970); and *Education for Critical Consciousness* (New York: The Seabury Press, 1973).

33. For example, Bruce O. Boston, "Conscientization and Christian Education," *Colloquy* 5 (May 1972): 36–41.

34. In 1975, the World Council of Churches met in Nairobi with the theme, "Jesus Christ frees and unites." A report on a preliminary dossier to the assembly is given by William B. Kennedy, "Education for Liberation and Community," *Religious Education* 70 (January–February 1975): 5–44. See also Letty M. Russell, "Women: Education through Participation," *Religious Education* 70 (January–February 1975): 45–53.

35. Iris V. Cully, *Change, Conflict, and Self-Determination: Next Steps in Religious Education* (Philadelphia: The Westminster Press, 1972).

36. Idem, *The Dynamics of Christian Education* (Philadelphia: The Westminster Press, 1958), pp. 84–87.

37. Cully, *Change, Conflict, and Self-Determination*, p. 88.

38. Pierre Babin, "J'abandonne la catéchèse?" *Catechiste* 76 (October 1968): 415–28.

39. Ibid., p. 421.

40. Ibid., pp. 422–23.

41. Pierre Babin, "Towards a Catechesis of Human Development: Does Catechesis Serve Human Development?" *Living Light* 8 (Spring 1971): 60–72. This article appeared first as "Pour une catéchèse du développement," *Catéchistes* 86 (avril 1971): 201–13.

42. Ibid., p. 62.

43. See Marshall McLuhan, *Understanding Media: The Extensions of Man* (New York: McGraw-Hill, 1964); Marshall McLuhan and Quentin Fiore, *The Medium is the Massage* (New York: Bantam Books, 1967). For a critical appraisal of McLuhan's doctrine, see *McLuhan: Pro and Con*, ed. Raymond Rosenthal (New York: Funk and Wagnalls, 1968).

44. Pierre Babin, "Audio-Visual Man," in *Audio-Visual Man*, ed. Pierre Babin (Dayton, Ohio: Pflaum, 1970), pp. 13–32. See also "L'homme audio-visual et son éducation," *Orientations* 35 (1970): 5–22, and "Le montage audio-visual en groupe de catéchese jeunes—options et méthods," *Vérité et Vie* 87 (1970): 629.

45. Gabriel Moran, *The New Community* (New York: Herder and Herder, 1970).

46. Idem, "Catechetics, R.I.P.," *Commonweal* 93 (18 December 1970): 299–302.

47. Idem, "Response to Professor Dulles 11," *CTSA Proceedings* 29 (June 1974): 118.

48. For example, Thomas Groome, "Shared Christian Praxis: A Possible Theory/Method of Religious Education," *Lumen Vitae* 21 (1976): 186–208, and "The Crossroads: A Story of Christian Education by Shared Praxis," *Lumen Vitae* 22 (1977): 45–70.

49. The study week had been initiated by CELAM, in conjunction with the EAPI, with Hofinger as usual at the helm. The spirit of "Medellín" has been disseminated by the review *Catequesis latinoamericana*, first published in January of 1969, and also by many catechetical institutes throughout Latin America.

50. "General Conclusions of the International Catechetics Week in Medellín, August 11–17, 1968," *Lumen Vitae* 24 (June 1969): 346. This statement can also be found, together with a selection of major papers presented at Medellin, in *The Medellín Papers*, ed. Johannes Hofinger and Terence Sheridan (Manila: East Asian Pastoral Institute, 1969).

51. "General Conclusions of the International Catechetics Week in Medellín, August 11–17, 1968."

52. James Michael Lee, "A University at the Service of Catholic Schools," *Catholic Educator* 38 (December 1967): 38.

53. James Michael Lee, "The Third Strategy: A Behavioral Approach to Religious Instruction," *Today's Catholic Teacher* (September, October, and November, 1969); and "The Teaching of Religion," in *Toward a Future for*

Religious Education, ed. James Michael Lee and Patrick C. Rooney (Dayton, Ohio: Pflaum Press, 1970), pp. 55–92.

54. James Michael Lee, *The Shape of Religious Instruction: A Social Science Approach,* (Birmingham, Alabama: Religious Education Press, 1971) and *The Flow of Religious Instruction: A Social Science Approach,* (Birmingham, Alabama: Religious Education Press, 1973).

55. James Michael Lee, ed., *The Religious Education We Need* (Birmingham, Alabama: Religious Education Press, 1977), p. 121.

56. Lee also included the theologians of Protestant Christian nurture, such as Miller, Smart, and Wyckoff, in his critique.

57. Lee, *The Shape of Religious Instruction,* p. 242.

58. Ibid., pp. 182–85.

59. Ibid., p. 227.

60. Ibid., p. 228.

61. Lee, *Toward a Future for Religious Education,* pp. 56–59.

62. Lee, *The Shape of Religious Instruction,* p. 56.

63. Lee, *The Flow of Religious Instruction,* p. 19. Lee distinguishes between structural content and substantive content. The former is the pedagogical procedure itself. In the religious instruction act it occurs inseparably from substantive content.

64. Paul M. Van Buren, "Christian Education post mortem Dei," *Religious Education* 60 (January-February 1965): 4–10. In this article he is applying the conclusions of his book, *The Secular Meaning of the Gospel: Based on an Analysis of Its Language* (New York: The Macmillan Company, 1963), to religious education. Van Buren has since regretted association with the "death of God" movement which he has referred to as "foolish exploits" and "journalistic nonsense." See *Theological Explorations* (New York: The Macmillan Company, 1968), p. 6. However, he has further pursued the question of religious language in *The Edges of Language: An Essay in the Logic of a Religion* (New York: The Macmillan Company, 1972). The theme of freedom continues to preoccupy him; see *The Burden of Freedom: Americans and the God of Israel* (New York: The Seabury Press, 1976).

65. Ian T. Ramsey, "Discernment, Commitment, and Cosmic Disclosure," *Religious Education* 60 (January-February 1965): 10–14.

66. Idem, "Christian Education in the Light of Contemporary Empiricism," *Religious Education* 57 (March–April 1962): 95–96. Ramsey's major work in this area is *Religious Language* (London: SCM Press, 1957; New York: Macmillan Paperback, 1963).

67. Randolph Crump Miller, *The Language Gap and God: Religious Language and Christian Education* (Philadelphia: Pilgrim Press, 1970), pp. 77–93.

68. Ramsay, "Christian Education in the Light of Contemporary Empiricism," p. 95.

69. Miller, *The Language Gap and God*, pp. 157–70.

70. Miller, "From Where I Sit: Some Issues," p. 105.

71. Gabriel Moran, *The Present Revelation* (New York: Herder and Herder, 1972), p. 13.

72. Gabriel Moran, *Religious Body* (New York: The Seabury Press, 1974), pp. 31–67.

73. C. Ellis Nelson, *Where Faith Begins* (Atlanta: John Knox Press, 1971).

74. Ibid., p. 18.

75. Ibid., p. 58.

76. Ibid., pp. 30, 34, 65.

77. John H. Westerhoff, III, and Gwen Kennedy Neville, *Generation to Generation: Conversations on Religious Education and Culture* (Philadelphia: United Church Press, 1974), p. 41.

78. Ibid., p. 16.

79. Ibid., p. 17.

80. John H. Westerhoff, III, *Will Our Children Have Faith?* (New York: The Seabury Press, 1976), p. 31.

81. "The General Catechetical Directory," art. 17, in Berard Marthaler, *Catechetics in Context* (Huntington, Ind.: Our Sunday Visitor, Inc., 1973), p. 46; "Message to the People of God," art. 1, in *Living Light* 15 (Spring, 1978): 86.

82. Not many of Audinet's writings have been translated into English. He has written the basic article on "Catechetics" in *Sacramentum Mundi*, 1:263–67. His only full-length work has been translated as *Forming the Faith of Adolescents* (New York: Herder and Herder, 1968). One of his many articles published in the French journal *Catéchèse* has been published in English as "Catechesis: The Church Building the Church within a Given Culture," *Our Apostolate* 24 (August 1976): 132–56. A summary of his theory, as well as some indications of his influence on "The Message to the People of God," can be found in Kenneth Barker, "Jacques Audinet: Catechesis as Pastoral Action," *The Living Light* 15 (Spring 1978): 128–40.

83. Bernard Guillard, "Evangelization and the Catechumenate in France," in *Concilium*, vol 22: *Adult Baptism and the Catechumenate* (New York: Paulist Press, 1967), p. 151.

84. The most mature statement of his position is found in Berard Marthaler, "Socialization as a Model for Catechetics," in *Foundations of Religious Education*, ed. Padraic O'Hare (New York: Paulist Press, 1978), pp. 64–92.

85. Ibid., p. 65.

86. Ibid., p. 73.

87. Ibid., p. 66. See Peter L. Berger and Thomas Luckmann, *The Social Construction of Reality: A Treatise in the Sociology of Knowledge* (New York: Doubleday and Company, Inc., 1966), pp. 47–183.

PART TWO

In Part One it was shown that the historical development of "catechetics" and "Christian education" has now entered a new phase. This new phase is characterized by a decisive turn to the human sciences to provide an adequate understanding of the dynamics of human growth. It was indicated that there is an issue of freedom underlying current trends in theory, since these trends emphasize that persons, to a large degree, are made or destroyed by environmental influences.

The thesis in Part Two is that theorists have three typical ways of understanding how education promotes freedom. While the typological study draws upon some of the theorists who have already been introduced in this work, the nature of the types precludes any previous categorization. The types expose the quest for an educational anthropology, and the issue of freedom, which, as the previous chapter indicated, lie beneath the surface of current theoretical trends.

Religious education theorists, implicitly or explicitly, presume that education promotes freedom when it promotes change toward greater humanness. Therefore, included within their understanding of education for freedom there is also a view of how education changes human beings, as well as an image of how human beings become more human within the world. It has already been noted that they attain this latter perspective from the human sciences. The type of human science they appeal to is closely related to the form their educational anthropology takes.

In turn, their educational anthropology is formed by, and informs, their theory of education for change, which, in turn, shapes what they mean by freedom as a goal in education. Therefore, for the sake of clarity, each type is presented under four general categories which, in fact, are interlocking aspects that cannot be entirely separated. The four categories are: (1) educational anthropology, (2) use of the human sciences, (3) education for change, and (4) education for freedom.

The first type, presented in chapter 3, is called the psychological type because it draws upon developmental psychology to understand how persons are formed or deformed within relationships. The second type, presented in chapter 4, is called the political type because it expands the realm of freedom to the enabling or disabling effects of sociopolitical institutions. The third type, presented in chapter 5, is called the cultural type because, in this approach, education for freedom means that persons are initiated into and shaped by their culture, so that they belong and can live creative lives.

The theorists who represent these various typical approaches differ on fundamental questions, such as whether there is a specifically *Christian* form of religious education, and whether specifically Christian faith has the power to promote freedom. These questions are bypassed in this section, not because they are unimportant, but because they do not bear *directly* upon *educational* anthropology, and the issue of freedom connected with it. To get behind, or below, the debate about the confessional character of "Christian education" or "catechesis," the author has chosen to distill and extract from the various theories what they say about *education*, and to display this under the four categories listed above. Because *education* is the common thread within the various theories, it enables a comparison between the types, without having to enter into the complicated tangle of definitional problems that arises when theorists variously describe the enterprise as "catechesis," "Christian education," "religious instruction," or "religious education." It will remain for a concluding section to suggest ways that the findings in the following section can be applied to catechesis as such.

Chapter 3
The Psychological Type

The two theorists chosen to represent the psychological type are Lewis Joseph Sherrill and Josef Goldbrunner. Sherrill is situated in the historical context of the Protestant nurture theorists. Goldbrunner belongs to the Catholic kerygmatic movement. Because of their historical context, both authors claim to come to the subject of education from within the Christian tradition, and not from outside of it. Both have turned to psychology in a radical way, in order to fill out their image of the human being as a person growing within dynamic relationships. Yet, they both claim that their use of psychology is subordinate to their theology of revelation, which stresses the uniqueness of the Christian *koinonia,* and hence, the uniqueness of Christian education.

The purpose of this chapter is not to judge the merits of such a claim. The author does not intend to discuss whether Sherrill and Goldbrunner's theological stance is adequate for dealing with the infusion of psychological insights into their theories. The focus of this chapter, rather, is upon the distinctive educational anthropology and educational strategy that arise from their appeal to psychology. It will be shown that this educational approach has human freedom, understood in psychological terms, as one of its primary goals.

Sherrill's three major works, which are most appropriate here, are *The Struggle of the Soul* (1951), *The Gift of Power* (1955), and *Guilt and Redemption* (1957).[1] These works represent his latest, and most mature, attempt to bring psychology into Christian educational theory. Sherrill draws heavily upon the neo-Freudian psychology and psychotherapy of Karen Horney, Otto Rank, and Harry Stack Sullivan.[2] From psychology, he gains a perspective on the root psychic conflict in human beings. From psychotherapy, he acquires the insight that relationships either make or break a person.

Goldbrunner's three principal works, as far as we are concerned, are *Holiness Is Wholeness* (1955), *Cure of Mind and Cure of Soul* (1958), and *Realization: Anthropology of Pastoral Care* (1966).[3] Goldbrunner has been influenced almost entirely by Jungian depth psychology.[4] Through this type of psychology he is able to describe the human being as growing toward integration under the powerful thrust of the emerging self.

The chapter begins by outlining the fundamental anthropology found in these authors. This is followed by a scrutiny of the type of psychology which informs their anthropology. Finally, their view of "education for change," and its implications for the growth of human freedom, will be expounded. Sherrill and Goldbrunner represent the beginning of a typical approach to "education for freedom," an approach that can be found, to a greater or lesser extent, in all religious educators who turn to psychology for an understanding of human growth.

EDUCATIONAL ANTHROPOLOGY

To understand the educational anthropology found in Sherrill and Goldbrunner it is necessary to make a mental distinction between intrapsychic dynamics and the dynamics of interpersonal relationships. However, both authors insist that such a distinction cannot exist in reality, since what happens in the interior world of a person is never isolated from what happens in the web of interpersonal relations within which a person exists.

For the purpose of clarity, this presentation will begin by discussing mainly intrapsychic dynamics and then show how, for both authors, interior conflict, stagnation, or growth occur within close interpersonal relationships.

Intrapsychic Growth

Sherrill develops a psychology of the "self" to describe the process of human being and becoming. He says there is an inner power within every human being, an energizing force within the psyche, which propels us towards realizing the fullness of personal potential. It is more than the will to survive; it is the will toward wholeness and completion. From the beginning of life, the self strives to protect its integrity by determining its activity from within. There is an integrating center within the human being, a thrust for wholeness. The mark of wholeness, says Sherrill, is that persons are fulfilling their destiny. Each human being has an inward destiny, which like a seed or an egg, is directed towards an appointed end. By becoming the self that we are truly meant to be, we fulfill this unique destiny, and attain wholeness. [5]

In a similar way, Josef Goldbrunner stresses that human beings are not static abstract essences. In the fluidity of their concrete existence, they have the task of *becoming* persons. In contrast to the anonymous mass, the person is an individual spiritual being, which is unique and irreplaceable. But personhood is not a given; it is a task. It must be realized. It is incumbent upon human beings to take possession of their nature, to take hold of existence. At the core of the human being, says Goldbrunner, there is a personal sphere which must become the unifying directing power of one's actions. To live personally is to live from within this mysterious, free, and creative center of one's being. It is to have discovered the center of inner motivation, self-determination, and responsibility, and to act always from within that center.[6]

This inner destiny is experienced by the person as the pull of the future. While the self is somewhat shaped by past environing determinants, the self can go beyond this by responding to the call to full self-realization. There is always the dread and fear of growth, a shrinking back from struggle, the risk of going beyond the present. This motive of "shrinking back" is experienced differently at different stages in life's journey. At each stage there is an inner struggle to overcome the determinisms of the past, to resist the temptation to settle down at that stage of development. There is always the challenge to heed the call to grow to the fullness of maturity.[7]

Sherrill points out that the thrust toward self-transcendence is activated and energized by God. He uses the biblical notion of the human being created in the image and likeness of God to explain this. The inward impulsion toward wholeness is not just a power belonging to the human self; it is first and foremost an empowering by God. It is a gift. It is the summons experienced within the depth of the psyche, calling human beings to the full realization of their potential.[8] Human beings, says Sherrill, have the capacity to say yes or no to their existence as creatures. If they affirm their creatureliness, they enter into the fullness of what it means to be human; and in realizing their inward destiny as creatures, they come to know God.[9]

Sherrill also speaks of the summons of God within the individual by referring to the biblical notion of the "name." Each person has been named by God. Each person is unique and irreplaceable, called by name to become what he or she is meant to be. The calling by name not only means the designation of the task of becoming a person, but also implies that the recipient of the name participates in the power of God, enabling the individual to respond through self-possession and fearless growth toward wholeness.[10]

Intrapsychic Conflict

Both Sherrill and Goldbrunner make the distinction between the potential one has for self-actualization and the internal inhibiting forces that operate to frustrate the emergent self. The actual self is divided. There is a fundamental conflict in the human being that threatens to render the person impotent, unable to grow. This conflict with its power for disintegration is found to some degree within every human being. Sherrill stresses that the human plight is not primarily located outside of the person in the blind forces of fate, or in the determining power of environmental influences. Any effort to try to locate the basic human conflict outside of the individual is considered by Sherrill to be another symptom of the basic human sickness itself. Both the origin of the conflict and the responsibility for a solution are to be found primarily within the deepest realm of the human psyche.[11]

The human self, according to Sherrill, is under constant challenge. It experiences a basic threat towards its very existence. The three fundamental emotional threats to the self are hostility, anxiety, and guilt. These emotions, says Sherrill, are deeply rooted in the structure of the human person from childhood. While we experience guilt on a superficial level when we break an established code, there is also a deeper level of primal guilt which is part of the make-up of our humanity.[12]

The guilt experienced at the deepest strata of the human person is intimately connected with hostility and anxiety. Hostility arises when love is thwarted. As with guilt, hostility occurs also on the superficial level. However, Sherrill postulates that there is a deeper level of less-conscious, all-pervasive hostility that a human being carries. Primal hostility arises in very early childhood when Eros love, with its desire to control, dominate, and possess, is necessarily thwarted. Invariably this hostility is not dealt with adequately, and therefore it spawns deep feelings of anxiety and guilt.[13]

Sherrill distinguishes "basic anxiety" from "situational anxiety." The latter arises in particular circumstances which are the occasion (but not the cause) of manifest anxiety attacks (e.g., the experience of stage fright). However, underneath these occasional manifestations of anxiety, Sherrill postulates that there is a deep, and painful, yet vague and diffuse, apprehensiveness of the self as endangered at the core of its existence.[14] This anxiety, and the hostility that engenders it, cut into the foundations of self-hood. They are the destructive powers that cause a split within the self, disabling the self, preventing it from reaching the fullness of its potential.

A further conflict within the self is described by Sherrill in terms of the "idealized self-image." The actual existing self, he says, usually constructs an image of itself which does not correspond with what the self truly is. Human beings usually create self-images that either outstrip their realistic capacities, or which fall far short of what they could realistically expect to become. In both cases there is a distorted image of the self, a discrepancy between what one is and what one sees oneself as being and a discrepancy between what one thinks oneself can become and what one really has the capacity to become.[15] The road toward wholeness is the road out of this blindness to one's real self; it is the road to self-understanding and self-acceptance.

Josef Goldbrunner associates the "ideal-image" with the Jungian concept of "persona." The "persona," or "mask," that a person wears is a facade which intervenes between the true self and the world. The true self, he maintains, is asleep behind the mask. To become an individual, to become authentic, to become self-determining, the human being has to courageously drop the mask and bare his or her real self to the world. [16]

Goldbrunner adds another dimension from Jungian psychology to describe the basic psychic conflict. He connects the fundamental aversion for growth, and penchant for the past, with the human being's need to integrate the creative powers of the unconscious into the process of development. The process of growth involves the ongoing challenge not to ignore the nonrational dynamism of the unconscious. He affirms that the vital energy of the unconscious, arising from the depths of the person, is a constructive dynamism, but, if it is ignored, it will turn into an inimical and virulent force for destruction. [17] The challenge is to embrace this vital flow of energy through the process of individuation. This is a Jungian concept which Goldbrunner has developed at great length. [18] Basically, it involves the synthesis between the conscious and the unconscious, holding them together in tension. The central unifying power in the developing synthesis is the emerging self. The temptation is to collapse one of the polar opposites, either by becoming totally ego-oriented, attempting to fence out the unconscious realm, or by becoming so captivated by the unconscious that one undergoes a psychotic break from the outside world. The first option is the perennial sickness of a rationally dominated society which holds prediction and control at a premium.

Interpersonal Relationships

At the outset it was stated that, for both Sherrill and Goldbrunner, interior growth and conflict are not isolated from personal relationships. For both these authors, the self comes to be through close personal relationships. They prefer not to talk in terms of mechanistic cause-effect relationships. Such language emphasizes the externality of the relationships, whereas these authors want to emphasize interiority. Rather than talk in terms of stimulus-response mechanisms, they prefer to talk in terms of the emotional intensity and the quality of acceptance within the relationships.

All that has been previously stated about intrapsychic growth and conflict must be put in the context of creative or destructive relationships. For Sherrill, psychotherapy has provided the basic insight.

> The self is formed in its relationships with others. If it becomes de-formed, it becomes so in its relationships. If it is re-formed or trans-formed that too will be in its relationships.[19]

For Sherrill, relationships are both disabling and enabling; they are both malignant and therapeutic. The degree to which the self is positively affected by a relationship depends on the degree of intimacy and affection in the relationship. And the degree to which the self is empowered to grow within a relationship is according to the quality of the relationship.

In early childhood, according to Sherrill, the motive of Eros love dominates—there is a powerful desire on the part of the self to capture, hold onto, and possess the loved one. However, this Eros love must be thwarted. The frustration of Eros love breeds a deep-seated resentment in the person. This hostility can only be offset in the self by the gift of unremitting Agape love bestowed by another. Agape love, unlike Eros love, has the motive of enhancing the status of the loved one. It gives rise to actions designed to liberate the loved one by means of the relationship, so the other may grow to the fullness of his or her potential. Especially in early childhood, and also throughout life, human beings are in need of this warm, accepting, nonjudgmental and nondominative love. It is only this type of love which can liberate the self from its fundamental hostility and, therefore, from accompanying anxiety and guilt.[20]

In Sherrill's perspective, then, defective love relationships condition the conflict within the self. This conflict can be healed through corrective, redemptive relationships. The paradigm for growth is the therapeutic relationship. The sense of guilt, with hostility and anxiety at its root, can be relieved by entering a dynamic, controlled relationship with a therapist. In therapy, the sufferer, who is simply a more acute case than the so-called "normal" person, discovers unconditional acceptance by the therapist. While the sufferer relives the part of experience that has been destructive, the therapist enters that person's private hell, accepting the person as he or she is without any advice or judgments. Through the experience of this Agape love, a new self comes into being. There is a "rebirth," as the previous self passes away and a new one is brought to life. The real self emerges through the experience of liberating Agape love.[21]

Goldbrunner, it should be noted, also emphasizes the role of healing relationships. He puts the category of "encounter" at the center of human growth. The actuation of the person depends on the person being "called forth" by the other. In encounter, the self is summoned to open up, to take a stand in regard to its existence, to respond to the call to reach towards the fullness of its potential.[22]

For both Sherrill and Goldbrunner, the community which comprises the context for growing selves is a network of I-Thou relationships, motivated by Agape love, which confirms selves in the impulse to grow. These relationships are redemptive, since they deliver a person from captivity to falsity and provide the opportunity for authenticity and wholeness.

INFLUENCE OF PSYCHOLOGY

Having presented the broad lines of the anthropology that underlies the typical educational approach taken by Sherrill and

Goldbrunner, we are in a position to state clearly what this educational approach is. However; before doing this, it is appropriate and instructive to show how these two authors use the human sciences to attain their image of human growth and, hence, their view of education for freedom.

Sherrill draws on psychoanalysis, psychotherapy, and existential reflection to describe the phenomenon which passes for human nature. To explain the split within the self, he acknowledges that he is appealing to clinical psychology, a generic term that he uses to include such diverse psychologists as Jung, Adler, and Rank.[23] His attraction to these psychologists is in direct contrast to his disdain for what he calls "academic psychology"—that is, any type of psychology that interprets the human situation as something imposed from without by external forces, consequently relieving the person of responsibility and freedom of choice.[24] Neo-Freudian and Jungian psychology view the basic conflict, and need for healing, in terms of the interior dynamism within the person. Such a view is in contrast to the view of the human being as an "animal-in-a-cage-adapting-to-the-environment," which he claims is propagated by the behaviorists.[25]

The concept of "basic anxiety," characteristic of the human predicament in Sherrill's thought, comes from psychologists such as Karen Horney, Harry Stack Sullivan, and Rollo May, as well as from existentialists such as Paul Tillich and Søren Kierkegaard. Horney, for example, has described it as "the feeling a child has of being isolated and helpless in a potentially hostile world."[26] Rollo May calls it a threat to the self's existence.[27] In a similar vein, Søren Kierkegaard writes of existential despair, "the sickness unto death," which is destructive of the self unless one yields in a relationship with God.[28] Sherrill also uses Tillich's analysis of the three types of existential anxiety—the anxiety of "fate and death," the anxiety of "emptiness and meaninglessness," and the anxiety of "guilt and condemnation."[29] For Tillich, if persons maintain the courage to take anxiety upon themselves, they can affirm their personal being and, hence, participate in the self-affirmation of being itself.[30]

The idea of an "idealized image" in Sherrill's writings is taken from Karen Horney. Horney describes it as an image created by the neurotic of what "he believes himself to be, or of what at the time he feels he can or ought to be."[31] The image, either conscious or unconscious, is out of contact with reality.

Sherrill's view of the self as developing within both creative and destructive relationships is also taken from psychologists such as Horney and Sullivan. However, his analysis of Eros and Agape love can be traced especially to Otto Rank.[32] Sherrill's contention that hostility arises from the thwarting of Eros love corresponds to Rank's observation that "love so frequently changes into hatred when the individual feels disappointed or hurt," a fact that indicates for Rank that there is a deep-seated relation between love and hostility.[33] In addition to Rank's influence, it is possible that Sherrill's idea of the self growing through tension toward wholeness is derived from Carl Jung's depth psychology. While Sherrill makes no explicit reference to Jung's writings in connection with this notion, he shows an acquaintance with, and sympathy for, Jungian psychology in general.[34]

Whereas Sherrill is mainly influenced by neo-Freudian psychology and psychotherapy, Goldbrunner is mainly influenced by Jungian depth psychology. The Jungian process of "individuation" is taken by Goldbrunner and used to describe the process of self-realization through interpersonal relationships. Wholeness is attained through the integration of opposites under the unifying activity of the emerging self. Goldbrunner identifies this psychological concept of the self with the existential concept of the dynamic person.[35] He summarily refers to many existential philosophers who have influenced him, including Søren Kierkegaard, Karl Jaspers, Martin Heidegger, and Gabriel Marcel, as well as theologians such as Romano Guardini and Karl Rahner.[36] From existentialism Goldbrunner also gained a profound sense of the importance of the individual. He quotes Kierkegaard: "To become an individual—that is the phase through which the world and Christianity must still pass! The individual is our great hope, he is the source and fountain head!"[37]

With Sherrill and Goldbrunner, we witness two of the earliest attempts to bring the insights of psychological development into the heart of educational theory within the church. It is not our purpose here to study how well they integrated theological insights with these psychological perspectives. These authors are presented here as typical representatives of those religious education theorists who fearlessly bring psychology into their system. This infusion of psychology creates a distinctive educational anthropology and a distinctive educational strategy.

Some explanation must be given of the above inclusion of "existentialism" as an influence on these authors. The influence of existentialism has been incorporated into this section dealing with the influence of psychology because both Sherrill and Goldbrunner were pathfinders in an approach to church education which appealed to "existentialism" precisely *within the context of psychology*. This is significant to note, since the appeal to existentialism, to a certain extent, gives a unique stamp to the psychological approach. Even though Sherrill and Goldbrunner used different psychological sources, their basic perspective on human growth is the same. A generic title that could be applied to the type of human science used by these authors, and also by so many contemporary church educationalists, is "existential psychology."[38] Rollo May explains that in psychology the term "existentialism" means "centering upon the existing person . . . the emphasis on the human being as he is emerging, becoming."[39] The existentialist posture in psychology opposes any tendency to treat human beings as machines, and takes a stand with the unique individual over against the forces for "massification" within society.

The "existentialist" stance is pervasive within humanistic American psychology, and informs much of current educational theory. This posture can be identified with the "third force" psychologists who emerged as a reaction against both behaviorism and Freudianism. They claim that both movements, revolutionary in themselves, were theories of mechanistic determinism. The "third force" theorists argue that neither approach left enough room for spontaneity, creativity, and responsibility. The "third force" was spearheaded by psychologists such as Alfred Adler, Carl Jung, and Otto Rank, who, each in his own way, broke away from orthodox Freudianism. It also includes in its ambit the theories of Abraham Maslow and Carl Rogers, who, each in his own way, broke away from behaviorism.[40]

The educational anthropology of Sherrill and Goldbrunner is situated within this broad stream of thought which continues to inform church-oriented educational theory. The main features characteristic of this approach can be summarized in the following way. These features, it should be noted, serve also as a summary of the view of humanity found in Sherrill and Goldbrunner:

1. The human person is not explained so much in terms of where it has been, but in terms of where it is going. This is a strong Jungian perspective, but it is shared by all humanists. The *forward-going* character of personality development is stressed. Human beings experience the pull of the future, the call to self-realization.

2. Even though the forward thrust has primacy, there is a *realism* about the inner forces that inhibit growth. Captivity to past heritage is a consistent theme of neo-Freudianism.

3. Primacy is given to the discovery of *inner meanings* and

purposes; coming into touch with the inner flow of experiencing within the human person.

4. The individual's *power to choose* is emphasized. They claim that Freudian undermining of autonomous will, and Marxian socio-economic critique, tend to play into the modern human neurosis—the undermining of the experience of self as responsible, the sapping of will and decision. No matter how great the forces victimizing the human being, existential psychology claims that any human being has the capacity to *know* that he or she is being victimized, and, therefore, can *relate* meaningfully to his or her fate. There is always a kernel of power within the person to take a stand, even if it has to be a solitary defiant stand, against the external deterministic powers of a technocratic society, or against the internal deterministic mechanism inherited from the past. The human being makes him/herself through decisions.

5. There is a concern for *authenticity*. The authentic person does not have to remain in the grip of a society which has provided a set of roles, or masks, for the person to wear. Growth to authenticity means deliverance from the masks, and the assumption of a new relation to the society. Individuals have it within their power to resist enculturation. They have the power of self-transcendence. The sociopolitical arena, in itself, is a source of inauthenticity, and cannot provide true values. Values can only emerge from within the experiencing of the unique human being.

6. The themes of dialogue, *encounter*, meeting are prominent. All emphasize the healing power of unconditional acceptance in a therapeutic relationship.

7. The human being is regarded as largely *unpredictable*. Humanists stress the spontaneity and creativity of human self-expression. What is most characteristic of the human being, they claim, is the creation of the new and unexpected, the breaking

out of any straitjacket imposed by the past. The self-actualizing person is characterized by the ability to create a new and alternative future.

EDUCATION FOR CHANGE

The preceding discussion provided a profile of the process of human development envisaged by Sherrill and Goldbrunner, and demonstrated how their view of human growth is dependent on a broad stream of humanistic American psychology. The task now is to specify what they consider to be the goal and means of education itself.

Education, for Sherrill, has the aim of changing people. It does so by seeking to align itself with the way people naturally develop. The changes that education hopes to facilitate are primarily changes within the interior life of the person. "The principal changes which are the subject of concern are changes in the depth of the self, instead of those which are at the periphery of the self."[41]

Sherrill is opposed to making the aims of education too specific; to designate specific cognitional, emotional, or behavioral outcomes would be a form of manipulation. He says that attempts to predetermine outcomes must destroy the freedom of the individual. Yet, while he opposes the determination of outcomes, he argues that there should be the general aim of "change" in the person toward greater self-realization and wholeness.[42]

Changes within the person toward wholeness, according to Sherrill's perspective, are promoted by dynamic therapeutic relationships. These relationships release the latent power within the individual for self-actualization, and liberate the individual from the powers of hostility, anxiety, and guilt which prevent the possibility of growth. Therefore, education for change occurs within the context of a community comprised of "I-Thou" relationships, motivated by Agape love. This education for change cannot be perfectly planned or predicted. All the same, people can deliberately engage in the enterprise of changing another, not by directly trying to alter another's interior life, but by indirectly offering warm, supportive, nonjudgmental love; thus confirming the other in the power to grow. The offer of Agape love delivers the other from deep-seated emotional blocks that prevent growth, and affirms the intrinsic dynamism toward self-realization and wholeness.

Both Sherrill and Goldbrunner consider education within a developmental perspective. Education for change has a different orientation as the age level of the individual changes. At each age level there are typical developmental tasks which face the individual and constitute a challenge to grow. In childhood, according to Sherrill, the person is faced with the challenge to become an individual "I"; in adolescence, the challenge is to become independent from one's parents; in young adulthood, the challenge is to find one's basic identifications in society and assume mature responsibilities; in middle life, the challenge is to achieve a mature philosophy of life; in later life, the challenge is to achieve simplification of life. Throughout this process, the self's growth to wholeness is facilitated by personal fellowship within the community, but because the growth needs of the self vary according to the stage of development, so the educational thrust ought vary accordingly. [43]

This developmentalist perspective can be seen clearly also in Goldbrunner, who relies totally upon the Jungian understanding of human development through individuation. Goldbrunner describes four stages of development, to which the educational effort must be tied. In real life, he says, these stages tend to interpenetrate; however, the typical problems that demand solutions at each stage do seem to have a special intensity at one age level rather than another.[44] The first challenge to the human being in childhood and adolescence is to become differentiated as an individual. The *persona,* or mask, that persons wear has been supplied by public opinion and the expectations of others. Education has the task of appealing to the true self behind the *persona;* its effectiveness depends on the personal authenticity and transparency of the educator.[45]

The second challenge to the human being, associated with early adulthood, is to open up one's individuality toward others. This transition is often initiated by an awakening to the other sex, which has special power to activate the capacity for encounter. The first attempts at love are usually motivated by Eros, and are fraught with ideal projections upon the loved one. Education meets the needs of this stage by creating an atmosphere of warmth and protection where encounter can occur, and a decision to respond to the call of the other can be made honestly and freely.[46]

The third challenge to the human being, associated with middle age, arises from the necessity to realize the depth of one's solidarity with all men and women in common creatureliness. The more deeply the individual becomes grounded in the authentic self, the more he or she becomes a true brother or sister in the human community. By coming in touch with one's creatureliness, the human being grows in awareness of the common plight shared with all people, and grows in compassion. Education, at this stage, is directed to the continued expansion of the self. The most important element is the existential depth of the educator. Confronted by a person whose existential depth calls to their own personal depth, people are challenged to enter more deeply into themselves, and hence discover human communion.[47]

The final challenge in human development, according to

Goldbrunner, is present in some way all along the road. It is the challenge to come into touch with the ultimate ground of one's existence. The religious question in the Jungian scheme attains greatest poignancy in the twilight years of adulthood. This opening up to the Transcendent Other, in a responding attitude of trust, is the highest actualization of the person. The person awakens to its full "name." To awaken to the sense of dependency on the Ultimate Other means to grow also in one's capacity to live from the center of one's being, to grow in the capacity for encounter with others, and to grow in the sense of solidarity with others. Educational efforts which invite and challenge the self to grow through close personal relationships are also efforts to invite and challenge the self to let go, and be grasped by the Transcendent.[48]

EDUCATION FOR FREEDOM

The typical educational approach, represented by Sherrill and Goldbrunner, is a deliberate effort to change selves through the medium of quality relationships. What significance has this approach for freedom? The freedom offered by this approach is a freedom *from* psychic disorder and *from* external impersonal forces, and a freedom *for* self-realization and wholeness. The locus, or arena, of freedom lies within the person. This approach takes for granted that every individual has the essential power to choose, the power to decide to grow or not to grow, the power to actuate one's personhood or to live as a pseudo-person at the mercy of public opinion and a collectivized society. Granted this essential capacity to make a decision for or against growth in each individual, education seeks to encourage a decision *for* growth, and to create the conditions whereby the internal and external forces inhibiting the exercise of this capacity will be minimized. By making a decision for growth, the person is exercising a capacity which is part of the essential structure of the human being. The person's essential freedom is activated and engaged by yielding to the inner thrust toward self-realization experienced as the pull of the future. This surrender is at the same time the beginning of a mastery over one's own existence vis-à-vis the threat of collectivization and anonymity.

In this approach, freedom is *from* psychic disorder. In Sherrill's terminology, this means freedom from excessive hostility, anxiety, and guilt; as well as freedom *from* an image of the self which is alien to its true nature. In Goldbrunner's language, it is freedom *from* the inhibition of social masks, and freedom *from* enslavement to Eros-motivated "projection."

It is also freedom *from* external forces. Sherrill refers to "vast impersonal forces" external to the self that seek to enslave it.[49] They are the forces of mass persuasion and manipulation that threaten the inward capacity of self-determination. Goldbrunner speaks of the almost inescapable slavery to numbers, the quantification of the human race.[50] Both have an aversion for mechanization and the technocracy. With their existentialist stance, they affirm the inner power of the unique individual to withstand all outward pressures and not submit to the persuasion and compulsion of others. Goldbrunner argues that by becoming one's true self, the anonymous mass is experienced freely and compassionately as one's brothers and sisters in the common human quest.

It is freedom *for* self-realization, for the fulfillment of one's inward destiny.[51] Positive freedom means to become whole. In this sense it can be claimed that their educational approach has the motif of freedom at the center of concern and all educational strategies are designed to enhance this human freedom through liberating relationships. As was shown above, liberating relationships, in this approach, are relationships characterized by unconditional acceptance. The therapeutic encounter is one that creates accepting space for the other, so he or she is enabled to grow. Freedom is not possible outside of the context of these *Agape* relationships. A community which is a network of creative I-Thou relationships is the best educational medium for promoting personal freedom. Deprived of this continuing affirmation, the person is abandoned to self-belittling torture and a life imprisoned within a psychic heritage of fear and guilt. The enabling relationships within the *koinonia* do not just support a person through affirmation of personal worth, but also challenge the person to transcend the confining influences of the past, to reach beyond the present stage of growth and enter a new level of freedom.

The ongoing quest for freedom which stirs within the core of a person's being is facilitated by accepting relationships. It is an insatiable hunger that is never fully satisfied. Education, in this approach, seeks to tap the power of this inner quest for freedom, to eliminate any relationship that would frustrate this quest, and to enable its ongoing fruition through confirming relationships.

NOTES FOR CHAPTER 3

1. Lewis Joseph Sherrill, *The Struggle of the Soul* (New York: The Macmillan Company, 1951) (hereafter referred to as SS); *The Gift of Power* (New York: The Macmillan Company, 1955) (hereafter referred to as GP); *Guilt and Redemption* (Richmond: John Knox Press, 1945) (hereafter referred to as GR).

2. See Maureen Murphy, *The Contribution of the Psychological Approach of Lewis Joseph Sherrill to the Twentieth-Century American Religious Educational Scene* (Ann Arbor, Mich.: University Microfilms, 1973).

3. Josef Goldbrunner, *Holiness Is Wholeness*, trans. Stanley Godman (New York: Pantheon, 1955); *Cure of Mind and Cure of Soul*, trans. Stanley Godman (New York: Pantheon, 1958) (hereafter referred to as CMCS); *Realization: Anthropology of Pastoral Care*, trans. Paul C. Bailey and Elizabeth Reinecki (Notre Dame, Ind.: University of Notre Dame Press, 1966) (hereafter referred to as *Realization*).

4. See Josef Goldbrunner, *Individuation: A Study of the Depth Psychology of Carl Gustav Jung* (New York: Pantheon, 1956).

5. Sherrill, *GP*, pp. 5 and 23; see also *SS*, p. 8.

6. Goldbrunner, *CMCS*, pp. 12, 15; see also *Realization*, p. 22.

7. Sherrill, *SS*, p. 10.

8. Idem, *GP*, pp. 191–92.

9. Ibid., pp. 6, 16.

10. Ibid., p. 21.

11. Sherrill, *GR*, pp. 13–61. In the first two chapters of this book Sherrill establishes that the ancient dilemma whether the conflict in man is from without (according to the fate of the gods) or from within (according to the split between mind and body) is similar to the modern dilemma between the behavioral psychologists, who want to place the conflict outside man, and the psychotherapists, who want to place the conflict within man. Sherrill opts for the latter.

12. Ibid., p. 78.

13. Ibid., p. 95–100.

14. Sherrill, *GP*, p. 29; see also *GR*, p. 101.

15. Sherrill, *GP*, pp. 35–40.

16. Goldbrunner, *CMCS*, pp. 43–56; *Realization*, pp. 61–90.

17. Idem, *Holiness is Wholeness*, p. 35.

18. His major presentation of this concept is found in *Individuation*. This book provides the details of the Jungian theory. The major focus in the present discussion is not upon the merits of Goldbrunner's early exposition of Jung, but upon his later attempt to use Jungian psychology for his own distinctive view of how the person develops.

19. Sherrill, *GP*, p. 45.

20. Sherrill, *GR*, pp. 98–100.

21. Ibid., pp. 142–59.

22. Goldbrunner, *Realization*, p. 19

23. Sherrill, *GR*, pp. 57–61.

24. Ibid., p. 45.

25. Ibid., p. 46.

26. Karen Horney, *Our Inner Conflicts: A Constructive Theory of Neurosis* (New York: W. W. Norton and Company, Inc., 1945), p. 41. Sherrill refers to this aspect of Horney's thought in *GR*, p. 102. For the same idea, see also Harry Stack Sullivan, *The Interpersonal Theory of Psychiatry*, ed. Helen S. Perry and Mary L. Ganud (New York: W. W. Norton and Co., Inc., 1953), p. 115.

27. Rollo May, *The Meaning of Anxiety* (New York: The Ronald Press Company, 1950), pp. 191–93. Sherrill acknowledges indebtedness to May in *GP*, p. 27. May is a proponent of "existential psychology." See "Recent Developments in Psychology and Their Significance for Religious Education," *Religious Education* 38 (May–June 1943): 142–52.

28. Søren Kierkegaard, *The Sickness unto Death*, trans. Walter Lawrie (Princeton: Princeton University Press, 1941). Sherrill refers to this aspect of thought in *GR*, p. 101.

29. Paul Tillich, *The Courage to Be* (New Haven: Yale University Press, 1952), pp. 40–54. Sherrill refers to this in *GP*, p. 28.

30. Tillich, *The Courage to Be*, p. 181.

31. Horney, *Our Inner Conflicts*, p. 96. Referred to by Sherrill in *GP*, p. 97.

32. See Otto Rank, *Beyond Psychology* (New York: Dover Publications, Inc., 1958).

33. Ibid., p. 190.

34. Sherrill refers to Jung in *Understanding Children* (New York: Abingdon Press, 1939), p. 57; in *GR*, pp. 48, 49, 51, 53, 148, and 212; and in two articles: "A Sense of Sin in Present Day Experience," *Religion in Life* 8 (1939): 513; "A Review of Modern Man in Search of a Soul," *The Register* 22 (1933): 16–17. The evidence is not strong enough to make anything but a tenuous connection.

35. Goldbrunner, CMCS, p. 30; see also *Realization*, p. 26.

36. Idem, CMCS, p. 17, fn. 2; p. 18, fn. 1; p. 19, fn. 1. See also *Realization*, p. 26, fn. 8.

37. Idem, *Realization*, p. 25.

38. The term "existential psychology" has its roots in the European psychologists, Ludwig Binswanger and Medard Boss, who were profoundly influenced by Martin Heidegger and Karl Jaspers. Hall and Lindzey present "existential psychology" as a discrete theory of personality, with Rollo May and Adrian Van Kaam as American representatives. See *Theories of Personality*, 3rd ed., ed. Calvin S. Hall and Gardner Lindzey (New York: John Wiley and Sons, 1978), pp. 311–45. In the American context, the term "existential psychology" takes on a broader connotation than its strict European origins. Hall and Lindzey point out that Gordon Allport, Abraham Maslow, and Carl Rogers have been influenced by existentialism. In the context of the buoyant American experience, there has been a tendency to overlook or to excise the more pessimistic elements of the existentialist outlook. Also, unlike the strict European interpretation of "existential psychology," which excludes all explanations of human existence in terms of self or the unconscious psychic processes, the term in this country includes those theories of the self, such as that of Carl Jung, which emphasize the creative internal energies propelling human growth. See Floyd W. Matson, "Introduction," in *Without/Within: Behaviorism and Humanism*, ed. Floyd W. Matson (Monterey, Calif.: Brooks/Cole Publishing Company, 1973), p. 5.

39. Rollo May, "The Emergence of Existential Psychology," in *Existential Psychology*, ed. Rollo May (New York: Random House, 1966), p. 16.

40. Floyd W. Matson, "Humanistic Theory: The Third Revolution in Psychology," in *Without/Within: Behaviorism and Humanism*, ed. Floyd W. Matson

(Monterey, Calif.: Brooks/Cole Publishing Company, 1973), pp. 11–12; see also Frank G. Goble, *The Third Force: The Psychology of Abraham Maslow* (New York: Pocket Books, 1971), pp. 3–22.

41. Sherrill, GP, p. 83.

42. Ibid.

43. Sherrill, SS, *passim*.

44. Goldbrunner, CMCS, p. 42. For an account of this development through age levels, see *Realization*, pp. 162–90.

45. Idem, CMCS, p. 56. This is developed in greater detail in *Realization*, pp. 78–80.

46. For an account of the general trend at this stage, see Goldbrunner, CMCS, pp. 59–72; *Realization*, pp. 91–117. The phenomenon of "projection" is a technical Jungian term. In the case of the male it is *anima* projection; and in the case of the female it is *animus* projection. The *anima* and *animus* are archetypes which one must come to terms with by objectifying them, thus differentiating oneself from them. See Goldbrunner, *Individuation*, pp. 128–29. For a description of "encounter" as an educational category, see *Realization*, p. 115, and Josef Goldbrunner, "Catechesis and Encounter", in *New Catechetical Methods*, trans. Sister M. Veronica Riedl (Notre Dame, Indiana: University of Notre Dame Press, 1965), p. 26.

47. For the challenge of this stage, see Goldbrunner, *Realization*, pp. 118–41; CMCS, pp. 72–84. For the educational approach through "authenticity," see CMCS, p. 106, and *Realization*, p. 138.

48. Goldbrunner, *Realization*, p. 145; see also CMCS. p. 96. Goldbrunner uses language that carries much more theological weight than the language used here. Within the limited parameters of this presentation, it is sufficient to note that human development for Goldbrunner, as indeed for Sherrill, opens up, at every stage, for participation in divine life.

49. Sherrill, GP, pp. 20, 30.

50. Goldbrunner, *Realization*, p. 130.

51. Sherrill, GP, p. 21.

Chapter 4
The Political Type

There is a long tradition in the United States which proposes social reconstruction as the outcome of good education.[1] In this tradition, education seeks to achieve nothing less than the transformation of society. In such an approach, education cannot be politically neutral; it necessarily is situated within a social context, and takes on certain institutional forms itself. In this perspective, education, to be liberating, has to promote social change toward the formation of a greater society, as well as undergo self-reformation to prevent stagnation and consequent emasculation of its transformative power.

The political[2] type of education for freedom is represented by the later writings of Gabriel Moran. Three of Moran's major works come under scrutiny in this chapter. The first is *Design for Religion* (1970).[3] In this work Moran argues that the catechetical enterprise in the Catholic church is wedded to a preaching model. It is concerned with transmission of a revelation which the church claims to possess. Furthermore, catechesis in the Catholic church is geared toward producing practicing church members. The church's catechetical efforts are more concerned with promoting institutional loyalty than with promoting the quest for the transcendent, which is common to all human beings. Moran claims that a truly religious education is ecumenical and cannot be bound to the imperialistic claims of any church. Religious education cannot be the possession of any partisan group; it is grounded in experience common to all human beings.

The concern of religious education coincides with the concern of all good education—the transformation of society.

The second work under consideration in this chapter is *The Present Revelation* (1972).[4] In this work Moran attempts to give a systematic presentation of what he means by "revelation." He says that the fundamental presupposition of Christian theology is that the church possesses a revelation which is not given to anyone else. This claim to a "Christian revelation" is false. There is one universal revelation founded in the breadth and depth of human experience. The Christian tradition represents one particular expression of this dimension of Mystery in human life. In this book, Moran is trying to take the word "revelation" from the possession of Christian theologians, and to invest it with new meaning so that it can operate as a comprehensive liberating metaphor.[5]

The third major source for this chapter is *Religious Body* (1974).[6] Here Moran again attacks "intramural" theologians within the church. The church, he says, cannot be judged by scripture, but must be reformed according to the tenets of human experience. Preaching must be replaced by good education, and concerns for institutional perpetuation must be replaced by good community. The valid religious body is where education and community join together to unfold the religious dimension of human life. Only the emergence of true community and true education can change the linguistic and institutional oppression found in the church and in the broader society.

In his writings prior to these works, Moran had sought to improve catechetics within the Catholic church. In these later works, he shows he has more in common with the Protestant religious education movement in the earlier part of this century than with the Catholic catechetical movement or the Christian education movement. His critique of catechetics and Christian education is reminiscent of Harrison S. Elliott's last-ditch stand against the new wave of neo-orthodoxy in 1940. The underlying issue is one of authority, or in other words, one of the ultimate criteria for the enterprise called religious education. For Moran, the ultimate norm of truth is common human experience, which is constantly unfolding and expanding. Scripture and church are human constructions that cannot be ultimate criteria of truth.[7] This chapter does not intend to discuss the merits or demerits of such a claim by Moran. It is sufficient to note, in this regard, that Moran's approach to religious education is strikingly similar to that taken by the early religious education movement. His confidence in education as a salvific remedy for society, his conviction that good education is necessarily religious, and his attack upon imperialistic, intramural forms of church education are all characteristics of the early religious education movement. In addition, his understanding of experience, which is the key category of his anthropology, comes from the educational philosophy of John Dewey.

This chapter will prescind from the methodological questions raised by Moran's neo-liberalism and will focus instead upon his educational anthropology, showing that Moran attempts to find a balance between individual and society, and between the rational and the nonrational. These two tensions are closely interrelated in his understanding of human growth toward freedom. It will be shown that he expands the psychological model of human growth presented in the previous chapter and subsumes it within a broader social and political context. Education for growth in intelligence is also education for social change. Education for freedom in this approach does not simply concentrate on changing hearts through loving relationships. It aims to change oppressive social structures which prevent the possibility of psychological freedom in the first place.

Moran has been chosen to represent this type because his

analysis of the social predicament and his solution to overcome it are distinctively North American. He has much in common with Paulo Freire, whose writings have made considerable impact on contemporary church education.[8] Moran considers Freire's contribution to be in the realm of pedagogy alone. Moran does not analyze society in the same way as Freire. While Freire grounds the basic social conflict in the class struggle between the wealthy minority and the oppressed majority, Moran grounds the basic social conflict in the over-arching bureaucracy spawned by a technological society. Given Freire's Latin American context, where the blatant injustice of economic structures perpetuates the poverty and ignorance of the masses, his education by revolutionary praxis is understandable. Moran also must be understood in his peculiar cultural context. The brand of bureaucratic superstructure, which, for him, is the *bête-noir* of all social ills, is a characteristic of a technological society. In addition, Moran's solution, unlike Freire's, is not "revolutionary" in the political sense of the word. Nevertheless, it *is* a political solution. Education, for Moran, should rebuild society; with that purpose, it cannot be politically neutral. However, education as a social liberating power, in Moran's writings, is more a process of evolution than a praxis for revolution.

EDUCATIONAL ANTHROPOLOGY

In his earlier writings, Moran had focused upon the unfolding of an individual's personal history.[9] Like Sherrill and Goldbrunner, he had emphasized the prereflective and prethematic summons of the individual who is called by name to the full realization of his or her potential. Moran concentrated on the relationship of salvation history to the struggle within the individual for truth and freedom.[10] The discovery of meaning in one's personal story and the power to make a decision affirming or denying some or all elements in the story were Moran's foremost concerns. His attention was riveted on the sphere of close personal relationships within which an individual develops, since he claimed that encounters with another mediate the inner summons to authenticity.[11] He was occupied mainly with the possibility of promoting interior change within individuals without undermining their quest for truth and without destroying the power of autonomous decision making.[12] At this stage, Moran's anthropology had a tendency towards *privatization,* the exclusive preoccupation with the internal life of the individual without cognizance of the socio-economic realities which shape the individual's consciousness in the first place.

New Social Awareness

With *Design for Religion,* Moran began to expand his vision of the individual within society. He remarks how much recent educational literature has dwelt almost exclusively on the I-Thou relationship between teacher and students, and explicitly acknowledges the major deficiency in his previous position.[13] He consciously broadens his educational anthropology to include a social dimension. Now he realizes that economic, social, and political elements function to either frustrate or create opportunities for mutual interpersonal relating. To build a paradigm of education in terms of I-Thou encounters, as if they are isolated from the powerful influence of social and political institutions, would be to construct an illusory basis for an education for freedom. Moran insists that the social dimension of education means much more than teaching individuals about social problems and how to cope with them. The social framework, he says, is formative of the person's consciousness; it is "at once his life blood and his constriction."[14] The matrix of relationships within which the person exists is not just comprised of I-Thou relationships, but includes, as well, economic, social, and political institutions which also structure the consciousness of the individual.

Moran points out that the individual's power to choose is not some impregnable fortress, from which the individual through sheer exertion of will can turn social disadvantage into social advantage. Facile pronouncements by those who have a vested interest in the status quo that social advancement is simply a matter of "making the right choices" ensure the perpetuation of the present order of things and keep some people in an oppressed situation. For some people, the options available are so limited by the oppressive social system that there is no possibility of making the "right choice" at all.[15] Moran argues that a person's quest for truth and freedom cannot be considered in a vacuum; this quest is intrinsically bound to the task of reconstructing the society as a whole.

Language

An important aspect of Moran's understanding of the socially structured human consciousness is his emphasis upon *language*. The human being is a being of language. It is obvious, he says, that knowledge determines speaking, but not so obvious that patterns of speech determine modes of thinking as well. The way a person speaks structures consciousness.[16]

Moran does not want to isolate language, as a set of abstract meanings, from language as a bodily expression of the human being. Language, he says, in its broadest sense, is a bodying forth of the human being in the world. Therefore, it is both verbal and nonverbal. The language of a society contains the objectified meanings that have been externalized by human beings. Language is authentic if it is a true expression of the shared life of a person, and, to remain authentic, it must undergo constant modification as the experience of the people changes.[17]

Language, according to Moran, functions to place agreed

boundaries on a community; it functions to keep the community together, and makes the community what it is. A language is handed down by a people, and it contains the common meanings of the people sedimented within it. Therefore, says Moran, how individuals will know, and what thoughts are possible for them, will be determined by the language that comes to them from within the tradition of their people.[18] Received language places limitations on a person's freedom by the simple fact that a person must learn to think within a given pattern of discourse. However, Moran does not consider this limitation, in itself, to be a form of coercion. Language is not necessarily alienating. Language becomes a form of enslavement only when it serves to legitimize built-in structures of oppression that prevent the ongoing regeneration of society, and hence prevent the growth of individual freedom.[19]

Moran considers language to be potentially liberating when it is simple, poetic, and paradoxical. Discursive statements do not have the power to open up the imaginative and symbolic dimensions of life. The language of story and myth, on the other hand, touch deeper levels of the human person and provide a way of integrating life within community. Rather than close off reality through rationalistic speech patterns that are insensitive to the whole of human experience, liberating education needs to provide a language which opens up reality in all its breadth and depth.[20]

The Crippling Power of Bureaucracy

Moran's later writings, we have noted, belong within the broad educational tradition in the United States that sees education as a lever for social reconstruction. However, he does not share the optimism of George Albert Coe that the "democracy of God" is almost inevitably unfolding under the intrinsic power of social evolution. There are serious impediments to social regeneration. The most powerful obstruction, he says, is the modern bureaucratic pattern of social organization which operates to control and domesticate the very forces that can humanize society. Bureaucracy, he says, is "simply the metaphor of the machine imposed on human relationships."[21] It moves relentlessly toward eliminating authentically human elements from society. Both political and economic life are bureaucratic in form. The threat of bureaucracy is that society will become an enormous "megamachine." As long as bureaucracy prevails, there is an inevitable drift toward the dehumanization of society.

According to Moran, bureaucracy resists changes toward humanization of society by controlling the sources of such change. The redemption of society can only be attained through the triple powers of education, community, and religion, which can operate as a counterforce to the crippling power of bureaucracy.[22] However, these three redeeming powers are conveniently kept in check. Moran indicates two basic modes of control used to domesticate these powers. First, the bureaucratic society controls the linguistic patterns, maintaining the fiction in people's minds that the present social system is entirely adequate. Second, the bureaucratic society promotes the illusion that rationality is the only worthwhile dimension of human existence.

Bureaucratic Control of Language

The bureaucratic social organization, says Moran, renders education, community, and religion ineffective by "blurring the language" used to describe them. Moran is convinced that whoever controls the dominant metaphors in society is the master of that society. Bureaucracy maintains control by making sure that the words "education," "community," and "religion" are overused and hence debased of all meaning. In addition, these words are extended to inadequate applications. Being vague and ill-defined, they are rendered impotent.[23]

The most devastating linguistic tactic of the bureaucracy, according to Moran, is not just to confuse the meaning of the terms, but also to use language so that community, education, and religion are each identified with a single institution (family, school, and church, respectively). The promotion of this linguistic pattern legitimizes the monopoly that these institutions have over the three liberating powers in society. It becomes a taken-for-granted reality that family is the paradigm for community, that school is the paradigm for education, and that church is the paradigm for religion. In addition, says Moran, each of these monopolizing institutions is identified with women and children, provinces of helpless minorities. This bureaucratic pattern of language, endemic within present society, not only segregates the three forces for liberation, with the implicit purpose of "divide and conquer," but also is divisive by setting up discrimination between men and women, and between old and young.[24]

Moran suggests that the way to unleash the liberating powers of education, community, and religion is to attain linguistic clarity by restoring their true meaning. However, the restoration of language is not enough. There must also be work to reform the institutions themselves and, at the same time, work for a diversification of forms so that the monopoly will be challenged. His ideal society is one where community, education, and religion intersect.[25]

Bureaucratic Rationalism

The second debilitating tactic which bureaucracy uses to tame community, education, and religion is to create the illusion that rationality is the only level of human existence. The bureaucratic system cuts off human life at its roots. Together with its ally, technology, the bureaucratic pattern of society is hailed as a liberator, since it brings order and control to human life and claims to eliminate chaos and fortuitous events. In the name of the order of the system, all kinds of nonrational human experiences are ruthlessly denied. The pretense is maintained that the nonrational and unconscious dimension of human existence is not there. When its existence is undeniably evident, it is dismissed as nonhuman. Community, education, and religion are defined by what society considers to be "reasonable," and this is nothing less than a program for unquestioning social conformity.[26]

Reconstruction Through Intelligence

To become human, for Moran, means to grow in *intelligence*. He distinguishes between intelligence and reason, between the intelligent and the rational. While bureaucracy promotes rationality, education, community, and religion promote intelligence. By intelligence he means the synthesis of the rational and nonrational within integrated adults, on both the individual and communal levels. Only growth in intelligence will ensure the reconstruction of society. Reason, he claims, is an inner component of intelligence, and has a controlling, systematic tendency. Divorced from its proper grounding in the nonrational subterranean region of the person, reason becomes an enemy of human freedom. When bureaucratic "reasonableness" prevails, authentic human life is denied.[27]

If individuals and communities grow towards intelligence, as Moran defines it, he claims that reason will not be inflated out of proportion to its true importance. With the emergence of intelligence, human beings will not succumb to the wiles of rationalistic legitimation of the status quo, and society can be saved from the inhibiting power of bureaucracy. Inflated reason destroys freedom; emerging intelligence creates freedom.

Experience as the Key Category

Moran's educational anthropology represents an attempt to subsume the psychological into the broader sphere of the social, and to subsume the rational into the broader sphere of the intelligent. He appeals to "experience" as the ultimate and comprehensive category capable of adequately accounting for human growth toward fulfillment. The notion of experience, he points out, has, since Dewey, dominated educational discussion in the United States. However, he deplores its trivialization in current religious educational literature, where "experience" is reduced to a technique, a jumping-off point to arouse interest. Experience cannot be manufactured artificially; it is not so much a matter of ensuring that people *have* experiences, but of realizing that people are already engaged in and enveloped by experience. People do not so much *have* experience as they participate with others *in* experience. Experience, according to Moran, is "the totality of interaction between organism and environment."[28]

The category of "experience" helps Moran understand individual development within the context of social reconstruction. Experience, he says, is a relational or social mode of being.[29] It has social, political, and institutional meaning. The meaning of the experience of a unique individual or group can only be grasped within the total matrix of relationships within which the individual or group grows. This matrix of relationships includes the inhibiting power of bureaucracy which has a stranglehold upon the humanizing forces in society, preventing social changes that could bring a redistribution of the means to live humanly. This broad matrix of relationships will only promote individual human growth when the present social institutions are reformed, and when there is a greater diversification of institutions claiming to be forms of education, community, and religion. It should be noted that Moran presumes institutions are not disabling in themselves. They are enabling bodies insofar as they are free of bureaucratic rationalism and continue to reform themselves and redress their linguistic definitions.

Intelligence Beyond Reason

The category of "experience" also helps Moran understand growth toward maturity as the ascendancy of intelligence over reason. Intelligence, he claims, is the ability to deal with experience in a way that leads to understanding; it is a practical relational and receptive capacity.[30] Moran indicates that there are three levels of experience within growth to maturity. The first level is the one most associated with childhood. Born into a social matrix, the child is in a position of passivity and dependence, open to direct unreflective encounter with the world. The second level is the one usually associated with adolescence. This is the level of reason, where analysis, control, and prediction of the world are highly prized. Revolting against passivity and dependence, human experiencing becomes a matter of actively seeking independence. However, if the experience of human beings remains fixated at this adolescent level, the rational reigns supreme and they are slaves to bureaucratic language and structures. True adulthood is attained when intellectual understanding emerges.[31]

Intelligence, says Moran, subsumes within it the rational and the irrational. It takes up within it elements of the first stage that reason, in its quest for scientific mastery, tends to ignore. Intelligence is an active/passive affair, an attitude or disposition toward reality which can best be summarized under the word "receptivity." It accepts dependence as an integral part of life, but maintains it in tension with independence. Intelligence, says Moran, is neither a matter of being submissive and fatalistic, nor a matter of being domineering and controlling. It is a matter of being responsive to the gift of life, a disposition of surrender to the mystery of life as well as a mastery over the forces that shape one's destiny.[32]

For Moran, human experience includes "more" than the human. There is a religious dimension to human experience. Awareness of mystery, or the transcendent, occurs within the matrix of relationships that comprise human experience, especially when life is experienced as a gift. The experience of life as a gift requires a surrendering, a "letting go" of the tight hold on life that reason tries to maintain, and an openness in humor and love to what the unknown future may bring. Men and women within community discover the divine in their relationship to themselves, others, and social institutions. This discovery is the fruit of intelligent receptivity to the truth and life unveiled in these relationships. To grow toward intelligence, therefore, means to become open to the Transcendent Other in an act of surrender which, Moran insists, includes within it an assertion of autonomy.[33]

USE OF HUMAN SCIENCES

Moran's educational anthropology has a more philosophical bent than the psychological approach taken by Sherrill and Goldbrunner. He affirms the importance of humanistic psychology to explain human growth, and also looks to social theory to help him understand the functioning of bureaucracy and the possibility of effecting social change.[34] However, the educational philosophy underpinnings of Moran's reflections owe much to

John Dewey. Moran uses John Dewey's definition of education as a starting point for his own thinking. Education, according to Dewey, is "that reconstruction or reorganization of experience which adds to the meaning of experience, and which increases ability to direct the course of subsequent experience."[35]

Moran contrasts his understanding of "experience" with the commonly accepted reduction of the term to refer to sense data and empirical facts. He argues that this reductionistic tendency is found in empirical sciences which claim to predict and control the flow of human life. He argues that experience cannot be fully subjected to empirical analysis and testing since it is not simply what human beings have, but also that by which human beings are embraced. We can never obtain a fully objective picture of it. Experience, he says, is a fundamental mode of being that undercuts the split between subject and object. He prefers to regard experience as having both a subjective and objective pole, neither of which can be separated out of it.[36]

The reconstruction of experience, according to Moran, occurs both at an individual and social level. In the flow of educational experiences for an individual, there is an ever-increased expansion of possibilities for further fruitful experiences, coupled with growing reflective capacity to determine the future course of experience. On the social level, since society is a growing organism, there should also be constant reconstruction. One sure instrument of social reconstruction is education.

While Moran's anthropology is indebted to Dewey, it should be noted that he departs from Dewey on at least two important counts. Moran does not have the same degree of optimism that is found in Dewey about the possibility of the new society coming about through scientific praxis. Nor does Moran have the same degree of optimism about the possibility of the school as an agent for social change.

Moran's reading in social theory, such as Max Weber's view

that the individual in modern society must become trapped by the bureaucratic machine, has made him less optimistic than his forebears in the early religious education movement.[37] In addition, his contact with the current literature critiquing the school has led him to relativize the importance of that institution in ongoing social life. Moran is sympathetic to the current attack upon the schooling paradigm, but is not so extreme as Ivan Illich who calls for the elimination of schools altogether.[38] For Moran, the struggle to destroy the institution in the name of individual freedom is doomed to play into the hands of the enemy. The aim should not be to destroy the institution, but to renovate it and to find alternative forms of education other than school.

Moran's awareness of the importance of human language has its source in philosophers such as Martin Heidegger, Ludwig Wittgenstein, and Susanne Langer.[39] In addition to these philosophical sources, he draws on the social theory of Peter Berger to explain how language is both an externalization of human interiority, as well as a set of cultural symbols which shape human consciousness.[40] From this background of philosophy and social theory, Moran develops the thesis, presented above, that an institution's control of language can destroy the possibility of human freedom, and that the broadening of intellectual horizons, both individual and communal, depends on the availability of the words to ask the right questions.

In summary, Moran's use of the human sciences is eclectic. He draws upon psychology and social theory insofar as they support his own distinctive philosophy of education, which takes the "reconstruction of experience" as its key category.

EDUCATION FOR CHANGE

Moran's view of education for change is an education that brings about social regeneration. In the section dealing with his anthropology, it was shown that, in addition to education, Moran believes that community and religion also have the power to rebuild society. This trio, according to Moran, is so intimately united that whenever an authentic manifestation of one is found, so also are the others. In fact, in Moran's scheme, these three powers are effectively reduced to two, since he believes that good community and good education are inevitably religious in character. Therefore, the powerful humanizing forces are "religious education" and "religious community." In keeping with the focus of this chapter, this section will not deal with Moran's view of the specifically religious dimension of community and education. The focus is upon Moran's educational approach in the light of his anthropology discussed above. However, it should be remembered that an account of Moran's idea of community and education, in his opinion, necessarily carries implicit within it statements about authentic religion.

Community

Education for Moran has a communal and social context. To describe what he means by education necessarily involves describing what he means by community and how community fits into the broader social patterns. By community, Moran means a small group of people bound together in common purpose, fulfilling the individual's need for identity and intimacy, and characterized by mutuality in close personal relationships. Community is the primary group within which the individual works. The group has a shared vision of an ideal community where there are no divisions and human unity is fully attained.[41] The actual existing community is an imperfect realization of the ideal and serves to demonstrate the possibility of the ideal being achieved. Within mutual relations of human love people grow in greater unity and diversity at the same time. The community attempts to minimize, and if possible eliminate, the divisions that bring oppression and destruction within human experience. These oppressive ruptures in human experience are economic, racial, national, generational, and sexual. By trying to overcome these divisions the community acts as a microcosm within the larger social organization, a protest against any form of oppression, and a demonstration that this form of oppression need not exist.[42] Without necessarily having to become a revolutionary cell with a consciously constructed political platform, communities by their nature become effective levers of social, economic, and political change. Authentic community is a prophetic voice announcing that the ideal society is coming, and an effective instrument to realize this society now.

Network of Basic Communities

The multitude of small communities, in Moran's scheme, is situated within broader social and political structures. These larger structures are impersonal, but not necessarily dehumanizing. As we have seen, they become destructive of human growth to freedom when they drift toward the pattern of the bureaucratic mega-machine. This bureaucratic superstructure operates to keep the political leverage of community and education in check, by trying to restrict these powers to exclusive identification with family and school, respectively. In Moran's scheme, the larger institutions are only intermediary, and serve a provisional function between the present imperfect times and the arrival of the new global community which will have no division and oppression. By forming new communities now, and by working to renovate existing institutions, the drift toward the bureaucratic mega-machine can be reversed.

In the present time, says Moran, the only liberating form that large institutions can take is the democratic form. Democracy, Moran explains, is opposed to unilateral exercise of power in which someone has the right to command and others have the duty to obey. He postulates that the democratic structure is the only alternative to authoritarian organization of power. The most suited democratic form for the overall superstructure of society is a federation of small communities carefully constructed into an institution. In this way authority is grounded in the exchange of power; power is worked out by interaction among the groups and is not absolutized anywhere.[43]

Education, in Moran's perspective, is at a premium within a communal context. It has its most intense form within the interpersonal relationships of the small community. However, these relationships cannot be considered outside of their context within broader social patterns. Individual and communal consciousness are determined by these larger institutional patterns, but individuals and communities also have the power to change these structures. Education itself builds up large institutional structures that go beyond the arena of personal relationships and can begin to operate to stifle human growth. These structures are not necessarily inhibiting. They are effective as expressions of authentic education to the extent that they embody the entire life of the people. Education as an institutional expression aims not only to reconstruct the society as a whole, but also, as an integral and necessary part of this venture, education aims to reform itself. The criterion of success for its self-reformation is the degree to which its institutional forms are authentic expressions of the life of the people.[44]

The School

Moran insists that education is not an authentic communal expression if it is locked into the schooling paradigm. It was shown above that, according to Moran, the rationalistic language of bureaucracy defines "education" as "schooling," and associates this monopolistic institution with women and children. School, as a monopolizing institution, becomes an instrument of oppression within society. Depriving education of its proper communal context, the current school serves to perpetuate structures of oppression. Rather than be a healing force for the economic, racial, national, generational, and sexual divisions within humanity, the school, Moran claims, becomes an imperceptible, but powerful, legitimation of the status quo. The result is a society that oppresses the elderly and handicapped, and is intolerant of racial and sexual differences.[45]

Moran does not deny the importance and necessity of the school. However, he advocates that it should take a more modest role within the overall educational endeavor. It is one educational institution among many and serves the specific function of instruction, which cannot be equated with education *in toto.* Education, for Moran, refers to the broad lifelong cycle of growth that occurs within the relationships that pattern social life. It involves "a continuous process of growth, adaptation, and realignment of oneself within the total environment."[46] Lifelong learning requires multiple forms for all different age groups. Education in its many institutional forms cannot be identified with a monolithic "formal education" called school.

Education for Intelligence

Education for social reconstruction, according to Moran, aims to foster intelligence.[47] It was shown earlier that by growth in intelligence he means the integration of the rational and irrational dimensions of the human person. It must be stressed that Moran does not perceive education's aim in individualistic terms. Growth in intelligence has political implications. His educational anthropology begins with the social matrix within which the individual exists, and only then considers capacities for learning. When intelligence emerges within individuals, and within communities, there is a capacity to act in appropriate relation to the total environment, which includes the social, economic, and political world in which persons live. This world, Moran says, has been succumbing to the stifling power of bureaucratic "reasonableness." Education toward intelligence grounds human beings in the deepest emotional strata of experience, giving them effective power to see through the social illusions perpetuated by such overinflated, ego-oriented rationalism.

However, education toward intelligence does not deny the importance of reason. Through the refining of rational powers, always in integration with the nonrational powers, education toward intelligence promotes a "critical" stance toward the present social system. The existing forms of social oppression are not taken for granted. They are exposed for what they are; and with this new power to name their world, individuals and communities have the effective power to transform their world toward the new community of brotherhood and sisterhood which is now only partially realized.[48]

Teaching

For Moran, this refining of "critical" powers, as a dimension of growing intelligence, becomes a special function of teaching. Teaching, he says, is directed toward reason, which is a more specific component of intelligence. Teaching occurs in all sorts of settings. Within the school, or outside of the school, teaching is a "moment" within the broad educational flow of life. For Moran, all educational activity has political implications, but it is especially in teaching that the political thrust of education becomes evident. It is a political activity, since it directly intends to change the lives of a people, not so much by attempting to bring about an interior conversion, but by working with the group to discover a pattern of language that will help the group get better control and understanding of their lives.[49]

According to Moran, language can be oppressive. It can operate to legitimize the social structures, maintaining the fatalistic attitude that existing structures are inevitable. In this situation people remain in false-consciousness, accepting the social system as immutable. They can only adapt to the present society; they have no power to change it. In this context, Moran refers to Paulo Freire's method of teaching illiterate adults to read. Freire's method was to enter deeply into the lives of the people, locating the generative words in their vocabulary, words that carry the most political meaning for the group. By means of posters or slides, these words were represented visually for the group. The ensuing dialogue increased awareness of the group's socio-economic oppression. As they begin to control the words that have previously shaped their lives, people acquire "critical consciousness," which is a new power to define the world on one's own terms, and not according to the definitions readily supplied by a powerful elite.[50]

Teaching, for Moran, is an "invitation to hone out a language" which adequately describes the common human experience of the group so that this language is freeing for all.[51] Moran implies that teaching offers the possibility of exposing the so-called "reasonableness" of given definitions of social reality by honing out a new language that is not in conformity with the meanings supplied by the ruling social definers. It unmasks the false definitions given by the bureaucratic pattern of society to key institutions and roles, and provides new patterns of speech that truly express the life of the people.

EDUCATION FOR FREEDOM

The typical educational approach, represented by Moran, projects education as a powerful lever in the regeneration of the social order. It provides the power for intelligent relating with the existing social structures, the ability to discern oppressive elements and to affirm liberating elements, and the power to change these structures towards greater humanization. The freedom promoted by this educational approach pertains to social and political life, as well as to the sphere of close personal relationships.[52] Education is not an attempt to protect a privatized sphere of freedom by fending off the impersonal powers of a collectivized society. It is not an attempt to promote self-actualization exclusively within the small community. Education takes as its fundamental premise that the possibility of growth of selves through decision making is conditioned by the social institutions which the society has constructed. To concentrate on changing selves in isolation from the broader social framework is to help perpetuate the very social illusion that bureaucracy intends to maintain—the illusion that "right decisions" are all that is necessary to overcome one's socio-economic plight.

Relativizing the School

Nor is education for freedom, in this perspective, simply a matter of tutoring individuals in the many social ills that afflict the present world, and then encouraging them to go out and change the world. In the past, schools have tried to reduce education for freedom to this type of individualistic enterprise. This approach ignored the fact that people cannot confront the truth of the social reality, within which they are formed, simply by talking about something "out there." Insofar as this sort of instruction went on within the school, it was, in fact, a counter-force against authentic freedom. It ignored the fact that schools themselves were part of the problem. Insofar as the school monopolizes education, it is a force for division and oppression, even when it professes to be shaping individuals for social action.[53] The school becomes an instrument for producing social conformity, since it deflects attention from its own endemic malady and directs attention to social conflict, as if this conflict is not in any way due to the schooling paradigm itself.

Education for freedom requires a relativizing of the school's role in social transmission. It requires that many educational institutions, appropriate to the age level and needs of particular groups, exist together with the school; and it requires that the school restrict itself to promoting basic body and linguistic skills. In this perspective, education for freedom is not possible unless the existing educational institutions undergo reformation, and unless the schooling paradigm ceases to govern the minds of people in the society.

If the presumption is maintained in society that there are those who have the "goods" because of their educational qualifications, and there are those who do not have the "goods," there is a level of fatalistic dependency maintained among the majority who think that they cannot govern their lives without the so-called "experts." A large group in the society are kept in a state of helpless childish dependency, clamoring to go to school so they will "learn" what is necessary to function better in the society. Adaptation to the existing order becomes the criterion of success for education. Unless the schooling paradigm is overcome, the inbred paternalism in present social structures will maintain certain groups of people in a state of oppression.

Overcoming Divisions in Society

Education for freedom asserts that *racial* division will not be overcome simply by concentration on desegregating the schools, since the schools are part of the problem. It asserts that *sexual* oppression will not be overcome simply by teaching courses on the male-female relationship, since the social environment carries within it a "hidden curriculum" instructing people that women are in some ways inferior to men. Education for freedom denies the possibility of facilitating *economic* liberation simply by concentrating on refining the power of individuals to make suit-able life-options. The economic patterns in society itself inhibit the power of the individual to choose, seriously limiting available options and instructing the individual that the present patterns are inevitable and immutable. Unless these patterns are modi-fied, the individual's power to choose is an illusion. Education for freedom, in this approach, seeks to help people find a way of articulating the racial, sexual, and economic divisions within their social existence. In the process of articulation, they become aware of the reality of their oppression. By beginning to name the powerful influences that shape their lives, they begin to gain some control over these influences. They begin to be shapers of their own destiny. The freedom attained is a freedom *from* racial, sexual, and economic oppression, and a freedom *for* the power to be shapers of the culture within which they live.

Forms of education are liberating when they promote authen-tic human growth. In this approach, human growth to freedom occurs not only within the matrix of close personal relationships, but also within the social framework which conditions these relationships. In a bureaucratic society, education for freedom takes on a distinctive character. On the one hand, the less bureaucratic, and more democratic, the larger structures become, the greater the possibility of authentic human growth. On the other hand, the greater the growth to intelligence, the more power the individual and community have to reshape the social and economic conditions in which they live. The freedom which this educational approach promotes is a freedom *from* oppressive bureaucratic structures and *from* linguistic patterns that legiti-mate these structures, and freedom *for* intelligent interpretation of ongoing experience by individuals and community alike.

Teaching for Freedom

Teaching, which is one moment within the educational enterprise, is the main activity which schools should attempt to perform. Teaching is geared toward liberation. Even though it is a directive and controlling activity, teaching is in the service of freedom. The issue is not *whether* it should be controlling, since individuals and groups are already under the powerful linguistic control of the present social system.[54] The issue is, rather, *what sort of control* teaching should exercise. Teaching must be a political activity, in the sense that it deliberately attempts to intervene in the taken-for-granted lives of people, seeking to unmask the social illusions which are perpetuated by vague and fatalistic language. It aims to challenge people to become aware of oppressive patterns of speech, and to change these patterns so that their language may operate to heal divisions within humanity, rather than exacerbate those divisions.

In this approach, education, and teaching as part of it, are not liberating unless they are political activities. They must intervene in the ongoing cycles of oppression in an effort to initiate critical and liberating dialogue with the oppressed. However, education is also not liberating if it is simply a matter of one group of people setting out to change another group through conditioning them to perceive the reality of their oppression, and providing them with instruments to overcome this oppression.[55] Such a paternalistic approach is regarded by both Moran and Freire as a subtle way of continuing the dependence of the oppressed, since it fosters the mentality that the "liberators" will do all. Freire argues that at all stages in the process of liberation the oppressed must see themselves as engaged in the historical vocation of becoming more human. This is possible only through critical dialogue. Any attempt to liberate the oppressed without their reflection, action, and dialogical participation would simply make them dependent on the self-styled "liberators."[56] Education for freedom requires a genuine solidarity with the oppressed, and a trust in their ability to reason and to grow in intelligence. Moran would see this in terms of the creation of democratic power structures within educational institutions, structures that would enable dialogue and mutual exchange as ways toward greater intelligence and liberation.[57]

NOTES FOR CHAPTER 4

1. Lawrence Cremin argues that early progressive education had its origin in the latter half of the nineteenth century "in an effort to cast the school as a fundamental lever of social and political regeneration" (p. 88). It grew out of a many-sided progressive movement which protested social ills and established programs for social transformation. For the social reformers, education through the schools held the promise of realizing the "American dream." John Dewey's ideas on education and democracy later provided the intellectual framework for this practical goal. Since then, social reconstruction has remained a central theme in United States educational theory. See Lawrence Cremin, *The Transformation of the School: Progressivism in American Education (1876-1957)* (New York: Alfred A. Knopf, 1961), pp. 85-89, 119-26. See also Robert E. Mason, *Educational Ideals in American Society* (Pittsburgh: Allyn and Bacon, Inc., 1960), pp. 99-110.

2. The term "political" is not being used here in the restricted, narrow sense, namely to refer to electoral matters, party activities, pressure groups, or the governing of the state. Political action refers here to "everything that contributes to the setting up, maintaining, reforming, and evolution of social structures and of the forms of justice in a lawfully constituted community". See Manuel Valazquez, "Faith, Hope, and Political Action" in *Lumen Vitae* 28 (Dec. 1973); p. 576. The properly political sphere is not, in the first place, the private world of the individual, nor the interpersonal world of close relationships—it is the arena of socio-economic realities. However, this does not rule out the political relevance of the personal and interpersonal spheres. An educational approach which aims to reconstruct society, and to do this especially by reshaping linguistic patterns, can appropriately be called political. Curriculum theorist Dwayne Huebner argues that education is necessarily a political activity since it is a deliberate and structural intervention in people's lives and an attempt to protect or to alter their modes of living together in

society. The political dimension of educational institutions raises questions about whether they simply reflect the dominant mentality of society or whether they have some critical thrust for social change. The political dimension of teaching raises questions about the exercise of power: "That which we are about as educators is politics: a struggle to maintain, maybe even change through destruction and reconstruction the world we make with others". Dwayne Huebner, "Poetry and Power: The Politics of Curriculum Development" in *Curriculum Theorizing: The Reconceptualists*, edited by William Pinar (Berkeley, California: McCrutchan Publishing Corporation, 1975), p. 272.

3. Gabriel Moran, *Design for Religion: Toward Ecumenical Education* (New York: Herder and Herder, 1970) (hereinafter referred to as *DR*). The three works treated in the chapter represent a major shift from Moran's early period which was discussed in chapter 2.

4. Idem, *The Present Revelation: The Search for Religious Foundations* (New York: Herder and Herder, 1972) (hereafter referred to as *PR*).

5. See Moran, *PR*, p. 29. In this work Moran explains that he is attempting to "reconnoiter a position somewhere between phenomenology and theology" (*PR*, p. 17). Recently he has reiterated that *PR* was not an attempt at Christian theology. He contends that his concern with "revelation" was educational, i.e., to wrench the word away from the institutional church, and its intramural theology, and to invest it with a meaning that will provide "linguistic bridges" between Christians and non-Christians. See Gabriel Moran, "Where Now, What Next?" in *Foundations of Religious Education*, ed. Padraic O'Hare (New York: Paulist Press, 1978), pp. 103–4. Despite his protestations to the contrary, Moran is in one sense doing theology in this book. If theology is understood broadly as the reflection upon God-given life, using as sources both the Christian tradition and broad experience of humanity, then Moran is doing theology.

6. Gabriel Moran, *Religious Body: Design for a New Reformation* (New York: The Seabury Press, 1974) (hereinafter referred to as *RB*).

7. In regard to scripture, Moran states that "experience is the ultimate guide and not the document." See *PR*, p. 33. In regard to the reformation of the church, Moran states that the new religious body should be modeled on the contemporary political experience of democracy. See *RB*, pp. 3 and 191.

8. Three of Freire's major works are: Paulo Freire, *Pedagogy of the oppressed*, trans. Myra Bergman Ramos (New York: The Seabury Press, 1968); *Cultural Action for Freedom* (Cambridge, Mass.: Harvard Educational Review and Center for the Study of Development and Social Change, 1970); and *Education for Critical Consciousness* (New York: The Seabury Press, 1973). Freire's theory of education has been mediated to North American catechists by authors such as John L. Elias and Malcolm Warford. See John L. Elias, *Conscientization and Deschooling: Freire's and Illich's Proposals for Reshaping Society* (Philadelphia: The

Westminster Press, 1976), and Malcolm L. Warford, *The Necessary Illusion: Church Culture and Educational Change* (Philadelphia: United Church Press, A Pilgrim Press Book, 1976).

9. These "earlier writings" include: Gabriel Moran, *Theology of Revelation* (New York: Herder and Herder, 1966), *Catechesis of Revelation* (New York: Herder and Herder, 1960), as well as two articles on his early theology of freedom: "The Freedom of the Sons of God," *Proceedings of the Twenty-fifth North American Liturgical Week* 25 (1964): 165–72, and "Freedom in Christian Revelation," *Proceedings, Eleventh Annual Convention of the Society of Catholic College Teachers of Sacred Doctrine* 11 (April 1965): 59–79.

10. See Moran, *Catechesis of Revelation*, p. 48. Moran was intent upon making the human subject an integral part of progressive revelation. See Mary C. Boys, *Biblical Interpretation in Religious Education* (Birmingham, Alabama: Religious Education Press, 1980), pp. 150–151.

11. See Moran, *Theology of Revelation*, pp. 158–59.

12. Moran, *Catechesis of Revelation*, pp. 70–71.

13. Moran, *DR*, p. 52.

14. Ibid., p. 51.

15. Ibid., p. 54.

16. Moran, *PR*, p. 135.

17. Ibid., p. 136.

18. Ibid.

19. This is the major theme running through the second chapter of *RB*, pp. 31–67. Moran has described this chapter as "the most important thing I have written." See Moran, "When Now, What Next?" p. 102.

20. Moran believes that religious language which the church monopolizes is under the control of rationalistic theology. He wants to rescue the word "revelation" from this fate. He claims it is a metaphor, not a theological term. The imaginative and symbolic dimensions of life are awakened by metaphorical language. The word "revelation" is a particularly powerful aesthetic category capable of liberating communities by appealing to the deeper dimension of the human being. It is a word that also gives a chance to comprehend the main divisions in the world; it is capable of synthesizing all of the complex relationships of life. See Gabriel Moran, "The Intersection of Religion and Education," *Religious Education* 69 (September-October 1974): 531–41; "Teaching within Revelation," in *Aesthetic Dimensions of Religious Education*, ed. Gloria Durka and Joanmarie Smith (New York: Paulist Press, 1979), pp. 153–64; "Response to Professor Dulles 11," *CTSA Proceedings* 29 (June 1974): 119; and "Peoples, Places, and Metaphors," in *Journeys: The Impact of Personal Experience on Religious Thought*, ed. Gregory Baum (New York: Paulist Press, 1975), p. 253.

21. Moran, *RB*, p. 33.

22. Ibid., p. 38. Moran's demand for reformation of catechetics and the

church stems from his conviction that the effectiveness of catechetics is limited by the linguistic and institutional pattern within which it operates. There is a failure to see how institutional structure and patterns of language are themselves educative or mis-educative. In light of this insight, he argues that as long as the academic study of religion remains in an ecclesiastical context, its structure and language will be controlled by theology. Hence, it should be conducted in the broad public sector of education. See Gabriel Moran, "Two Languages of Religious Education," *The Living Light* 14 (Spring 1977): 7–15.

23. Moran, *RB*, p. 39.

24. Ibid., pp. 51–53.

25. Ibid., pp. 47–50 and 56–57.

26. Ibid., pp. 40–41; see also Moran, *DR*, pp. 58–59.

27. Moran, *RB*, pp. 169–71; and idem, *DR*, pp. 68–69.

28. Moran, *PR*, p. 79; and idem, *DR*, p. 63.

29. Moran, *DR*, pp. 64–66; and idem, *RB*, p. 168.

30. Moran, *RB*, pp. 169–70. Moran is not relying on empirical research for these observations. His reflections on human growth are those of an insightful philosopher of life.

31. Moran, *DR*, pp. 69–70.

32. Moran's description of adulthood is in terms of strong contrasting forces finding a synthesis in the human being: rational/irrational; control/letting go; independence/dependence. The adult is marked by the relaxed receptive attitude and capacity to respond to the gift of life. Moran, *DR*, p. 132. See also idem, *Education toward Adulthood* (New York: Paulist Press, 1979), pp. 17–35.

33. For Moran, there are three stages in religious development which occur, to some degree, in individual history and in the history of the race. The first is the nonrational, magical experience of being confronted by a divine power. The second is the controlling rational experience of turning revelation into a thing. The third is the experience of communities of men and women discovering the divine in relationships. It is this third stage which is associated with intelligence which recaptures the best of two previous stages and holds them in tension. See Moran, *RB*, p. 99.

34. In *DR* and *PR* Moran utilized insights from the humanistic psychology of Maslow, Rogers, and Allport, and from the neo-Freudian psychology of Fromm, to describe growth to adulthood. However, by the time of *RB* (1974), he was including more references to social theorists such as Robert Merton and Max Weber.

35. Quoted by Moran, *DR*, p. 74. See John Dewey, *Democracy and Education* (New York: The Free Press, 1966), p. 76; also *Experience and Education* (New York: Collier Books, 1938), p. 89.

36. Moran, *PR*, p. 79.

37. Moran is not as pessimistic as Weber, but the sort of critique provided by

Weber has sobered the social reconstructionist fervor displayed by early religious educationists. See Moran, *RB*, p. 36; also Max Weber, *Politics as a Vocation* (Philadelphia: Fortress Press, 1965).

38. Illich argues that not only education but social reality itself has become schooled. This is a form of institutional paternalism which discourages and disables the poor from taking control of their own learning. The schooling paradigm perpetuates the worst of a consumer society intent upon casting all relationships in terms of production and demand, and intent upon instructing people that they are dependent upon a larger institution to bring them fullness of life. See Ivan Illich, *Deschooling Society* (New York: Harper and Row, 1970). Illich's opinions can be found together with opinions both supporting and opposing his views in *After Deschooling What?* ed. Alan Gartner, Colin Greer, and Frank Riessman (New York: Harper and Row Publishers, 1973).

39. In *PR* (p. 135), Moran refers to Martin Heidegger, *An Introduction to Metaphysics*, trans. Ralph Mannheim (New Haven: Yale University Press, 1959); in *RB* (p. 20), he refers to Ludwig Wittgenstein, *Philosophical Investigations* (Oxford: Blackwell, 1953), p. 47; in *PR* (p. 141), he refers to Susanne Langer, *Philosophical Sketches* (Baltimore: The Johns Hopkins University Press, 1962), pp. 26–53.

40. In *PR* (p. 136), Moran refers to Peter Berger, *The Sacred Canopy* (New York: Doubleday and Company, Inc., 1967), pp. 3–28.

41. Moran, *RB*, p. 111. This ideal community is a "universal sisterhood/brotherhood which would include both humans and nonhumans in a relation which cultivates differences in unity." See ibid., p. 142. Moran does not want the existing microcosm and the universal ideal to be separated. The actual community now is already an embodiment of the ideal being realized.

42. Moran, *RB*, p. 125. For a description of nonfamilial communal forms, see Moran, *Education toward Adulthood*, pp. 95–102.

43. Moran, *RB*, pp. 193–96. Moran does not believe it is possible to form a "pure democracy," where all persons have the same degree of participation in government. He is also critical of the language of "decentralization," when it is used by an institution which is pyramidal in structure, and hence without a center in the first place. See ibid., pp. 201–6. An earlier work on community was a prelude to the discussion. See Gabriel Moran, *The New Community: Religious Life in an Era of Change* (New York: Herder and Herder, 1970).

44. Moran, *RB*, p. 155.

45. Ibid., p. 157. For the distinction between school and education, see Moran, *Education toward Adulthood*, pp. 37–53.

46. Moran, *RB*, p. 173.

47. Ibid., p. 166.

48. To the extent that Moran stresses the positive function of reason, in its power to take a critical stand in regard to oppressive structures, he comes close

to Paulo Freire's perspective. Freire sees "conscientization," consciousness-raising, as the aim of education. The educational enterprise endeavors to aid the process whereby people, as knowing subjects, become more deeply aware of sociocultural reality that shapes their lives and acquire the effective power to transform that reality. Education is both an unmasking of the social illusions, as well as active intervention by participants in the social process to build new structures. See Paulo Freire, *Pedagogy of the Oppressed,* pp. 67–74. A very clear presentation of Freire's "conscientization" can be found in "Conscientizing as a Way of Liberating," *LADOC* II, 29a (April 1972): 1–8.

49. Moran, *RB,* pp. 162–66.

50. The term "critical consciousness" is studiously avoided by Moran. He considers that the term in its popular usage is open to a new form of individualism. He also argues that the concept of learning through expansion of consciousness presumes a linear development in individuals and community. He argues, from a Jungian perspective, that real development is a synthesis of dialectical opposites, between rational and nonrational, conscious and unconscious. To concentrate on "critical consciousness" as the end of education is too rationalistic. See Moran, *RB,* pp. 93–94.

51. Moran, *RB,* p. 164. The alienating and liberating function of language is a favorite theme of Dwayne Huebner, a curriculum theorist from Columbia University. Huebner shares Moran's concern that the political and economic nature of education be exposed and that curriculum design be geared toward building a more just society. Moran refers to an article by Huebner in *DR,* pp. 110, 116. See Dwayne Huebner, "Curricular Language and Classroom Meanings," in *Language and Meaning,* ed. James B. Macdonald and Robert R. Leeper (Washington, D.C.: Association for Supervision and Curriculum Development, 1966), pp. 8–26. For further reading in Huebner, see "Curriculum as Concern for Man's Temporality," in *Curriculum Theorizing: The Reconceptualists,* ed. William Pinar (Berkeley, Calif.: McCrutchen Publishing Corporation, 1975), pp. 237–49; "Poetry and Power: The Politics of Curriculum Development," in *Curriculum Theorizing,* pp. 271–78; "The Tasks of the Curricular Theorist," in *Curriculum Theorizing,* pp. 250–69; "Toward a Remaking of Curriculum Language," in *Heightened Consciousness, Cultural Revolution and Curriculum Theory,* ed. William Pinar (Berkeley, Calif.: McCrutchen Publishing Corporation, 1974), pp. 36–53; "Curriculum as a Field of Study," in *Precedents and Promise in the Curriculum Field,* ed. Helen F. Robinson (Columbia University: Teachers College Press, 1966); "Education in the Church," *Andover Newton Quarterly* 12 (January 1972): 122–29; "The Language of Religious Education," in *Transformation and Tradition in Religious Education,* ed. Padraic O'Hare (Birmingham, Alabama: Religious Education Press, 1979), pp. 87–111.

52. Moran, *DR,* p. 52.

53. Illich makes the point that schools can provide courses on "liberation"

but as long as schools are credited with the principal function of forming critical judgment, they perpetuate a lie by claiming to be liberating agencies. As long as schools exist, learning will remain a commodity. Illich, *Deschooling Society*, pp. 68–69.

54. Moran, *RB*, p. 165.

55. For Moran, "mutuality" is the hallmark of education. In this context, he refers to Paulo Freire's "banking model" of education as the antithesis of a mutual arrangement. See Moran, *RB*, p. 159. The "banking model" of education has the effect of integrating people into the existing structures of oppression. It is wedded with paternalistic social welfare systems which treat people as objects of care and assistance, and not as intelligent beings who have the power to master their own destiny and participate in the shaping of history. It preserves the status quo, engendering attitudes of fatalism, resignation, and docility in its recipients. See Freire, *Pedagogy of the Oppressed*, pp. 57–65.

56. Freire, *Pedagogy of the Oppressed*, p. 53.

57. Moran, *RB*, p. 184.

Chapter 5
The Cultural Type

The cultural type focuses on the community as a bearer of cultural heritage. Culture is understood as a way of life and a world view which are held in common by the members of the community and are transmitted with conviction to the next generation.[1] The community's common perspective on life is expressed in a symbol system which must be maintained to keep a strong sense of identity. Also, it must be faithfully transmitted in order to initiate new members into this common world view. Education in this approach becomes a conscious and deliberate effort on the part of the community to have its members adopt its symbols and internalize their meanings.

The cultural type is represented by C. Ellis Nelson and John H. Westerhoff. Their writings can best be understood in the context of the meeting of cultural anthropology and general educational theory within the United States. The discovery of cultural anthropology by educationalists gave further impetus to the quest for the social foundations of education. Cultural anthropology assisted educationalists to become more aware of the large range of cultural influences that shape individuals. Educationalists gained further confirmation that the school or classroom is not a special zone of immunity from the broad enculturation process. Cultural anthropology gave educational theorists more tools for understanding education as a process of cultural transmission.[2]

Nelson's major work, used in this chapter, is *Where Faith Begins* (1967).[3] In this book, he establishes that the social sci-

160

ences provide a "clue" to understanding human development by showing that the basic personality structure of children is shaped by culture, and that social-interactional processes among adults serve to deepen them in understanding the world and to strengthen them in conviction and action.

Westerhoff's major works that are relevant for this chapter are: *A Colloquy on Christian Education* (1972), a collection of articles originally published under his editorship in the journal of the same name; *Generation to Generation* (1974), co-authored with Gwen Kennedy Neville, a cultural anthropologist; *Will Our Children Have Faith?* (1976), a tract in which he intends to propose an alternative framework for evaluating, planning, and engaging in Christian education; and *Learning through Liturgy* (1978), another work co-authored with Gwen Kennedy Neville.[4] Over the years Westerhoff has collaborated with Neville, whose particular anthropological stance has influenced his theory of education. Both Nelson and Westerhoff turn to cultural anthropology to fill out their understanding of how human beings develop in community.

Both men seek to advance the Protestant Christian nurture theory by using the social sciences. As was mentioned in chapter 2, they have much in common with Berard Marthaler, a contemporary Catholic advocate of a "socialization" model of catechesis.[5] Marthaler draws upon the socialization theory of Berger and Luckmann to explain how the community initiates new members and maintains a sense of coherence and identity. Marthaler's writings provide constructive suggestions which supplement the approach taken by Nelson and Westerhoff.

The choice of these two theorists to represent this approach is governed by the type of educational theory which is contained within their works. As with previous chapters, to distill out their distinctive way of approaching education for freedom, it is necessary to prescind from a number of other issues present in their writings. While they use cultural anthropology to *describe* the process of communicating the faith within a Christian community, they use "theology" to establish the *normative* criterion of uniqueness for this community.[6] "Theology," they maintain, explains what is truly distinctive about this Christian community vis-à-vis any other community engaging in cultural transmission. This chapter does not elaborate upon or evaluate such a claim. Nor does this chapter investigate the claim made by Nelson and Westerhoff that distinctively Christian faith brings a power to be individually and collectively free.[7]

As with previous chapters, the modest aim here is to show how Westerhoff and Nelson have an underlying educational anthropology that derives from their use of cultural anthropology. This view of human development informs their theory of education for change and determines how they envisage the liberating function of education.

EDUCATIONAL ANTHROPOLOGY

In this approach the themes of social *belonging* and social *identification* are central. To be human means to belong to a particular group, to have roots in the tradition of this group, and to gain one's identity from reference to the foundational symbols that express and constitute the life of the group. The community, which is the locus and means of all growth, shares a common memory, a common view of the world, common ways of life, and common goals and purposes. Westerhoff and Nelson both point out that such a primary group should be small enough to maintain meaningful interactions among its members, and large enough to include the presence and interaction of three generations. It is a community that encourages a wide diversity of roles, but which manages to maintain a united vision of what the various role expectations should be.[8] Westerhoff acknowledges how difficult it is to designate boundaries to communities within contemporary society, but he insists that "to understand persons is to locate their 'meaningful communities.'"[9]

Self/culture

Both Westerhoff and Nelson see the community, or primary group, as the most important communication medium for culture. While they agree that culture can be considered as a wider phenomenon than the *communitas*, their concern is with how each community, with its own tradition and vision of the world, perpetuates itself through the transmission of its own peculiar culture. Culture, Westerhoff explains, implies a common way of life, a common understanding of life, and a common set of values.[10] The peculiar culture of a community carries the objectified meanings that express how the community defines itself and how the community envisages its role in the world.

Nelson emphasizes that cultural reality, the product of past human learning, is, in one sense, over against the individual. We are born as unfinished human beings, and begin to swim in the culture of our community prior to any ability to reflect upon it. The selfhood of individuals, he says, is *shaped* by culture. Even though individuals do eventually build their own selfhood, they can only do this in relation to those around them. The self is, in large measure, an extension of the nurturing group. Individuals accept the self-definition assigned to them by the group; they accept the perspective on the world that is shared by the group; and they acquire the beliefs and values that are cherished most strongly by the group.[11]

Nelson describes three processes that operate within cultural transmission to shape individuals. Each of these processes, he says, leaves powerful mechanisms within individuals, making them, in turn, agents for transmitting what they have already received. The first process of transmission described by Nelson is the formation of a perceptive system in the individual. By teaching language, the cultural group imparts to the individual a way of interpreting reality. Newcomers to the group, especially the very young, see what they are taught to see, and then, in the act of seeing it, they receive confirmation that this is the way reality is.[12]

The second process that Nelson describes is the formation of conscience. He considers that the rewards and punishments within society, especially those associated with parental control, which are first experienced as external threats or inducements, are gradually internalized by the individual. When the external authorities are successfully internalized, the individual experiences guilt after violating society's code.[13]

The third process is that of self-identification. Nelson points out that a person's self-understanding emerges only with reference to the group. The primary social group has, in its collective memory, a self-definition of what it means to belong to this group. Individuals take on this social identity through the process of imitation, or role-modeling.[14]

Culture, then, according to Westerhoff and Nelson, is a powerful formative influence on individuals. Human persons cannot be understood outside of their cultural context. While both authors stress that early childhood identification with significant others, such as parents or teachers, shapes the person, they also point out that cultural formation is a *lifelong* process. Even though individuals may gain some distance from cultural symbols as they pass through a critical evaluative stage of development, they are never able simply to slough off the shaping influences of culture. A change from early uncritical affiliations to a later, more critical stance may mean changing one's community of nurture, and accepting a whole new set of symbols. Westerhoff stresses that human change cannot be sustained in a cultural vacuum. Human beings cannot live and grow outside of communities of shared meanings and values, communities which provide for them the fundamental symbols that give sense to their lives.[15]

Storytelling

Both Nelson and Westerhoff emphasize the function of the tradition-bearing community in patterning a person's self-understanding according to the self-understanding of the group. In passing on the tradition, according to the mode of cultural transmission, Nelson says that the community delivers the meanings that are constitutive of its life. Once received, these meanings become constitutive of the individual's life. It is not a matter of learning *about* a tradition. It is a matter of entering into the symbolic narrative of a people so that the understandings and ways that are received become "unargued assumptions," the only way of interpreting reality and of understanding oneself.[16]

At the heart of community life, says Westerhoff, there is a *story* which explains the community's understanding of the world, the place of persons in that world, and the ways of life they should pursue.[17] It is important for the ongoing life of the community that the community's story be agreed upon and that it become *our* story. By telling the story, the community seeks to activate its memory, not simply by cerebral recollection, but by living again the past events which gave rise to the story initially. The past is evoked in such a way that it still has power over people today.[18]

Ritual

According to Westerhoff, the story of the community is best communicated within ritual. The meanings that express the community's life are stored in ritual. Human beings, he says, are made for ritual, and rituals make human beings.[19] The stories and ritual of a culture are closely connected because they are symbolic expressions, in narrative and action, respectively, of the shared meanings and values of the community. Rituals sustain and transmit the community myths. The stories and ritual of a community, says Westerhoff, help the members to know and to remember who they are. Otherwise, in a pluralistic society, with many competing visions of reality, life can become fragmented and compartmentalized. Rituals, he says, have an integrating function. They bring wholeness and at-one-ness, knitting together the community in common purpose and action, thwarting the threat of lostness in a broken world.[20]

Logos/mythos Levels of Consciousness

Because this approach emphasizes story and ritual as fundamental human activities that constitute life in community, there is an appeal to the *intuitive* mode of consciousness.[21] Prior to any reflection upon experience the individual is already, from earliest years, informed by primordial symbols which operate on the intuitive level of consciousness. These symbols, which are evocative of the deeper and more primal levels of the human being, are carried in the story and ritual of the community. Westerhoff holds that individuals do not change their perspective on life and their own self-definition through the exercise of critical reason alone. Even though they need to go through a time of critical judgment upon the understandings and ways of the community in order to discover and affirm their own identity, persons can only undergo and sustain such a change by the integration of new symbols into their lives. If people begin to become disenchanted with the understandings and ways of their nurturing community, they have already begun to assimilate new symbols. Conversion, according to Westerhoff, does not occur by autonomously think-

ing about it, but by surrendering to the possibility of new awareness; this happens by intuitively beginning to integrate a new set
of cultural symbols.[22]

USE OF THE HUMAN SCIENCES

It has been mentioned above that both Nelson and Westerhoff
use cultural anthropology to establish that the human person is
formed by a wide range of varying cultural patterns transmitted
within a particular society.[23] Before elaborating on how this
approach to human growth views education for change, some
indication must be given of how these authors regard cultural
anthropology, and what sources they use to arrive at their understanding of culture, society, and the individual.

While acknowledging the contribution of attempts at empirical investigation of social reality, Nelson points out that this
approach is limited to describing human *conduct*. It is unable to
analyze understandings, motivations, or attitudes. He argues that
experimental observation of behavior, such as that conducted by
Watson and Skinner, only deals with one aspect of the total
environmental formation of the person.[24] Nelson is attracted,
rather, to the social scientists who do not rely on empirical data
alone, but who bring an inquisitive, intuitive mind to the
analysis of human actions. While these social scientists gather as
much empirical data as possible, they are not chained to the
results of experimental tests alone. They bring "the imagination
and educated guess of a mind grappling with a wide range of
observations." Nelson identifies these social scientists as "cultural anthropologists" and "sociologists concerned with the way
culture is internalized by persons."[25]

The "clue" that Nelson gains from cultural anthropologists
and sociologists of knowledge is that the self is "trained" by

culture through internalizing a given world view and given set of values. His major source for this fundamental notion that culture has primacy over the individual is Ralph Linton's *The Cultural Background of Personality*.[26] Linton describes culture as a "way of life" of a particular society, a set of behavior patterns, understandings, and values of a people that are communicated to the next generation.[27] Individuals imbibe cultural reality before ever being conscious of it. According to Linton, society survives by transmitting its culture. Each primary society, situated within the broader social organization, tends to develop its own set of shared cultural patterns which it communicates to new members of the society, so that the social order may be maintained.[28]

Nelson also appeals to field studies in cultural anthropology, especially those dealing with the communal life of various native and ethnic American groups, and those dealing with prevailing values in the current North American technological society. In each case, his references serve to reinforce the basic thesis that the individual self is shaped within a culture and has no meaning outside of this cultural immersion.[29]

Westerhoff, for his part, is dependent upon cultural anthropologist Gwen Kennedy Neville, with whom he co-authored *Generation to Generation* and *Learning Through Liturgy*. Neville has been concerned with applying "the old ethnographic methods of field study and participant observation to the new context of city and town life in present day communities."[30] She views contemporary society as a collection of myriad ethnic groups. By "ethnic" she means a group with a distinctive cultural heritage, shared traditions, and way of life. It is a group with a "sense of peoplehood."[31] The group maintains this sense of belonging and identity by shared institutions, clearly defined social roles, and shared stories and rituals. For this group to survive, it must transmit its culture to the next generation.

Westerhoff has also gained his understanding of the function of ritual from Neville. Neville describes ritual as an intense "tele-scoping" of the meanings and values most cherished by the culture. She also describes two types of rites—communal rites and rites of passage, a distinction which Westerhoff has adopted. Communal rites are those celebrated at timely moments by the people. These rites serve to maintain the community in its shared vision of reality. They intensify group commitment and revive flagging loyalties. They protect against the threat of disintegration and chaos, offering a stable identity to the group, reaffirming its common interpretation of the past and articulating its common expectation of the future.[32]

Rites of passage, on the other hand, are rites that protect against disintegration of the individual in crisis times of life. These rites serve to provide meaning at crucial times in human development, such as birth, adolescence, marriage, and death. These transitional rites also consolidate a support group for the individual. Neville and Westerhoff both follow the classic description of Arnold van Gennep who pointed out that a transition ritual has three important phases—separation, transition, and reentry. The individual is symbolically set apart from former companions, thus entering a liminal phase of existence which often includes intense training for the new role that is to be adopted, and finally the individual symbolically reenters the community at a new level of competence and status.[33] Westerhoff argues that education, which intends to initiate and nurture persons within a community, must necessarily take account of these findings about ritual from cultural anthropology.

From collaboration with Neville, Westerhoff has also acquired the insight that enculturation often forms rigid convictions at the implicit or unconscious level. Neville refers to Edward T. Hall's *The Hidden Dimension,* which describes how culture is transmitted in hidden ways.[34] There is a "silent language" that instructs individuals in beliefs, values, and ways of acting, often without a word being spoken. This type of cultural instruction accounts for the stereotypical attitudes that cause barriers between races, sexes, and all ethnic groups.

Westerhoff has also called upon cultural anthropology to understand the relationship between religion and culture. He has not articulated clearly what this relationship is; however, he agrees with Neville that any religious group is a carrier of culture. It has its own peculiar culture, but the understandings and ways that comprise its culture are intertwined with, and not entirely distinguishable from, the cultural beliefs and values of the larger society. Because it is a *religious* community, it sanctions beliefs and values with an appeal to ultimate authority. Therefore, it is possible that the religious institutions, religious language, and sacred ritual of a group could serve to legitimize stereotypical understandings and divisive practices. The religious community, he says, is asked and induced by the wider society to bless the way things are, to support the status quo by giving religious legitimation to prevailing values, institutions, and lifestyles.[35] The religious community is in danger of simply mirroring and blessing the dominant culture's beliefs, attitudes, and values.[36]

Westerhoff maintains that there have been many cases in history when religious institutions have not succumbed to the status quo, but have become agents of change within the culture. He argues that, even though religious institutions normally exert a conservative influence on culture, they are a powerful means for cultural change because the impulse to change comes from a "transcendent reality."[37]

EDUCATION FOR CHANGE

According to this approach, education for change involves shaping selves through cultural transmission. Education is considered a distinct aspect of the enculturation process conducted by the community. Persons are shaped by culture regardless of any consciously organized efforts on the part of others. Education makes this process explicit and intentional. According to Westerhoff, education consists of "deliberate, systematic, and sustained efforts to transmit or evoke knowledge, attitudes, values, skills, and sensibilities in persons."[38] Education aims to enable persons and groups to evolve particular ways of thinking, feeling, and acting.

This approach does not intend "education" to be understood as another form of behavioral modification. Even though there is a strong emphasis on the shaping of persons, there is a passionate disavowal of the "schooling-instructional paradigm." Education is a *community* project. The life of the community itself is the medium for communication of beliefs and values. The community itself educates as it becomes itself by retelling its story and celebrating its rituals. Westerhoff rails against the prevailing assumption that improving techniques and resources of schooling and instructing will solve educational problems. That approach simply perpetuates the "schooling-instructional paradigm" which ignores the whole range of unseen cultural influences on the person.[39]

Westerhoff points out that only an education which makes the whole life of the community part of the "deliberate systematic and sustained efforts" can bring the hidden dimension of enculturation into view. There is a "hidden curriculum" which consists of all the factors in the physical and social environment that are normally taken for granted and considered of neutral educational value. This "hidden curriculum" is operative in the structuring of space and ecology, the interior decorative design of buildings, the roles assigned by the community, the peer group, the lifestyle of members in the community, etc. Education intends to bring all these cultural influences into view and to utilize them in the initiation of persons into full life within the community.[40]

Education for change in this approach has two aims: intentional socialization of the young and the resocialization of adults. When human beings are born they are unfinished; they have no social identity, and no way of interpreting the world. The community, through its educational efforts, delivers to the individual its own self-definition and world view. As a result, the individual is united to the group by a powerful social bond. The individual becomes more human through belonging to the group.[41]

Education also aims to resocialize adults by providing them with new knowledge of what is expected of them in terms of beliefs and values, new skills to fulfill these understandings and ways, and new motivation to live according to the way indicated.[42]

In this approach, the quality of what is communicated to the young depends on the quality of adult beliefs and practice.[43] As adults are educated, the children also grow. The effectiveness of the communication of culture to the next generation depends on the cohesion of the adult system of beliefs and values, and upon the degree and quality of the commitment which adults have towards these beliefs and values. As Nelson points out, education as cultural transmission is first and foremost the responsibility of adults to each other, since they are the leaders of the community and the chief socializing agents for the young.[44]

In this approach, the whole life of the community is the agent of education and the whole life of the community benefits from education. Educational efforts, says Westerhoff, should concentrate upon three dimensions of community life—ritual, experience, and action. *Ritual* embodies the community's shared meanings and values. Ritual can become a more deliberate attempt to focus on, communicate, and reinforce the community's way of looking at the world and its way of life. Westerhoff does not intend ritual to be used solely as an instrument for education, but, rather, he encourages the community, and those engaged in specific educational ventures, to realize how ritual is a powerful educative medium, helping to sustain and transmit the common way of life.[45]

The second specific concern of the community and its educators, according to Westerhoff, should be the *quality of experiences* that are provided for people. A way of interpreting reality and finding meaning in life cannot be transmitted abstractly. It must be transmitted by creating opportunities for persons to experience the cherished beliefs and values of the community in the challenges of their own life-situation. Educators, Westerhoff insists, do not hand over abstractions, but create the conditions whereby people experience firsthand the message that is to be conveyed, and also have room for reflection upon the experience, as well as ways of sharing these reflections with others.[46]

In this approach, the community is both the message and the medium. Therefore, both Nelson and Westerhoff insist that the *primary* experience essential for good education is the experience of real community, to gain the sense of being a people together, and to have opportunities for critical reflection upon this experience.[47]

The third concern of the educating community is *action*. Education is not only geared toward the cognitive and emotional levels of human beings; education is geared primarily towards promoting a change in patterns of action. Human beings, Westerhoff insists, learn through engagement in action; they are not divided into thinking, feeling, and active components. The cognitive, affective, and lifestyle domains are helpful for scholarly analysis, but they are not independent in action. When the whole body-person becomes engaged in specific tasks, the thinking, feeling, and active dimensions of the human being are integrated, and learning occurs. Furthermore, the only true test of beliefs and values are individual and corporate actions in the world. The *lifestyle* of individuals and communities is the only authentic indication of the quality of their learning.[48]

EDUCATION FOR FREEDOM

Education, in this approach, is a deliberate and purposeful activity geared towards changing persons. However, Westerhoff cautions that, in one sense, education is not a matter of some people doing something to effect change in others. The enculturation process should not be collapsed into an instructional model which, he claims, implies that some people assert power over others to effect their "learning."[49] Westerhoff emphasizes that the whole community, and every person within it, are both teaching and learning at the same time. He urges that the authentically educating community is a community which is built by the ongoing "interaction" of its members.

Indoctrination?

By appealing to an "interactionist" model, Westerhoff provides some rebuttal of the claim that the "cultural" type is a veiled form of indoctrination. Some advocates of "freedom" claim that this approach indoctrinates individuals by incorporating them into an institutional reality without possibility of accepting or rejecting what has been given them.[50] They claim that this approach dooms the individual to become a passive sponge soaking up the culture of the group without any possibility of creatively questioning and searching for truth. They see the "cultural" type as a form of domestication, where the individual is inducted into a taken-for-granted world without any opportunity to come to terms personally with the definitions of reality delivered authoritatively by the elders. Implied in this claim is a second accusation that the "cultural" approach works most effectively if the cultural reality remains unchanged. The cultural perspective, opponents argue, precludes any possibility of the community reforming itself or altering its structures, roles, and lifestyles which are part of its cultural heritage.

Westerhoff's approach would answer the first charge by stressing that the authentic community is one where "interaction" occurs on all levels, allowing individuals to pass beyond an early stage of uncritical affiliation with the nurturing symbols into a more critical stance and then beyond this to a more mature acceptance of the symbols of the community. According to this approach, maturity is not attained by reaching a stage of independence, autonomy, and critical judgment in regard to the inherited symbol system. Maturity is attained by passing through this "critical fire" to a new stage of surrender to the nurturing foundational symbols of the community.[51]

Westerhoff would answer the second charge by appealing to the concepts of "resocialization" and the "maypole dancers." The first concerns the possibility of internal reform of communities of nurture; the second concerns the possibility of forming new communities comprised of dissidents from the traditional communities of nurture. Resocialization of adults, described in an earlier section, is necessary to offset the powerful forces of immobility and apathy that beset any community.[52] It can generate new perspectives and new styles of living. However, Westerhoff points out that a few people, because of physical separation from their nurturing communities and because of new challenging experiences, find themselves as "outsiders," no longer sharing the same world view or value system of their traditional communities. They are estranged, "wanderers," unable to feel "at home" in the local ritual, or to participate meaningfully in local community action. A new perception has dawned on them; they have a new awareness. Following Gwen Kennedy Neville, he calls them "maypole dancers," because, even though they have lost their original supportive community, they are united by longer strings of unity and dance to celebrate their new-found autonomy.[53]

Westerhoff points out that no one can maintain new perspectives alone. Adults who are resocialized need a supportive community which carries the new perspectives they have acquired. Likewise, "maypole dancers," after their first fleeting moments of independence, will either float back and be absorbed into the original mothering community or they will gather together to form a new community. He suggests that the "maypole dancers" may well be the architects of an alternative future for traditional communities and hence for education within these communities.

This presentation of Westerhoff's attempt to deal with the question of freedom as it is posed by opponents of the cultural approach does not include everything he has written to address the problem. In fact, most of his explicit references to freedom in this context are to specifically "Christian" freedom.[54] Consistent with the focus of the present study, these references have been ignored. While one can say that Westerhoff deals with the issue, at least in the faltering way outlined above, Nelson does not deal with it at all. Both these authors tend to retreat into theology before dealing with the issue at the level of the human sciences.[55]

Freedom "from" and Freedom "for"

Westerhoff's stress upon education as an *intentional* activity is designed to draw attention to the degree of *unintentional* socialization that is effected within the community. Education aims to expose the "hidden curriculum," and hence deliver persons from captivity to the powerful persuasion of stereotypical cultural patterns. Education, in this approach, aims toward freedom *from* the "hidden curriculum" and freedom for *fuller* involvement in the life of the community. Education for freedom involves reshaping the community as much as it involves reshaping individuals. It is not a choice between the community or the individual. The individual can only grow in freedom if the community, and in particular the adult leaders of the community, are becoming more aware of the beliefs and values embodied in the structuring of space and the ordering of relationships within the community. The community can educate toward freedom of the individual only be evaluating and changing institutions, roles, architecture, rituals, art, and all the other numerous cultural symbols that structure the consciousness of persons. Human beings are formed within culture, and there are no elements of the culture that are of neutral educational value. The more the community reflects upon its life as a bearer of culture, the more it can become responsible in imparting this culture to the next generation. The community reflection will necessarily involve some reshaping of its present cultural patterns, so that they become a true expression of the professed communal beliefs and values. Rather than be subject to the control of powerful but hidden persuasion, individuals will be subject to responsible educative efforts that work towards their deeper inclusion in the authentic life of the community.

Education for freedom, in this approach, has an even more fundamental meaning than freedom from the "hidden curriculum." Education initiates persons into the community through story and ritual. It builds the selfhood of persons by establishing a sense of identity and a sense of belonging. Through story and ritual it allows persons to discover meaning, especially in those times in the life cycle when there is a threat of disintegration. Education also welds the community together, maintaining the communal sense of identity, and the communal definitions of reality. Through story and ritual the communal life is protected from disarray and disintegration.

The freedom that education as cultural transmission offers is a freedom *from* chaos, confusion, and fragmentation and a freedom *for* creative living together. Being truly human is to live in a community sharing common meanings and values. By celebrating communal rituals, sharing in common experience, and engaging in authentic action together, human beings grow toward greater freedom. Education, as initiation and nurture, is an intensifying the community's effort to maintain the common symbol system which expresses its shared meanings and values. It is also an intensifying of the community's effort to transmit this symbol system to the next generation. Ideally, education's interest is to free persons from the dark fear and alienating loneliness of separation from communal life. It aims to provide the liberating experience of belonging to community and of engaging fully in the ongoing life of community. When there is a coherent symbol system, people can securely establish their own self-definition, and can have room for their own creative exploits without fear of chaos.

CONCLUSION

The chapters in Part Two exposed three typical ways that religious education theorists deal with education for freedom. We have avoided discussing specifically Christian education, or even, for that matter, religious education. The exposition of the four types has centered around the category of education itself, and the approach that education takes to promote freedom. Education proved a suitable category to use, since it enabled comparison of theories whose authors have different views on the extent to which the adjectives "Christian" and "religious" qualify the noun "education" when defining religious education.[56]

The theories that have been analyzed under this focus are multifaceted and have a more complex structure than is evident from the classification used here. Nevertheless, the categories chosen, namely, educational anthropology, use of the human sciences, education for change, and education for freedom, provide questions one can ask in order to distill from these theories the essential components of their approach to the issue of freedom. The categories themselves clarify the issue of freedom by pointing up theoretical options available to pastoral planners and curriculum designers in education within the church today.

The exposition of the educational anthropologies characteristic of each type identified three different approaches to human development discernible within current religious education theory. Hence, education for freedom means a different thing for different authors. They all claim to promote human freedom, but there are variances in what they understand by that claim.

These three typical approaches to an education for freedom are not mutually exclusive. While they can be clearly distinguished and compared, using the categories mentioned above, each approach benefits from incorporating insights from the other two approaches. They are not necessarily incompatible. When they are brought into dialogue the three approaches complement one another. The following discussion points out the merits and liabilities of the distinctive educational anthropology of each approach, indicating the need for insights from all three approaches for a religious education which promotes freedom.

The Psychological Approach

The educational anthropology underlying the psychological approach to an education for freedom has the advantage of stressing the interior pull toward self-transcendence in the human person. It jealously guards the uniqueness of the individual over against an amorphous and anonymous collectivity. It values the healing of interior wounds and opens the way for contemplation as a quest for the authentic self. This approach also establishes the priority of the I-Thou encounter in human growth.

On the debit side, however, the psychological approach, of itself, restricts the scope of human interaction to the interior and subjective dynamism within close personal encounters. In this perspective, the human subject exists in a secluded and protected zone of close interpersonal relationships, ideally immune from the influence of broader social cultural forces. The existential stance of this approach makes it seem as if the person exists in "a no-man's land of free-floating interpersonal relations"[57] and not in a society that operates according to laws of its own. There is no appreciation that social reality has an objective side—that it has "a drift, a momentum, a weight of its own."[58] In the psychological approach, human development is described in terms of development of the individual psyche. There is no evident understanding of the necessity to change social structures that determine the capacity of an individual to decide and act, and which also determine the possibility of relating interpersonally. The psychological approach, of itself, is inadequate since it does not recognize the enabling and disabling forces in the social, political, economic, and religious institutions.[59]

Both Goldbrunner and Sherrill, representatives of this approach to an education for freedom, seek to protect the individual from the massification of society. Goldbrunner does not envisage social action to change the causes of this external threat; rather, he argues that the individual by an exercise of will, can bestow meaning on any situation regardless of the inhumanity of the social conditions.[60] This implicit acceptance of the status quo is what the political approach aims to overcome. Goldbrunner's idea of social roles also betrays a lack of appreciation for the objectivity of social reality. He sees social roles as facades assumed by the individual in order to hide the authentic self. Becoming human means to drop the roles, or masks, and be fully genuine.[61] This way of thinking is contrary to social theory which presents the positive function of social roles, and denies the possibility of social activity without them.[62]

Both Sherrill and Goldbrunner see social reality as an annoying and troublesome external factor which threatens freedom of the individual. They do not perceive that human enslavement or liberation occurs in and through social mediation. They fail to see that a person's interior life is shaped not only by I-Thou relationships, but also by the institutions, roles and language of a society at large.

The Political Approach

The great advantage of the political approach is that it seeks to change those institutional and linguistic structures which inhibit personal growth. It repudiates the implicit assumption in the psychological approach that human beings can become authentic without an accompanying transformation of society. It draws attention to the function of language in structuring human consciousness, and points out how language can serve to legitimate the status quo. The political approach presents human beings as active agents in social change. If people passively succumb to enculturation they become less human, since they are not fulfilling their historical vocation to take part in the remaking of society. Moran describes this state as a loss of intelligence for the sake of the over-inflated rationality promoted in the institutions and language of a bureaucratic society. Only by critical intelligence, he maintains, will people be able to name the many forms of social, cultural, and political oppression and be able to do something to change them.

A weakness of the political approach, at least as it is expounded by Moran, is that it is highly speculative. Moran draws from many different sources from varying disciplines. Then, from this assortment of ideas he welds together a theory of religious education. While he does use insights from the social sciences he has a more philosophical bent than the other authors considered. His theory would be strengthened if he advanced more empirical evidence for his theoretical arguments.

The political approach, of itself, is also inadequate because it emphasizes social transformation and de-emphasizes cultural transmission. As presented by Moran, the political approach maintains that bureaucracy, the product of a technological society, is the fundamental social ill breeding conformity to the dictates of "reasonableness."[63] The only way out of this morass, says Moran, is through growth to intelligence which occurs when the current oppressive language and institutions are transformed. The presumption is that bureaucracy is evil, that the language and institutions of society need reform. This is only a half-truth. Language and institutions are benign as well as malignant.[64] If the whole thrust of an educational system is to transform the society, the aspect of cultural transmission is overlooked. An equally important task of education is to transmit the culture, the common understandings, values, ideas, and language of the community.

The goal of transforming the society should not, in the view of this author, supplant the other goal of maintaining and transmitting cultural symbols. To recognize the inherent conservatism of culture, its resistance to change, and the need for continual innovation is to deal with only half the problem. In terms of freedom, the primary educational aim is to provide people with the means to think and decide for themselves. Assimilation of a culture is a prerequisite of this.[65] Culture is a medium supporting thought and growth to intelligence. By learning a culture we acquire the knowledge, attitudes, values, skills, and sensibilities that enable us to develop critical and intelligent responses to social reality. Once again it is a matter of emphasis. The political approach is inadequate of itself because it focuses first on the crippling and disabling forces in society at large and sets up strategies to overcome them. An equally important task is that of induction into a common culture. Here the importance of dialogue between the political and cultural approaches becomes evident. While one emphasizes transformation, the other emphasizes transmission. An education for freedom requires both aspects.

The Cultural Approach

The cultural approach has the advantage of stressing the importance of a cohesive symbol system and of a strong commitment to common beliefs and values for effective communal transmission of these beliefs and values to the next generation. It demonstrates that the truly educational community has a strong collective identity and a coherent world view which can be internalized by new members of the community.

This approach develops the concern in the political approach for liberating language. It subverts the technological world view which is usually dominant in industrialized societies like the United States.[66] The great advantage of the cultural approach is that it stresses the symbolic consciousness of human beings. Human beings are seen as symbol-making adults—discovering meaning in a diaphonous universe and bestowing meaning through their own constructive activity. In this approach, meaning emerges from human interaction with the environment, and all human interactions can become revelatory of the dimension of mystery in life. The communal myths are formulated out of the perennial existential situations of human living and dying. They serve to mediate the transcendent. They shape the religious imagination of the community and open up the possibility of new modes of being in the world together. Through telling and retelling of sacred stories the community discovers and rediscovers its relatedness with the ultimate make-up of reality. Through storytelling the imagination of the community is awakened for the future action.[67]

The emphasis on storytelling is one way that the symbolic imagination is shaped. Ritual is another. Human beings are ritualizers. The meanings that express the community's life are stored in ritual. Ritual functions to reinforce the communal identity, and to maintain relatedness with the Ultimate. In ritual celebrations the capacity to wonder is expanded and the narrow confines of a technocratic society are superseded. Both story and ritual function to free persons and communities from the flat, one-dimensional world of rationalistic endeavor and to open up new imaginative possibilities for human living.

The weakness in the cultural approach lies in an inherent tendency to domesticate individuals by making them "good practicing members" of the community.[68] The story and ritual can become fixed and no longer provocative of an imaginative response. If left unchecked, the community can become apathetic in relation to changing its own structures. The taken-for-granted world constructed and maintained by the community can be delivered to newcomers as the only belief system which is unquestionably valid for all time.

The cultural approach needs the political type for its completion. Without the sharp edge of prophetic critique, any tradition-bearing community suffers from fatigue and ossification of linguistic and structural forms. Critical prophetic groups within the community help to keep it honest in its construction and maintenance of reality. The social constructions need to be challenged. The critique comes both from intuitive, insightful charismatic figures and groups, as well as from cool-minded social programmers and reformers. Unfortunately, advocates of the cultural approach sometimes want to tame the more critical members of the community since challenges to the status quo are perceived as a threat to continuity with the past. Theorists of the cultural approach need to include within the dynamics of cultural continuity some room for effective marginal dissent which is not just an optional extra or a tolerable appendage but an absolute necessity for the up-building of the community.

The Concept of Community as the Nexus

The three approaches to an education for freedom are mutually interdependent. Each approach centers on a different aspect of human development and hence of education for freedom. Religious education theories which have neo-Freudian psychological underpinnings promote freedom *from* internal psychic conflict and *from* external depersonalizing forces. They promote freedom *for* self-realization and wholeness. Religious education theories which have a political bent, such as Moran's, promote a freedom *from* racial, sexual, and economic oppression, and a freedom *for* the power to be shapers of the culture within which we live. Religious education theories which center on the concept of cultural transmission promote freedom *from* chaos, confusion and fragmentation, and a freedom *for* fuller involvement in the life of the community.

In each approach to an education for freedom a community of face-to-face relationships occupies a central place. However, each approach conceives of the function of community in a different manner. In the psychological approach, community is a network of interpersonal relationships that enable individuals to realize their personal potential. In the political approach, community functions as a prophetic critique of an overly-bureaucratic society. In the cultural approach, community functions as the transmitter of common meanings kept in its stories, beliefs, rituals, values, and lifestyles. While the perspectives are different, there is agreement that liberating education occurs in and through community.

This common strain through the three approaches suggests to religious educators that a theory of education for liberation should embrace all three aspects of communal activity—the psychological, the political, and the cultural. The liberating community is a psychological community since it provides an atmosphere of unconditional acceptance within which persons can discover their own uniqueness and celebrate their individual gifts. Yet it is not just a *koinonia* of affective relationships. The liberating community must also be constantly reforming itself, and have a transformative influence in the broader society within which it exists. Only in this way will the stifling powers of bureaucratic reasonableness be overcome. It is a political community engaged in prophetic action to change patterns of oppression in society. It is also a cultural community, in that it seeks to maintain its own identity and way of life, initiating the young into its distinctive stories, rituals, beliefs, and practices.

The model emerging from a dialogue between the three approaches gives primacy to the concept of community—a group small enough to enable face-to-face relating, a group extended enough to enable intergenerational interaction, and a group localized enough to have common stories and rituals. The evidence from our elaboration of the psychological, political, and cultural approaches indicates that education for freedom can be best conducted by fostering such communities. These communities provide opportunities for people to grow in their experience of new interpersonal relationships. They stabilize identity through a common symbol system which is handed down from generation to generation. And they offer opportunities for a greater commitment to justice within the social milieu that surrounds them. Communal activity of this kind, if developed into a practical model, could foster freedom at all levels—the psychological, the political, and the cultural.[69] The inadequacies of any particular approach could be overcome by the complementary effects of the other two. No one approach can be absolutized without losing an important aspect of education for freedom. If the three approaches are kept in dialogue then they complement one another and together comprise a theory of religious education for freedom that addresses their weaknesses and enhances their strengths.

NOTES FOR CHAPTER 5

1. A. L. Knoeber and Clyde Kluckhohn, after considering over 150 definitions of culture from anthropologists, sociologists, and psychologists arrive at a working definition that combines most of the elements of this highly complex reality. "Culture consists of patterns, explicit and implicit, of and for behavior acquired and transmitted by symbols, constituting the distinctive achievement of human groups, including their embodiments in artifacts; the essential core of culture consists of traditional (i.e. historically derived and selected) ideas and especially their attached values; cultural systems may, on the one hand, be considered as products of action, on the other as conditioning elements of further action". See A. L. Knoeber and Clyde Kluckhohn, *Culture: A Critical Review of Concepts and Definitions*, (New York: Vintage Books, 1963), p. 357. A strikingly similar definition was made by Charles Ellwood in *Dictionary of Sociology*, edited Henry Pratt Fairchild, (New York: Philosophical Library, 1944), pp. 80–81. In this article Charles Ellwood says "As culture is transmitted by processes of teaching and learning, whether formal or informal, by what has been called inter-learning, the essential part of culture is to be found in the patterns embodied in the social traditions of the group, that is, in knowledge, ideas, beliefs, values, standards, and sentiments prevalent in the group." It is important to note that cultural transmission occurs dialectically—we are both

the products of culture and the shapers of culture. Culture cannot be reduced to the purely psychological domain, since it includes all the institutions, artifacts, and human products that distinctively belong to this community. On the other hand, culture cannot be totally reified since it includes common patterns of thinking and valuing.

2. See George D. Spindler, "Anthropology and Education: An Overview," in *Education and Anthropology*, ed. George D. Spindler (Stanford: Stanford University Press, 1955), pp. 1–23. For a revised edition of some articles in this volume, as well as further articles dealing with the meeting of educational and anthropological theory, see *Education and Culture: Anthropological Approaches* (New York: Holt, Rinehart and Winston, 1963). For other works along the same lines, see George F. Kneller, *Educational Anthropology: An Introduction* (New York: John Wiley and Sons, Inc., 1965); and *Anthropological Perspectives on Education*, ed. Murray Lionel Wax et al. (New York: Basic Books, 1971). In 1968 the Council on Anthropology and Education was formed to discover and promote ways that anthropology can be applied to research and development in education. The council publishes the *Anthropology and Education Quarterly*.

3. C. Ellis Nelson, *Where Faith Begins* (Atlanta: John Knox Press, 1967) (hereinafter cited as *WFB*).

4. A *Colloquy on Christian Education*, ed. John H. Westerhoff, III (Philadelphia: United Church Press, 1972); John Westerhoff, III, and Gwen Kennedy Neville, *Generation to Generation: Conversations on Religious Education and Culture* (Philadelphia: United Church Press 1974); John H. Westerhoff III, *Will our Children Have Faith?* (New York: The Seabury Press, 1976) (hereinafter cited as *WOC*); and Gwen Kennedy Neville and John H. Westerhoff, III, *Learning through Liturgy* (New York: The Seabury Press, 1978).

5. Marthaler's publications include the following: *Catechetics in Context; Notes and Commentary on the General Catechetical Directory Issued by the Sacred Congregation for the Clergy* (Huntingdon, Indiana: Our Sunday Visitor, Inc., 1973); "Catechesis and Theology," in *CTSA Proceedings* 28 (1973): 261–70; "A Traditional and Necessary Ingredient in Religious Education: Hagiography," *The Living Light* 11 (Winter 1974): 580–91; "Total Religious Education: A Blueprint for a Learning Society," *The Living Light* 11 (1974): 267–92; "Socialization as a Model for Catechetics," in *Foundations of Religious Education*, ed. Padraic O'Hare (New York: Paulist Press, 1978), pp. 64–92.

6. "Theology," for these authors, is used synonymously with "faith." Westerhoff, in particular, does not distinguish the discipline of theology, and its possible contribution to education, from his own inspiring and prophetic vision of faith. He argues that the role of the professor is to *profess* what he or she believes at the moment, in order to stimulate further thinking. The so-called "theological" aspects of his writings are highly personalized. See *WOC*, p. x.

7. Nelson describes "revelatory experiences" which allow individuals to

break through any captivity to tradition. By an experience of the in-breaking word of God, individuals find a new center of being, no longer living according to the authority of their socializers, but now living from a new authority which has taken charge of their inner being (*WFB*, p. 87). Westerhoff talks about a new existence "in Christ," both individually and collectively. This also results from a conversion experience whereby a person or community becomes obedient to the will of God alone and disavows former obedience to the will of culture or to obsolete tradition. See Westerhoff, "Reshaping Adults," in *Generation to Generation*, pp. 154, 158. Westerhoff employs "liberation theology" to establish that the church's unique mission in the world is to be an agent of cultural change, and that individuals who are also immersed "in Christ" can likewise be agents of historical change. His explicit language of liberation is derived from his vision of faith. While these perspectives are important, they do not bear directly upon his educational anthropology which is the subject of this chapter. See *WOC*, pp. 31, 42, 44–45.

8. Westerhoff, *WOC*, pp. 52–54; Nelson, *WFB*, p. 34.

9. Westerhoff, "Religious Education for the Maypole Dancers," in *Generation to generation*, p. 75.

10. Ibid., p. 77.

11. Nelson, *WFB*, pp. 39–42.

12. Ibid., p. 60.

13. Ibid., p. 62.

14. Ibid., p. 65.

15. Westerhoff, "Reshaping Adults," pp. 149–51.

16. Nelson, *WFB*, p. 82.

17. Westerhoff, "Liturgy and Catechesis: A Christian Marriage," in *Learning through Liturgy*, pp. 96–97;

18. Idem, "Spiritual Life: Ritual and Consciousness," in *Learning through Liturgy*, p. 121; see also *WOC*, p. 71.

19. Westerhoff, "Liturgy and Catechesis: A Christian Marriage," p. 94.

20. Ibid., p. 103.

21. Westerhoff's notion of the "intuitive mode" is not clearly defined in his writings. Intuition is a mode of thinking which is prereflective and prethematic. At certain stages of psychological development symbols are interpreted more at the intuitive level of conscious; at other stages they are interpreted more at the critical level of consciousness. For a variety of philosophical options, see Richard Rorty, "Intuition" in *The Encyclopedia of Philosophy IV*, edited by Paul Edwards (New York: The Macmillan Company and The Free Press, 1967): 204–212.

22. Westerhoff, "Christian Initiation: Nurture and Conversion," in *Learning through Liturgy*, pp. 152–53. Westerhoff describes the development of faith as a movement from early childish unquestioning affiliation to the symbols of the

nurturing group, through adolescent searching and critical questioning, to mature faith which is capable of making a conscientious decision against community norms. However, he insists that mature faith has found a new way of being at home in the nurturing community. This developmental perspective which he attempts to incorporate into his theory is not well integrated with the emphasis on enculturation. See WOC, pp. 94–99.

23. Cultural anthropology is the study of human culture. Its key concept is culture. The scope and principal methods of cultural anthropology are implied in the definition of culture (see footnote 1). Cultural anthropologists strive to maintain a wholistic perspective of a culture while at the same time researching specific patterns of behavior. They do not stand apart in isolated objectivity, but enter into the culture for an inside viewpoint. They focus on patterns of behavior that may be convenient units of measurement. They make comparisons between various groups to ascertain similarities and differences in cultures. They build theories from the empirical evidence gained through participatory observation—their theories, therefore, derive from humanistic insight as well as from scientific objectivity. See David G. Mandebaum, "Cultural Anthropology" in International Encyclopedia of the Social Sciences Vol. 1, edited David L. Sills, (New York: The Macmillan Company and the Free Press, 1968), pp. 313–319.

24. Nelson, WFB, p. 16. Following Max Weber, and influenced by the phenomenology of Husserl, many social theorists, such as Alfred Shutz and Maurice Natanson, deny that the type of objectivity found in the natural sciences is possible within the social sciences. They point out that social reality is made up of the meanings which actors give to their actions. Therefore, a social action can only be understood by grasping the meaning which the action has for the actor who performs it. This is different from the meaning which the action has for a neutral observer. The mode of interpreting social reality, then, is Verstehen, that is, according to Shutz, the way that commonsense thinking finds its bearing within the social world and comes to terms with it. The scientific procedure of the Verstehen school involves utilizing reflective experience within the investigation to a larger degree than is possible in natural science investigation. See Alfred Shutz, "Concept and Theory Formation in the Social Sciences" in Philosophy of the Social Sciences, edited Maurice Natanson, (New York: Random House, 1963), pp. 231–49; and Maurice Natanson, "A Study in Philosophy and the Social Sciences," in Philosophy of the Social Sciences, ed. Maurice Natanson, (New York: Random House, 1963), pp. 271–85. Shutz's position can be found contrasted to that of B. F. Skinner in Philosophical Problems of the Social Sciences, ed. David Braybrook, (New York: The Macmillan Company, 1965).

25. Ibid., p. 32.

26. See Nelson, WFB, pp. 18, 36–43. His major source is Ralph Linton, The

Cultural Background of Personality (New York: D. Appleton-Century Company, 1945).

27. Nelson, *WFB*, pp. 19, 30.

28. Ibid., p. 24.

29. For example, Clyde Kluckhohn, *Navaho Witchcraft*, abridged from part II, sec. 3, by J. Milton Yinger, in *Religion, Society and the Individual* (New York: The Macmillan Company, 1957); Allison Davis, et al., *Deep South: A Social Anthropological Study of Caste and Class* (Chicago: The University of Chicago Press, 1941); and Ralph H. Gabriel, *Traditional Values in American Life* (New York: Harcourt, Brace and Company, 1960).

30. See the Preface of *Generation to Generation*, p. 15.

31. Gwen Kennedy Neville, "The Sacred Community—Kin and Congregation in the Transmission of Culture," in *Generation to Generation*, p. 54.

32. Gwen Kennedy Neville, "Rites and Rituals for a Double World—Private and Public Meanings," in *Generation to Generation*, p. 94.

33. Ibid., pp. 95–102. See also Neville, "Baptism: A Life-Crisis Liturgy," in *Learning through Liturgy*, pp. 58–70; Westerhoff, "Identity and the Pilgrimage of Faith," in *Learning through Liturgy*, pp. 170–81, and *WOC*, pp. 56–58. Neville and Westerhoff rely upon the classic work of Arnold van Gennep, *Rites of Passage* (Chicago: University of Chicago Press, 1960). They also refer to Victor Turner's concept of "liminality." See Victor W. Turner, *The Ritual Process* (Chicago: Aldine Publishing Co., 1969).

34. See Neville, "Sex and Socialization," in *Generation to Generation*, p. 176, and "Rites and Rituals for a Double World," p. 94, fn. 2. Hall has written a number of books dealing with the structure of human experience as it is molded by culture. The two most significant are: Edward T. Hall, *the Silent Language* (New York: Doubleday and Company, Inc., 1959), and *The Hidden Dimension* (New York: Doubleday and Company, Inc. 1969).

35. Westerhoff, *WOC*, p. 45; see also idem, "Liturgy and Catechesis: A Christian Marriage," p. 99.

36. Westerhoff, "Reshaping Adults," p. 153.

37. See Westerhoff's comment on Neville's discussion of "Continuity and Change in Human Culture," in *Generation to Generation*, pp. 163–72 (especially p. 171). This is a rare reference by Westerhoff to the creative function of *religion*. Usually, as we have mentioned earlier, he sees religion as a conservative force within culture that can only be offset by authentic *Christian faith*. Only authentic *Christian* existence over against the status quo can enable communities and individuals to become counterculture agencies. One cannot be nurtured into this Christian existence which enables one to act on behalf of God's will to change the social order. It is a matter of Christian *conversion*, which Westerhoff sees more in terms of supernatural intervention than as part of the process of enculturation. This chapter, it will be remembered, does not

deal with this issue (see fn. 7). See also Westerhoff, "Liturgy and Catechesis: A Christian Marriage," pp. 100–101.

38. Westerhoff, "What is Religious Socialization," in *Generation to Generation*, p. 38; see also "Toward a Definition of Christian Education," in *Colloquy*, pp. 63–70, and "A Socialization Model," in *Colloquy*, p. 82.

39. See Westerhoff, *WOC*, pp. 6 9, 49 50. Westerhoff argues that the most significant learning takes place outside school. See "Religious Education for the Maypole Dancers," p. 82; see also Nelson, *WFB*, pp. 183–84, 189.

40. Westerhoff, "What is Religious Socialization?" p. 42; *WOC*, pp. 16–19; "Toward a Definition of Christian Education," p. 64.

41. Nelson quotes Kurt Lewin to the effect that "learning is first a new belonging"; see *WFB*, p. 187. See also Westerhoff, "A Socialization Model," p. 82, and "What is Religious Socialization?" pp. 38–39.

42. Westerhoff, "Reshaping Adults," p. 150.

43. Ibid., p. 152; see also Nelson's comment in *WFB*, p. 211.

44. Nelson points out that adult group life is essential for effective socialization. In communal life adults find themselves, obtain emotional security, reinforce and reinterpret the world-view and value system of their tradition. In community, they find strength to resist other interpretations of life, and are trained to play their role as socializers. See Nelson, *WFB*, p. 96.

45. Westerhoff, *WOC*, pp. 54–60; "Religious Education for the Maypole Dancers," pp. 83–84; "A Socialization Model," pp. 84–87.

46. Westerhoff, *WOC*, pp. 60–64; "Religious Education for the Maypole Dancers," pp. 84–86; and "A Socialization Model," pp. 87–88.

47. Idem, *WOC*, p. 101; and Nelson, *WFB*, pp. 200–201.

48. Westerhoff, *WOC*, pp. 64–69; "Religious Education for the Maypole Dancers," pp. 86–88; "A Socialization Model," pp. 88–89.

49. Idem, *WOC*, pp. 78–80. For a similar perspective, see Berard Marthaler, "Total Religious Education: A Blueprint for a Learning Society," *The Living Light* 11 (Summer 1974): 266–93.

50. J. Gordon Chamberlin's attack on the Christian nurture theory, recorded in chapter 2 of this book, was an early example of this type of objection to enculturation. A more recent example, from a "political" perspective, is Thomas Groome, "The Critical Principle in Christian Education and the Task of Prophecy," *Religious Education* 72 (May-June 1977): 263–66. The literature on "indoctrination" is extensive. Most of it has been written by educational philosophers who possess an epistemology that is inadequate to account for the social context of the individual. They discuss the question in terms of the transmission of information from teacher to learner. For a good summary of some positions on "indoctrination" vis-à-vis "education," see Barry Chazan, "Indoctrination and Religious Education," *Religious Education* 67 (July–August 1972): 243–52.

51. James Fowler, who is one of Westerhoff's sources, has devised a stage-theory of human development which includes a tentative description of how persons and communities grow in their interpretation of traditional symbols. At the conventional stage a person still swims within the surrounding culture like a fish which has no control over the water which supports and engulfs it. The person grasps and is grasped by the symbols on the passional level more than on the rational level. Transition to a new critical awareness of symbols requires the availability of an ideologically potent world view which is either an alternative to the one shared by the original nurturing community, or a presentation of this community's common story in such a way that a clear choice can be made in relation to it. In this new stage of "critical-consciousness" the evocative power is no longer in the symbol itself, but in the meaning that the critical mind can extract from the symbol. However, the next stage in Fowler's scheme involves the "postcritical" rejoining of irreducible symbolic power and ideational meaning. The person in this stage becomes more in touch with the unconscious psyche; the person therefore allows nurturing symbols to elicit deeper responses than any conscious attitude that might be brought to bear upon the symbols. A second naivetè is possible and desirable. An integration is possible between the outside symbol system that is handed down within the culture and the interior powers within the person.

Much of Fowler's work is found in unpublished papers. His published articles include: James Fowler, "Toward a Developmental Perspective on Faith," *Religious Education* 69 (March-April 1974): 207-19; "Stages in Faith: The Structural Developmental Approach," in *Values and Moral Development*, ed. Thomas Hennessy (New York: Paulist Press, 1976); "Life/Faith Patterns: Structures of Trust and Loyalty," in *Life Maps: Conversations on the Journey of Faith*, ed. Jerome Berryman (Waco, Tex.: Word Books, Publishers, 1978), pp. 14-101; "Psychological Perspectives on the Faith Development of Children," in *Catechesis: Realities and Visions: A Symposium on the Catechesis of Children and Youth*, ed. Marianne Sawicki and Berard L. Marthaler (Washington, D.C.: U.S.C.C. Department of Education, 1977), pp. 72-86.

52. See Westerhoff, "Reshaping Adults," *passim*.

53. See Westerhoff, "Religious Education for the Maypole Dancers," *passim*.

54. See footnote 6. Nevertheless, Westerhoff has honestly struggled with the problem. He agrees with Joseph Fichter that "socialization" can too readily carry the assumption that human behavior is determined. Contrary to any deterministic assumption, he insists that "we are more than mere players of pre-existent or determined roles; we are meaning makers and value choosers." See John H. Westerhoff, III, "A Changing Focus: Toward an Understanding of Religious Socialization," *Andover Newton Quarterly* 14 (1974): 128-29. The reference is to Joseph Fichter, "The Concept of Man in Social Science: Freedom, Values, and Second Nature," *Journal of Scientific Study of Religion* 11 (June

1972): 110–21. In his most recent books, Westerhoff continues to struggle with the problem. However, he resorts to theological concepts rather than to social science concepts to try to explain freedom and social change. See John H. Westerhoff, *Tomorrow's Church: A Community of Change*, (Waco, Texas: Word Books, Publishers, 1976) and *Inner Growth/Outer Change: An Educational Guide to Church Renewal*, (New York: Seabury Press, 1979).

55. A tentative suggestion of a way the social sciences can throw light on the problem of "internalization" has been made by Hervè Carrier and Berard L. Marthaler. Both authors stress that internalization of social meanings is not a one-sided mechanical process, but an interaction whereby the individual selectively and interpretively takes on roles and attitudes of others. Internalization, they say, is a dialogical process in which the socializer is an active participant. Marthaler takes the socialization dialectic of Berger and Luckmann as his starting point. See Hervé Carrier, *The Sociology of Religious Belonging* (New York: Herder and Herder, 1965), and Berard L. Marthaler, "A Socialization Model of Catechesis," in *Foundations*, pp. 66–70.

56. See Introduction, footnote 9.

57. Russell Jacoby, *Social Amnesia: A Critique of Conformist Psychology from Adler to Laing*, (Boston: Beacon Press, 1975), p. 64.

58. Ibid., p. 65.

59. Gregory Baum has pointed out that there has been a trend in neo-Freudian psychology to de-privatize psychoanalysis. The "Freudian left," he says, attempt to add social analysis to analysis of psychic misery. They disagree with the readiness of some therapists to regard the social world to which patients belong as the reality to which they must learn to adjust. Left wing therapists speak not only of adaptation to a given social reality, but also of creativity which enables people to have greater power to engage in social action to change structures of their world. See Gregory Baum, *Religion and Alienation*, (New York: Paulist Press, 1975), pp. 227–237. Neither Sherrill nor Goldbrunner show evidence for being aware of the political implications of Freudian psychology.

60. Goldbrunner, *Realization*, p. 130.

61. Goldbrunner, CMCS, pp. 43–56.

62. See Robert J. Havighurst and Bernice L. Neugarten, *Society and Education*, (Boston: Allyn and Bacon, Inc., 1967), p. 127.

63. Moran, RB, pp. 40–41.

64. This is the point Johannes Metz has been making in regard to the church considered as a social institution. He calls the church an "institution of social criticism." See Johannes B. Metz, "The Church's Social Function in the Light of a 'Political Theology'" in *Concilium* 36 (May 1968), p. 10.

65. Lawrence Stenhouse, *Culture and Education*, (London: Thomas Nelson and Sons Ltd., 1967), pp. 9–10.

66. See Theodore Roszak, *The Making of a Counter Culture*, (New York: Doubleday and Company, Inc., 1969), pp. 1–22. Roszak's idea of "technocracy" is fundamentally the same as Moran's idea of "bureaucratic reasonableness."

67. See John Shea, *Stories of God: An Unauthorized Biography*, (Chicago: The Thomas More Press, 1978), pp. 7–39.

68. Thomas Groome has been a consistent critic of an absolutization of this approach. See Thomas H. Groome, "The Crossroads: A Story of Christian Education by Shared Praxis" *Lumen Vitae* 22 (1977), pp. 49–50, and "The Critical Principle in Christian Education and the Task of Prophecy" in *Religious Education* 72 (May–June, 1977), pp. 262–266.

69. Within the church, especially in the Third World, "basic communities" are providing this sort of liberating education. The definition of a "basic community" given by the General Conference of Latin American Bishops at Puebla, Mexico, describes in theological and liturgical language the reality of the psychological-political-cultural community: "As a community the CEB [base-level ecclesial community] brings together families, adults, and young people, in an intimate interpersonal relationship grounded in faith [psychological] . . . . It celebrates the Word of God and takes its nourishment from the Eucharist. . . . It fleshes out the Word of God in life through solidarity and commitment to the new commandment of the Lord [cultural]. . . . United in a CEB and nurturing their adherence to Christ, Christians strive for a more evangelical way of life . . . work together to challenge the egotistical and consumeristic roots of society . . . . Thus they offer a valid and worthwhile point of departure for building up a new society [political]." See *Third General Conference of Latin American Bishops: Evangelization at Present and in the Future of Latin America: Conclusions*, (Washington, D.C.: National Conference of Catholic Bishops, Secretariat, Committee for the Church in Latin America, 1979), pp. 126–127.

PART THREE

Chapter 6
Catechesis and Freedom

Human freedom has been a perennial issue in religious education and catechetics. Part One of this work surveyed the historical background of the contemporary religious education theory.
It showed that the intellectual ferment surrounding the emerging
catechetical movement in the Catholic church and Christian
education movement in Protestantism contained the seeds of a
dilemma for catechetical theorists. On the one hand, there was
an urgency to communicate the faith. On the other hand, there
was the necessity of respecting that faith is a free response. In the
late sixties and early seventies, religious educational and
catechetical theorists turned more and more to the human sciences to understand those factors that facilitated or impeded
freedom. The quest was for an adequate anthropology that would
ensure a free response. Part Two examined current religious education theory and concluded that it yields at least three distinct
but interrelated approaches to an education for freedom. Now,
Part Three takes recent documents of the Catholic church and
asks how they relate catechesis and human freedom.

The four documents chosen are the *General Catechetical Directory (GCD), Sharing the Light of Faith (SLF)*, which is the National Catechetical Directory for Catholics in the United States,
the *Message to the People of God (MPG)*, and *Catechesi Trandendae (CT)*. [1] A study of these documents in the light of the three
types reveals that the "cultural" approach predominates. The
other two approaches, insofar as they are evident, are included
within the comprehensive perspective of the "cultural" model.

The church documents are not used here to bless the cultural approach, and thus attempt to legitimize it through appeal to a "higher authority." The chapter simply argues that the cultural approach is the operative model of education for freedom in these documents.

The chapter aims to validate this claim from the texts themselves. If indeed it can be shown that the cultural approach is truly the integrating model underlying catechesis, it will be helpful to point out the strengths of such an approach with reference to human freedom, and to warn of certain inherent dangers.

THE DOCUMENTS

The four documents under consideration were generated in different circumstances and to meet different needs, but they are all situated within the mainstream of Catholic pastoral theology which has been shaped by the kerygmatic scriptural and liturgical movements and given impetus by the decrees of the Second Vatican Council. The *General Catechetical Directory*, for instance, was mandated by the decree on the Pastoral Office of Bishops.[2] Finally published in 1971, the GCD's formation was influenced heavily by the six International Study Weeks convened by Johannes Hofinger from 1959 to 1968. It was the result of wide consultation with episcopal conferences and catechetical experts, especially those from European countries. The expressed intention of the directory was to "provide the basic principles of pastoral theology . . . by which pastoral action in the ministry of the word can be more fittingly directed and governed" (*GCD*, Foreword). The directory drew its inspiration more from theological reflection than from educational principles. Pastoral activity was defined first and foremost from theological premises and only secondarily from principles derived from the human sciences.

The purpose of the GCD was to present guidelines for the

production of national and regional directories as well as to enumerate principles for the development of catechetical materials.[3] Having outlined the basic principles governing the nature and objectives of catechesis, the GCD left it to national hierarchies to apply these principles to their own concrete cultural circumstances (GCD, Foreword). In the United States, after a lengthy process of consultation at all levels of the church's life, the National Conference of Catholic Bishops approved the *National Catechetical Directory* in November 1977.[4] The bishops gave it the more popular title *Sharing the Light of Faith*. This document was reviewed and finally approved by the Sacred Congregation for the Clergy on October 30, 1978. Because of the extensive consultation with many diverse groups within the church, the *SLF* can claim to be a consensus document which represents the majority opinion of the church in the United States. Its distinctiveness is found especially in the importance it gives to sacramental catechesis, to catechesis for social justice, and in the way it addresses the problem of cultural diversity within the United States itself.

The third document is the *Message to the People of God*, delivered by the assembled bishops at the 1977 synod.[5] This synod was convened with the theme "Catechesis in our time, with special reference to the catechesis of children and young people." The deliberations of the synod occurred in the wake of renewed fervor for propagation of the gospel message aroused in the three years following the previous synod which dealt with evangelization. In 1974 the bishops had pondered the problems of proclaiming the Good News within the contemporary world. As a follow-up to this synod, Pope Paul issued an exhortation entitled *Evangelii Nuntiandi*.[6] This magisterial statement provided a backdrop for the 1977 synod. Catechesis was discussed within the context of evangelization, and was defined as an integral part of the church's ministry of the word.

The *Message to the People of God* was issued at the close of the synod. It is a statement of general conclusions addressed to the universal church. At the same time the synod also approved another document, consisting of thirty-four propositions, which was sent to the Holy Father along with nearly 1,000 amendments.[7] These "thirty-four points" were a confidential report to the Holy Father of the trends in the bishops' deliberations. They were forwarded to Pope Paul with the recommendation that they be incorporated into a magisterial statement to come later. This statement finally came in October 1979 from Pope John Paul II in the form of an apostolic exhortation with the title *Catechesi Trandendae.*

In his exhortation, the Holy Father endeavored to remain faithful to the ecclesial-evangelical thrust of the synod.[8] He admitted the limitations of his document and sought to discuss "only a few of the most topical and decisive aspects" of catechesis (*CT*, 4). He did not intend to make "a rigorous formal definition of catechesis." He referred to the *GCD* as providing an adequate definition and called "for specialists to clarify more and more its concept and divisions" (*CT*, 18).

The four documents, therefore, are interconnected. They build upon one another.[9] Together they comprise an authoritative summary of the principles, goals, and methods of catechesis in the Catholic church. They represent the maturing thought of a catechetical movement that has been buoyant with energy and enthusiasm for over half a century. They illustrate an emerging consensus among Catholics about the nature and purpose of catechesis. For this reason they are significant material worthy of examination and appraisal by theoreticians from any religious tradition.

There are various features of the cultural approach that are major principles within the documents. These features are usually described in theological or liturgical language. However, the language can be penetrated to perceive the basic structure of the cultural approach. Catechesis is defined in terms of increasing bonds of religious belonging and strengthening a sense of communal identity. Its hallmarks are initiation and nurture within the Christian community. There is a deep concern for the integrity and communication of the symbols of the faith. Human growth is perceived in terms of interaction within a tradition-bearing community. The ongoing conversion of adults is the measure of catechetical success. All these features belong to the cultural approach. The following presentation exposes these characteristics more fully, validating the claim that catechesis as understood by the official documents of the Catholic church is based on the cultural model.

CATECHESIS AS AN ECCLESIAL ACTIVITY

Catechesis is defined as an activity of the local community initiating and nurturing its members and building a strong sense of identity and belonging. It is an ecclesial task, a pastoral activity conducted by the church, in the church, and for the church.

By the Church

According to the documents, catechesis is an indispensable form of the ministry of the word which is integral to the pastoral mission of the church in the world (CT 1, 15; GCD 17, 21). Because catechesis is an ecclesial action "all Christians, according to the circumstances of their own lives and their special gifts or charisms, are really involved in it" (MPG, 12). While some members of the community of believers are called to share in the catechetical ministry in specific roles such as teachers, parents, coordinators, etc., the documents are clear that the community itself is the agent of catechesis (SLF, 204). There is a differentiated but shared responsibility in the catechetical action of the church. As Pope John Paul puts it, "... Catechesis always has been and always will be a word for which the whole church must feel responsible and must wish to be responsible..." (*CT*, 16).

By emphasizing that catechesis is a common task shared by all members of the believing community, the documents assume that the community ought to have a common understanding and interpretation of its symbols. Catechesis will only be an ecclesial activity, as the documents propose, when there is a strong collective identity, especially among the adult members, and a deep allegiance to communal goals and aspirations.

In the Church

These documents broaden the concept of catechesis, disengaging it from exclusive identification with any one educational institution such as the school, and putting it within the communal life of the people of God. "The normal place or setting of catechesis is the Christian community" (*MPG*, 13). The local parish is called the "prime mover and preeminent place for catechesis" (*CT*, 67).

The family is recognized as the first community in which a person is educated, but we are reminded that "the entire faith community is an important part of the experience of children and youth" (*SLF*, 18 ii), and that "the total learning environment of the parish is an important factor in motivating adults to grow in their faith" (*SLF*, 189). The community of believers in its life, language, rituals, and structures is itself a powerful and persuasive message that nourishes faith (*SLF*, 181 v).

The school is seen by the documents as a "community within the wider community, contributing to the parish upon which it depends and integrated into its life" (*SLF*, 232). The necessity of the school is affirmed, but any tendency for it to monopolize education is denied. The ecclesiastical community, we are told, not only provides opportunities for formal training of its members but also welcomes its new members into an environment where they can live as fully as possible the ideals, values, and beliefs which they share with the community (CT, 24).

While the structure of parish, family, and school is emphasized, there is also clear recognition that the "community of believers" need not be manifest only in these three forms. Other forms of ecclesial communities, such as *communautés de base*, [10] youth groups, family clusters, etc., are also seen as catechetical situations (MPG, 13; SLF, 9; CT, 47).

The effort to bring all Catholic educational institutions under the umbrella of community education is a trait of the "cultural" approach to education for freedom. The purpose of the Catholic school is understood only within the more comprehensive framework of the goals of the Catholic Christian community. No educational institution is absolutized. Rather, there is an attempt to rediscover that the community of God's people is a total learning situation. It is both "ecclesia discens" and "ecclesia docens."[11]

For the Church

The documents describe catechesis as a process of building up the community of believers. The church finds in catechesis "a strengthening of her internal life as a community of believers and of her external activity as a missionary church" (CT, 15). Catechesis is concerned with fostering the "authentic experience of Christian community" which always includes witness and committed action in the world (SLF, 210, 209). Catechists have the task of "making the ecclesial community come alive, so that it will be able to give a witness that is authentically Christian"

(*GCD*, 35). Catechesis is authentic only if it serves to make the Christian community a more lucid sign of credibility by the individual conversion of its members and the transformation of any structures that obscure the witness of justice and love in the world (*GCD*, 35; *SLF*, 38).

Catechesis as an enterprise that builds the church is not a narcissistic endeavor. In these documents the mission of the church in the world is intrinsically linked with its being. If the church is becoming itself through the pastoral action of catechesis, then the church is becoming the "universal sacrament of salvation." Commitment to justice, and the new lifestyles and structures that express it, arise out of the church being true to itself. A catechesis which authentically builds up the church cannot be introverted and intramural in its thrust but is always a call to individual and communal conversion. As Christians are educated to take their full place in the community of the disciples of Jesus Christ, they of necessity become more identified with the authentic gospel mission for justice and peace in the world. (*MPG*, 10).

A catechesis which builds the church means that the community of believers is challenged to undergo a reevaluation of what it means to be Catholic Christians in today's world. There is an implicit challenge in the documents for Catholics to find a new cultural idiom in which the profession of faith in Jesus Christ can be made today. This involves a search for roots in a concrete cultural community, as well as an attempt to discover a new self-definition as Catholics in the language of today.

THE RITE OF CHRISTIAN INITIATION OF ADULTS

The growing conviction in the Catholic church that catechesis is an ecclesial process can be attributed in large measure to the *Rite of Christian Initiation of Adults (RCIA)*, published in 1972 by the Sacred Congregation for Divine Worship.[12] The *RCIA* has been responsible, at least in part, for the vision of catechesis found in the documents under study. As indicated above in chapter 2, the *RCIA* was the result of early experimentation in the restoration of the adult catechumenate. In the document itself, and in the recent flourish of pastoral initiatives prompted by it, there has been an attempt to recapture an ancient vision of catechesis.

In the early church the catechumenate offered a step-by-step initiation into the faith community. The community had the vital role of welcoming and assisting candidates in their journey of faith. The neophytes were led gradually to accept the story of the community as their own story. At each stage in the initiation process there were appropriate ritual celebrations. The emphasis was not on instruction, but upon the experience of mysteries at the prethematic level of consciousness. Having been nurtured by the powerful language, rituals, and witness of the community, the newly baptized were invited to undergo "mystagogical" catechesis. The mysteries into which they had already been immersed were now explained. This exploration of the meanings of the Christian symbols was an ongoing learning experience throughout adult life. All these features of the ancient catechumenate have been restored in the *RCIA*. They are all characteristic of the "cultural" approach to an education for freedom.

The *MPG* insists that "through an ordered and progressive education in the faith it (catechesis) leads to a continual process of maturing in the same faith" (*MPG*, 1). Catechesis is defined as an ongoing process of conversion:

The model for all catechesis is therefore the baptismal catechumenate, that special formation which prepares an adult convert for the profession of his baptismal faith during the paschal vigil. During this preparation, catechumens receive the gospel (sacred scriptures) and its ecclesial expression the creeds (*MPG*, 8).

Catechesis as a deepening in the mystery of Jesus Christ is seen as an entry into the passover mystery as it is experienced, lived, and celebrated by the community of believers. Catechesis is an activity occurring at the heart of the church's life and worship, at the center of the church's being, as it corporately passes in Jesus Christ from death to life by the Spirit.

SLF takes up this theme when it states:

> Full initiation into the church occurs by stages. The *Rite of Christian Initiation of Adults* (Roman) provides a norm for catechetical as well as liturgical practice in this regard. . . . Such catechesis will involve many members of the parish community who support and pray with the catechized, besides instructing them so that they may grow in understanding of the Christian message (*SLF*, 115).

In this model of catechesis the individuals are invited to join the journey of faith of the entire community. Individuals are not called simply to a private conversion of their personal beliefs, values, and world view. In this process the community also undergoes constant unsettling of some of its cherished assumptions and reevaluates its basic structures as it experiences again the transforming power of its foundational symbols. The ongoing conversion of the community is the *sine qua non* of Christian initiation.

The group of catechumens are not just recipients of a one-way ministry. Their very presence, enthusiasm, and quest for truth is a stimulus to conversion for the rest of the Christian community. Likewise, as the catechumens enter step by step into full participation in the community life they are challenged to put aside old ways and to embrace the symbols of new life. They are called upon to reinterpret their own history in terms of a new symbol system which expresses the story of the Christian community they are now joining.

A COMMUNITY OF COMMON MEMORY[13]

In the process of Christian initiation, liturgy and catechesis become intimately connected. Both are expressions of the church's faith, and both strengthen the faith and summon Christians to conversion (*GCD*, 25; *SLF*, 36, 113; *CT*, 23). The *MPG* points out that the intimate link between liturgy and catechesis is grounded in the experience of *anamnesis*. The Christian community is united in common memory of the Lord Jesus which it relives in the living word of the tradition and in the living celebration of the liturgy (*MPG*, 9). In the daily life of the church, liturgy and catechesis cannot be separated. The creeds and scriptures are read and interpreted with deepest meaning within the liturgical setting. In addition, liturgy is itself a form of experiential education in the faith. Even though liturgy has a distinctive purpose, the documents insist that "every liturgical celebration has educative and formative value..." (*SLF*, 36).

The documents stress that the living tradition of the Christian community is the communal story which holds the meanings that constitute the life of the community. This story is told and retold in order that the community may reaffirm its collective identity and discover new ways of expressing itself in today's world. The story has special poignancy in the liturgical context, since it is already woven into the fabric of the communal rituals, which are nonverbal expressions of the life of the community, serving to affirm religious identity while also calling for conversion of heart and renewal of communal structures. Catechesis, therefore, involves a telling and retelling of the communal story which is not some piece of information that can be passed on like a family heirloom. The story is embodied in the life of the community, in its whole symbol system, its beliefs, practices, documents, moral ideals, physical and social structures.

The papal document states it most clearly:

> Authentic catechesis is always an orderly and systematic initiation into the revelation that God has given of himself to humanity in Jesus Christ, a revelation stored in the depths of the church's memory and in sacred scripture, and constantly communicated from one generation to the next by the living, active "traditio" (CT, 53).

CATECHESIS AS THE TRANSMISSION AND MAINTENANCE OF THE SYMBOLS OF THE FAITH

Catechesis, according to the MPG, occurs within the living tradition of the church and can be described as the "transmission of the documents of the faith," that is, the creeds and sacred scripture (MPG, 9). Within the context of an initiation process, the tradition-bearing community hands on the symbols of the faith from one generation to the next.

> Catechesis is the manifestation in our day of the "mystery which was hidden in God before all times." This is why the first language of catechesis must be sacred scripture and the creeds. Catechesis is for this reason the authentic introduction to the lectio divina, that is, the reading of sacred scripture, but "according to the Spirit" which dwells in the church, both supporting apostolic ministries and acting in the faithful. The scriptures make it possible for Christians to speak a common language . . . . Believers should also make their own those expressions of faith, the living fruit of the reflection of Christians

over the centuries, which have been gathered in the creeds and the principal documents of the church (*MPG*, 9)

The creeds and sacred scripture are held to be fundamental symbols that shape the identity of the Christian community. All four documents stress that catechesis "must be impregnated and penetrated by the thought, the spirit, and the outlook of the Bible and the gospels" (*CT*, 27). This is to be achieved most of all through a richer reading of the texts within the heart of the church, and especially within the church's liturgical life. Steeped in the imagery of the parables, nourished through the affectivity of the psalms, enlightened by the wisdom literature, stirred by the Exodus story, challenged by the Sermon on the Mount—the Christian community lives and grows by the scriptures. This common language shapes the attitudes, values, behavior, and expectations of the community.

As with the scriptures, so also with the creeds. The latter express the common faith in formulas honed out of the living language of the people. Adherence to the creed is a mark of belonging to this particular religious tradition. Pope John Paul points out that the "traditio symboli," the symbolic handing over of the creed in the adult initiation rite, is a peak liturgical expression of what is happening in catechesis (*CT*, 28). Catechesis means transmitting the symbols of the faith. To become a member of the Christian community means to appropriate the symbols of this community to oneself.

While sacred scriptures and the creeds are the first language of catechesis, the documents indicate that there are other ways that faith is articulated and communicated. What Christians believe is expressed in liturgy which stores the constitutive meanings of the community's life. The content of faith is also embodied in the various lifestyles of service which build up the community and witness to the world. *SLF* states:

The church also gives witness to its faith through its way of life, its manner of worship, and the service it renders. The lives of heroic Christians, the saints of past and present, show how people are transformed when they come to know Jesus Christ in the Spirit. The forgiveness and reconciliation experienced by repentant sinners are signs of the church as a healing community. Concern for and ministry to the poor, disadvantaged, helpless, and hopeless are signs that the church is a servant. Uniting in love and mutual respect people from every corner of the earth, every racial and ethnic background, all socio-economic strata, the church is a sign of our union with God and one another effected in Jesus Christ. Every Christian community, characterized by its stewardship, is meant to be a sign of that assembly of believers which will reach fulfillment in the heavenly kingdom. Such a community catechizes its members by its very life and work, giving witness in a multitude of ways to God's love as revealed and communicated to us in Christ. (*SLF*, 45).

The beliefs of Christians are also expressed and communicated in a multitude of cultural modes such as "visual arts, in poetry and literature, in music and architecture..." (*SLF*, 59). According to the documents, the ongoing communal life is objectified in common symbols which are both the medium and the message of catechesis. To become a Christian means to enter into the living tradition of the people of God, and to express one's identity in terms of the fundamental symbols of this community.

There is a concern for maintenance of the symbols of the faith, or, to use the language of the documents, for "integrity of content" (*CT*, 30). They insist that the Christian mystery is an organic whole, centered in the salvific event of Jesus Christ, represented and effective in the community of believers today (*GCD*, 39; *CT*, 30; *SLF*, 53, *MPG*, 7). All the other symbols cohere around this one foundational symbol, Jesus Christ who discloses the hidden unseen God, and draws humankind into communion with him. The Christian community now in its life and worship continues the redemptive presence of Jesus Christ. To become incorporated into the community means to profess that "Jesus the Son of God, the Christ, lives and is our Savior" (*MPG*, 8). In this profession of faith, articulated in the language of the symbols of the faith, Christians attain a strong sense of identity and belonging.

The documents are also careful to insist upon the harmony and interrelationship of the beliefs which the church receives, serves, and hands on (*CT*, 31; *SLF*, 47; *GCD*, 39). This concern for the integrity of the belief system and the interconnection of its parts is a concern for maintaining a strong sense of communal identity with reference to the foundational symbols.

While catechesis has the concern for communicating and transmitting the belief system, theology has the task of establishing the precise way "for ordering the truths of faith according to an organic plan in a kind of synthesis" (*GCD*, 36). The documents point out that catechesis must be distinguished from theology. Theology has the task of systematically investigating and analyzing the symbols of the faith found in scripture and the creeds. Catechesis, on the other hand, has the task of maintaining communicating and interpreting the symbols within the life of the community for the purpose of maturing faith (*GCD*, 17, 36, 38, 112; *SLF*, 37; *CT*, 61).

IDENTITY, BELONGING, WELCOME, AND NURTURE

The documents possess a keen awareness that Catholic Christians today live under the pressure of comprehensive symbol systems, both religious and secular, which conflict with their own internalized beliefs and values. This awareness adds sharpness to Pope John Paul's insistence that "Christians must be educated to a sense of their own identity" (*MPG*, 15). It is a recurrent theme already mentioned above. Catechesis is meant to ground Christians in a clear sense of who they are, adherents of Jesus Christ, who belong to this particular community and with roots in this particular tradition.

The documents recognize the need for a new sense of what it means to be and become a Catholic Christian in today's world. They do not call for a retreat into the "fortress" church and a reinstitution of an old apologetic where the catechism was learned against other groups. In the spirit of the Second Vatican Council, these documents see catechesis as fostering an openness to the world. However, they stress "an authentic openness supposes and demands a profound awareness of our own Christian identity" (*MPG*, 16). *SLF* provides a pithy statement of the aim of catechesis in the following words: ". . . Catechesis refers to efforts which help individuals and communities acquire and deepen Christian faith and identity through initiation rites, instruction and formation of conscience" (*SLF*, 5).

In the face of fragmentation due to rapid technological changes, the resulting religious indifference, and the breakdown of family and community life in a mobile society, the documents call for a catechesis that offers forms of welcome and modes of initiation. Catechesis offers authentic community for the alienated, isolated, lonely, and confused. Referring to the "climate of uncertainty" among many Christians today due to the difficult circumstances of a rapidly changing world, Pope John Paul concludes that these conditions demand that "catechesis should strengthen them in their identity and that it should continually separate itself from the surrounding atmosphere of hesitation, uncertainty and insipidity" (*CT*, 56).

Elsewhere the papal document points out the need for consolidation in the faith after one has given an initial adherence to

Jesus Christ. The community bears the responsibility of strengthening this allegiance:

> Catechesis runs the risk of becoming barren if no community of faith and Christian life takes the catechumen in at a certain stage of his catechesis. That is why the ecclesial community at all levels has a twofold responsibility with regard to catechesis: It has the responsibility of providing for the training of its members, but it also has the responsibility of welcoming them into an environment where they can live as fully as possible what they have learned (CT, 24).

There is a recognition here that catechesis is a form of welcome into and nurture within the Christian community. It takes its cue from the adult catechumenate. The total environment is crucial for education in the faith. Language, documents, social roles, meetings, rituals, practices, architecture—all are symbols conveying meanings to the catechumen. The community in all these symbolic expressions is expected to bespeak profound hospitality for newcomers. Catechesis includes a ministry of welcome, of inviting and leading one another to come further on a common journey of faith.

Catechesis also includes sharing the experience of communal life. *SLF* states:

> The catechist is called to foster community as one who has "learned the meaning of community by experiencing it." Community is formed in many ways. Beginning with acceptance of individual strengths and weaknesses, it progresses to relationships based on shared goals and values. It grows through discussion, recreation, cooperation on projects, and the like. Yet it does not always grow easily; patience and skill are frequently required. Even conflict, if creatively handled, can be growth-producing, and Christian reconciliation is an effective means of fostering community. Many people

have had little experience of parish community and must be gradually prepared for it (*SLF*, 209).

Sharing of communal experiences, in the context of the catechumenate, includes telling personal stories of faith experiences, listening to the common story of the community, celebrating the communal rituals, and living within the daily interactions that maintain the social fabric.

CATECHESIS FOR MATURITY OF FAITH

Catechesis as initiation and nurture within the Christian community, according to the documents, aims to foster mature faith. The *GCD* defines catechesis as "that form of ecclesial action which leads both communities and individual members of the faithful to maturity of faith" (*GCD*, 21). Whereas the "transmission and maintenance of the belief system" emphasizes the *fides quae* aspect of the act of faith, the "maturity of faith" theme emphasizes the *fides qua* aspect. The *GCD* treats them separately. Yet it insists that "these two aspects are by their very nature inseparable, and a normal maturing of faith assumes progress of both together" (*GCD*, 36).

All the documents agree that the life of faith is dynamic and grows through various stages or levels. Faith is a relationship with God the Father in Jesus through the Spirit. The quality of this relationship can improve as it becomes more like the relationship Jesus has with the Father (*SLF*, 173; *GCD*, 18, 22, 75).

The documents relate the life of faith as it grows and develops to the patterns of human development. Since human beings pass through various stages of growth, they develop in their capacity to respond in faith to God's invitation to friendship (*GCD*, 30; *SLF*, 175). The documents, in various ways, employ a psycho-social model of human development. They draw upon developmental psychology to provide a framework for a catechesis according to age levels, but they do not have an individualistic tone about them. They are not only concerned with the interior life of the individual, but also describe various social and cultural tasks that are presented at each stage of life as challenges for the person to grow. This model of human growth is a characteristic of the cultural approach to an education for freedom. It is an "interactionist" model. There is a dialectical relationship between social reality and individuals as they grow to maturity.

The social world with which a person interacts to attain a higher level of maturity expands progressively throughout the early years of the life cycle. In infancy and early childhood, "healthy growth is most likely in a positive, nurturing environment—normally, the immediate family" (SLF, 177). Family relationships provide powerful models for developing attitudes and values, and hence foster or hinder human and Christian growth (GCD, 78; CT, 36). At the later childhood stage, "other people" now include a "community much larger than the immediate family." The social world has expanded to include the new tasks that face the youngster at school, the role-modeling of members of the larger community, and the influence of the mass media, especially television (SLF, 178; GCD, 79; CT, 37). At the preadolescent stage, not only the home and school but also the peer group begins to assume a determining influence over attitudes, values, and behavior (SLF, 179).

The documents describe adolescence as a time of uncertainty, confusion, deep inner questioning, and reevaluation of one's past socialization. They see adolescence as a culturally defined time of transition which gives young people the space to make decisions based on their own discovery. It is a time when the adult community best facilitates growth by being patient and standing as fellow travelers with young people, confident in their fundamental generosity and their desire for truth (*GCD*, 82; *SLF*, 180; *CT*, 38).

Early adulthood is described by the documents as a time when persons face the challenge of making crucial vocational decisions, translating ideals into practice, and making tangible commitments within their religious tradition (*SLF*, 183). Middle adulthood is seen as a time of crisis brought on through the experience of defeat and disappointment at not having achieved major goals in life. This challenge provides the opportunity for accepting one's limits and moving into a new level of maturity. The person in middle life is challenged to attain an integrated vision of life, "to reduce to a unified whole all the experiences of his personal, social, and spiritual life" (*GCD*, 94; *SLF*, 184). The documents recognize later adulthood as a special area of attention for catechesis. As life expectancy increases, the existence of large numbers of elderly becomes an increasing cultural phenomenon. Old age constitutes the challenge of serenely and wisely accepting one's death (*SLF*, 186; *CT*, 45; *GCD*, 95).

While it is not stated explicitly in these documents, there is sufficient evidence to conclude that the model of growth is one where the self at each stage of life makes choices and constructs a personal world out of the possibilities and constraints given in the social and cultural environment. The documents warn against absolutizing any school of psychology or sociology in describing human development (*SFL*, 175). They avoid being tied to any one school, but, in general, they endorse an approach which unites in a dynamic synthesis the unfolding of the individual self and challenges and inhibitions given to the self by society. [14]

This assumption of an "interactionist" model of enculturation has important implications for the possibility of human freedom in the process. These implications will be explained below.

THE IMPORTANCE OF ADULT CATECHESIS

Another characteristic of the "cultural" approach found in the documents is the importance of adult catechesis. It also has implications for the possibility of human freedom during enculturation. The aim of catechesis is "maturity of faith," to lead persons into a responsible adherence to the beliefs and values of the Christian community. If "maturity of faith" is the aim, then adult catechesis becomes the norm. The catechesis of children and adolescents, while having its own distinctive features, is treated in the light of the movement toward maturity in adult years.

The primacy of adult catechesis is a constant theme in the documents, as expressed in *GCD:*

> . . . Catechesis for adults, since it deals with persons who are capable of an adherence that is fully responsible, must be considered the chief form of catechesis. All other forms, which are indeed always necessary, are in some way oriented to it (*GCD,* 20).

Persons who are adults by chronological age are more likely to have the capacity for critical reflection and the power to make responsible decisions in the society. They have the ability to attain psychological maturity and to make a mature response to God in faith. Adults have the capacity to understand and critically interiorize the whole of the Christian message embodied in the symbols of the believing community. Therefore, the catechesis of adults is described as the summit of catechetical endeavor. This point is underlined by *SLF:*

> The act of faith is a free response to God's grace; and maximum human freedom only comes with the self-possession and responsibil-

ity of adulthood. This is one of the principal reasons for regarding adult catechesis as the chief form of catechesis. To assign primacy to adult catechesis does not mean sacrificing catechesis at other age levels; it means making sure that what is done earlier is carried to its culmination in adulthood (*SLF*, 188).

SLF disavows the notion that adult catechesis gains its importance from its relationship to the catechesis of children. While arguing the case strongly for parental and teacher education, it stresses that these forms of catechesis do not provide its *raison d'être*. "Rather, the prime reason for adult catechesis—its first and essential objective—is to help adults themselves to grow to maturity of faith as members of the church and society" (*SLF*, 40).

The profound concern here is for a free appropriation of the symbols of the faith. Growth to adult maturity involves an intelligent interiorization of the meanings that were earlier accepted unquestioningly. It means a critical appraisal of and recommitment to values and beliefs imbibed earlier from the cultural milieu and reinforced by the affective intensity of attachment to significant others. The measure of success of catechesis is not the allegiance of children, but the adherence of adults who have personally appropriated the meanings objectified in the community symbols. The documents do not desire to keep adults of chronological age in a position of "first naiveté." The act of faith envisaged for adults is a knowing surrender to the revealing God, manifest in Jesus Christ, who is the foundational symbol of the Christian community.

The maturity of faith is never fully attained. Therefore, catechesis for adults aims to assist their ongoing conversion. Since adults hold the key positions of responsibility in the community, the expansion of adult horizons is intimately connected to the renewal of the entire community. If adults remain complacent and fixed in their ways, the whole community remains stagnant. The documents present adult catechesis as a way of converting the leaders of the community, and also the adult organizations and institutional life, to a deeper adherence to gospel values, providing stronger conviction and loyalty to the gospel, and greater generosity in participating in the pastoral mission of the church (GCD, 22–26, 28–29, 92, 94, 97; SLF, 99, 125–26).

The documents are keenly aware that adults strongly influence the faith-perception of children and catechumens. Parents especially are singled out as the most powerful nurturing influence upon small children. Pope John Paul states: "I cannot insist too strongly on this early initiation by Christian parents in which the child's faculties are integrated into a living relationship with God" (CT, 36). Similarly, SLF points out that

> God's love is communicated to infants and young children primarily through parents. Their faith, their confidence in human potential, and their loving and trusting attitude toward God and human beings strongly influence the child's faith (SLF, 177).

Since the impact of parents is decisive for the catechesis of children, the documents regard preparation for parenthood and parent education as an important subsidiary reason for adult catechesis (SLF, 25).

Adult catechesis, according to the documents, has the effect of strengthening the community of faith. Adults are considered more responsible than other members of the community for the coherence of the communal system of beliefs and values and for the delivery of these to the new generation. The effectiveness of the transmission of the symbols of the faith depends on the degree of adult commitment and the consistency with which it is translated into action. Therefore, adult catechesis ensures that the witness of adults through individual words, attitudes and actions, and also through institutional forms, will foster faith in the young (CT, 43; SLF, 40; MPG, 3; GCD, 35).

The documents further maintain that adult catechesis keeps the external mission of the church vital and active. For the church to be present in the world as a "leaven in the midst" working to build up the kingdom of justice and peace, there is a need for enthusiastic, idealistic, and informed adult Christians (SLF, 170 (13), 185 a; GCD, 26, 92; CT, 43, 29).

While adult catechesis is crucial for the communication of the faith, the documents keep it within the context of communal catechesis. There is a mutuality within the community of believers. Everyone is both catechist and catechized. There is no group that has exclusive rights to teaching. As John Paul puts it:

> Adults have much to give to young people and children in the field of catechesis, but they can also receive much from them for the growth of their own Christian lives. It must be restated that nobody in the church of Jesus Christ should feel excused from receiving catechesis (CT, 41).

The cultural approach to an education for freedom undergirds contemporary catechesis. The emphasis is on catechesis by, within, and for the ongoing life of the local community of believers. The community of common meaning and value is the context of all growth. This is a community that relives the great events of the past which shaped its origins. It does this through *storytelling* and *ritual* celebrations. It is a community that bears a common culture since its faith is always being expressed in symbols. This symbol system has as its foundation the central, unifying myth of Jesus Christ, who is the fundamental sacrament of encounter with God. The documents of the faith, especially the scriptures and the creeds, are also fundamental symbols to which members of the community adhere. In addition to fundamental symbols such as these, there are a multitude of secondary symbols, such as art, architecture, music, devotions, etc. Through allegiance to these symbols, members of the community know and express their identity and are able to confidently perform acts of service. Confident of their own identity, they are able to enter into mutual dialogue with other religious traditions, and are also open to contributions from secular symbol systems.

Catechesis, therefore, aims to strengthen religious belonging, to provide a strong sense of identity as Catholic Christians in continuity with the Church of the Apostles. It does this by ensuring the coherence of the symbol system and by transmitting this symbol system to the new generation. Catechesis places great value on adult education since the quality of cultural transmission depends on the degree of commitment of adults, and the extent to which adults themselves are turning over their lives and making them more visible witnesses of gospel values.

EVIDENCE OF THE PSYCHOLOGICAL AND POLITICAL APPROACHES

The "cultural" approach is undeniably prominent. Before discussing the implications of this for human freedom, the following section indicates how elements of the psychological and political approaches are present in the documents. These elements are subsumed within the all-embracing cultural paradigm.

The Psychological Approach

An indication of the psychological approach can be found in the emphasis on warm protective relationships in the family which can provide a person with a fundamental sense of trust in self, others, and the world.

> Healthy growth is most likely in a positive, nurturing environment—normally the immediate family. Family relationships and interaction provide young children with the most powerful models for developing attitudes, values, and ways of responding to external influences which foster or hinder Christian and human growth (SLF, 177).

This theme, which is fairly pronounced in the documents, is subsumed into the cultural approach. For example, SLF states:

> Education, broadly defined, includes the entire process by which culture is transmitted from one generation to the next. Educational research supports the view that the home is the critical educational institution (SLF, 25).

In addition to family catechesis, the documents often view the Christian *koinonia* as a close interpersonal community empowering others to grow in self-respect and dignity. The preference for the group model of catechesis, especially with adolescents, arises from a desire to respect the free inquiry of individuals in their personal search for truth. Referring to youth ministry, SLF states:

> The community dimension will usually be expressed in a preference for small groups within which relationships can develop. Weekend prayer, "search," encounter, or retreat experiences provide liturgical experiences in a communal setting of acceptance and exchange (SLF, 228 b).

The GCD also endorses the group experience as a mode of mutual support in the quest for freedom:

> For adolescents and young adults, the group must be considered a vital necessity. In a group, the adolescent or young adult comes to know himself and finds support and stimulation. In the case of adults, the group can today be considered a requisite for catechesis which aims at fostering a sense of Christian coresponsibility (*GCD,* 76).

The directory continued by linking the small group experience with the whole of the church's life, thus subsuming the psychological approach within a broader ecclesial perspective: "A group which has achieved a high degree of perfection in carrying out its task will be able to give its members... an excellent experience of ecclesial life" (*GCD,* 76).

Both the emphasis on the family as the basic Christian community which nurtures faith, and the stress on group catechesis as a vital experience of *koinonia,* carry assumptions from the psychological approach. However, the documents have placed these forms of catechesis in the broader context of the local church. The broader community through its structures, planning, and deployment of personnel supports and encourages these more intense opportunities for growth to maturity of faith.

The Political Approach

Elements of the political approach are evident in the documents when they promote a catechesis for social ministry. *SLF* highlights this dimension of catechesis much more than the other documents. It quotes a poignant text from the statement of the Synod of Bishops in 1971 on *Justice in the World:*

> Action on behalf of justice and participation in the transformation of the world fully appear to us as a constitutive dimension of the preaching of the gospel, or, in other words, of the church's mission

for the redemption of the human race and its liberation from every oppressive situation[15] (*SLF*, 160).

SLF goes on to point out that the responsibility of the church to work for justice in the world begins with the reformation of its own structures and the individual conversion of its members:

> Any group or institution which ventures to speak to others about justice should itself be just, and should be seen as such. The church must therefore submit its own policies, programs, and manner of life to continuing review . . . the plight of the many millions of hungry people in our world today calls seriously into question the morality of typical lifestyles and patterns of consumption in our affluent society. We are all—bishops, priests, religious, and laity—called to an ongoing examination of conscience in these matters (*SLF*, 160).

The document points out that responsible social action necessarily includes participation in political enterprises to change unjust structures. Therefore, one of the aims of catechesis is "to awaken a critical sense, leading to reflection on society and its values and to assessment of the social structures and economic systems which shape human lives" (*NCD*, 170 iv). Catechesis, the document continues, should involve people in "vital contact with the reality of injustice" and hence "empower people to exercise more control over their destinies and bring into being communities where human values are freely respected and fostered" (*SLF*, 170 x).

This political dimension of catechesis which underlines the need for social transformation is integrated into the central unifying idea that catechesis is by, with and for the church. The aim of building the church toward "maturity of faith" does not conflict with the demands of a catechesis for social justice. The documents point out that the development of a conscious, active, and critical group of adult leaders, people who have really been challenged by the transforming symbols of the faith, will ensure that the pastoral mission of the church in the world denounces sinful social structures and announces the coming of the kingdom of justice and peace.

THE PROBLEM OF FREEDOM

There is an inherent danger in the approach to catechesis taken by the documents. Catechesis is the transmission and maintenance of the symbols of the faith. It seeks to socialize persons into a symbol system so that they begin to understand themselves in terms of these symbols. Insofar as it is an educational enterprise, catechesis is geared toward shaping selves by cultural transmission. Therefore, catechesis can become simply the preservation of a taken-for-granted culture. It can degenerate into a delivery system, which channels established beliefs and values without stimulating critical thinking with regard to their validity. It can lull the members of the community into a sense of false security, assuring them of safety and not challenging them to change. It can hand on a received heritage without questioning its authority.

Catechesis may fail to perceive that hidden assumptions in the traditional world-view and practices do not square with gospel values. It can breed a form of provincialism by socializing people into a given religious denomination, creating strong bonds of belonging, and blinding them to their common bond with all men and women. It can settle for an ecclesiastical culture that is comfortable for the majority but blatantly unjust for the minority. It may even bear the contradiction of denouncing injustices outside ecclesiastical boundaries, but perpetuating similar injustices within its own structures. Its conservative instinct may try to domesticate groups that are critical of the status quo, preferring uniformity of language to the pain of conflicting world views.

AMBIGUOUS ASSERTIONS OF FREEDOM

The documents do not face the danger of domestication directly. When the language of freedom appears, it is usually related to issues other than the problem of domestication as such. For instance, the papal document asserts that "every human being has the right to seek religious truth and adhere to it freely" (CT, 14); but the context of the statement indicates that the concern is for "religious freedom" vis-à-vis the oppressive machinery of totalitarian states.[16] The GCD announces that ". . . adherence on the part of those to be taught is a fruit of grace and freedom . . ." (GCD, 71), but the context in this case is the degree of active intervention permissible for a teacher.

Both these documents make it plainly understood that catechesis aims to elicit assent to church teachings. For instance, while warning against overburdening the consciences of adolescents by exerting physical or moral pressure to obtain religious behavior, CT insists that Catholic education must nevertheless make adolescents understand that the call, embodied in "the commandments of God and the precepts of the church," is binding upon conscience (CT, 69). The document asserts freedom, but stops short of allowing for dissent from church teaching as a possible, even if undesirable, outcome of authentic catechesis.

The GCD states categorically that "the conscience itself of Christians must be taught that there are norms which are absolute, that is, which bind in every case and on all people" (GCD, 63). In another passage the GCD drifts dangerously close to an explicit endorsement of domestication. While encouraging adult questioning, it rules out any possibility of dissent. Adherence to "the faith" is the only possible outcome envisaged.

> Thus they should be asked how they understand the Christian message and how they explain it in their own words. Then a comparison should be made between the results of that questioning and what is taught by the Magisterium of the church, and only those things which are in agreement with the faith should be approved (GCD, 75).

SLF represents an improvement upon the GCD and CT, insofar as it explicitly acknowledges the possibility of dissent from noninfallible teachings of the church. On the one hand, SLF agrees with the other documents that "it is the task of catechesis to elicit assent to all that the church teaches, for the church is the indispensable guide to the complete richness of what Jesus teaches" (SLF, 190). On the other hand, in the following sentence SLF acknowledges the possibility of dissent and refers to the U.S. Bishops' statement Human Life in Our Day for principles that would make this dissent viable.[17] Nevertheless, this solitary sentence in SLF is little more than a suggestion of the possibility of deviation from church teaching, and we are quickly reminded that in such cases "presumption is always in favor of the magisterium" (SLF, 190).[18]

In the conclusion to Part Two, it was pointed out that the cultural approach will simply perpetuate the status quo unless it makes room for effective marginal dissent. Critical prophetic groups keep the community honest by challenging its previously unargued assumptions. The perennial temptation for the pilgrim people is to pitch their tents and to sink into a tepid, fatalistic mind-set. They are passive, docile, and contented, willing to accept unquestioningly pronouncements of the ruling social definers. Catechesis, according to the cultural model, remains an instrument for such domestication unless there is some built-in provision for creative dissent.

SOME SAFEGUARDS AGAINST DOMESTICATION

Despite their avoidance of the issue, the documents do have certain features that serve as safeguards against the possibility of individual inertia or communal stagnation. These characteristics are not sufficient in themselves to address the problem. However, their presence in the documents indicates a respect for a person's own appropriation of the message and an implicit, even if unwitting, recognition that some built-in corrections are needed to avoid domestication.

1. Freedom is attained through growth to maturity. *SLF* develops the theme more explicitly than the other documents. As persons grow through the life cycle, they increase in maturity and freedom. In early childhood,

> self-acceptance, trust, and personal freedom undergo significant changes... the expression of personal freedom being modified by recognition that other people, too, have rights and freedom (*SLF*, 178).

In preadolescence, *SLF* continued,

> puberty also adds a new dimension to the practice of personal freedom: increased responsibility for directing one's actions, together with increased readiness to accept their consequences (*SLF*, 179).

Adolescence also brings a new growth in freedom:

A new sense of responsibility matching their expanded capacity for independent action often leads adolescents to reject, or seem to reject, laws and rules which they regard as arbitrary, external restrictions on their personal freedom. Many substitute a kind of inner law or norm of behavior based on personal ideals (SLF, 180).

There is a general acceptance in the documents that adolescence and early adulthood is a crucial turning point. The challenge to reflect upon communal meanings and make them one's own is uppermost. *SLF* suggests that at this time,

catechesis seeks to encourage faith-inspired decisions and close identification with the adult faith community, including its liturgical life and mission (SLF, 183).

"Identification" does not mean slavish imitation or unthinking adherence to cultural symbols. Earlier it was shown that the documents employ a psycho-social model of growth, an interactionist model. Persons are not rubber stamp copies of significant others. Children and adolescents are not understood by the documents as clay to be molded by their elders. In a text already quoted earlier, Pope John Paul stresses the mutuality of catechesis:

Adults have much to give young people and children in the field of catechesis, but they can also receive much from them for the growth of their own Christian lives. It must be restated that nobody in the church of Jesus Christ should feel excused from receiving catechesis (CT, 45).

Children and adolescents do not passively imbibe meanings from the adult world. They are themselves a stimulus for adults to change.

2. The stress upon adult catechesis is the best safeguard against communal captivity to a dead tradition. This point was made above and deserves reiterating. *SLF* states:

> As people mature, their increased knowledge and proper love of self make it possible for them to enter more deeply into self-giving relationships with others. Their courage, honesty, and concern increase. Their practical experience grows. They come to enjoy higher levels of personal freedom. (*SLF*, 186).

If adults are helped to grow to maturity and to exercise their own freedom in relation to the symbols of the faith they will deepen in conversion to the gospel. As leaders of the community, they will seek to change many of the structures that perpetuate injustice. The communal forms will be reevaluated in the light of their rereading of the scriptures in the context of the contemporary situation.

3. Catechesis is not intended by the documents to put boundaries around individual or communal horizons. It is a call to conversion, the expansion of intellectual, moral, and religious horizons. Catechesis calls the church, and especially the adult community, to continually modify its world view, and to reevaluate its system of beliefs and values. The documents measure the success of catechesis in terms of whether it produces mature adults who have made a conscious decision to commit themselves to the foundational symbols of the Christian community.

AN UNRESOLVED QUESTION

These features of catechesis, presented by the documents, show that the intention is not to indoctrinate or domesticate.

However, for the critical mind, there remains a lingering suspicion that this approach has a hidden agenda. The expected outcome is persons fully incorporated into a given community, committed to its unifying symbols. Is this a subtle tactic, assuring "allegiance to the party," while creating the fiction that one is free? It is true that the documents do not see the community as a stable, unchanging entity with a doctrinaire ideology, solidified rituals, and fixed practices. They insist that the community must grow. But protestations alone do not ensure freedom. The question remains. Given the human propensity for settling down comfortably where we are, what is the principle that ensures ongoing conversion? Is there a transforming impulse within the faith-community that generates new insights and opens new worlds? These questions were put earlier to the cultural approach at the end of chapter 5; they now can be put to the church documents.

From a theological point of view, one could answer that the Holy Spirit is the transforming power at work within the church ensuring its ongoing renewal. However, there is a need for catechetical theorists to go behind that language, since it could simply be functioning as a sacral legitimation of the status quo. The use of social sciences helps theorists to study how a foundational symbol, such as the Holy Spirit, in the Christian community has transforming power, releasing new meanings and subverting fixed patterns of thought and action. In the search for *the* fundamental symbol in Christian tradition which has inexhaustible meaning for every age, the critical theorist is led to Jesus Christ, who is the promise, anticipation and realization of the kingdom of God. The symbol of the kingdom coming in Jesus Christ, a kingdom of justice and peace, expresses what the Christian community is about. Moreso, it stimulates the religious imagination, subverting taken-for-granted worlds and opening up the possibility of new modes of being together as a people.

However, all symbols, no matter how potentially subversive, can be evacuated of meaning through disuse and neglect. It is incumbent on the faith community to continually recapture its tradition, to discover again the root symbols by which it was born. This is a process of interpretation, since in every age the horizon by which the scriptures are approached will be different. On the other hand, the scriptures themselves will interpret the present beliefs, values, and practices of the community. In this hermeneutical dialectic the Christian community hones out a new idiom—the language, stories, rituals, structures, and life-styles which it maintains and transmits to the new generation.[19]

CONCLUSION

The four documents analyzed in chapter 6 represent an official endorsement of the modern catechetical renewal described in Part One of this study. They are an attempt to channel the energies of this movement for the benefit of the whole church. For the most part, pastoral principles are cast in theological-liturgical categories. Post-Vatican II pastoral theology emphasizes the role of the local *ecclesia* in the ministry of the word. Catechesis is therefore a central task of the local church and aims to facilitate ongoing conversion within the community. Catechesis as a process of initiation and nurture includes step-by-step liturgical celebrations throughout the life cycle of the individual. It passes on the tradition, handing on and interpreting the symbols of the faith.

In chapter 2 of this study it was pointed out that the trend in catechetical theory has been changing in the last decade. There has been a decided turn to the human sciences. The official documents have to a certain extent reflected this new interest in secular disciplines. They have incorporated insights from psychology and sociology when describing faith development. As was shown above, they have a penchant towards a psycho-social model of human growth. Nevertheless, the overall perspective of these statements is theological-liturgical. Having acknowledged the importance of the secular sciences in clarifying fundamental issues in catechetics, the documents have left it to theorists to pinpoint these issues and to indicate the contribution that the human sciences can make. The problem of freedom is one such issue.

For Catholics, it is especially pertinent that the official church documents place catechesis fairly and squarely within the local community. While the documents stress the culture-bearing function of community, they include ample references to the psychological and political functions. Thus, they point catechetical theorists in the direction of ensuring that all three dimensions of education for freedom are operative in catechesis. Since catechesis is seen by the documents primarily in terms of the cultural approach, catechetical theorists need to be in dialogue with religious educational theorists who espouse the political approach. This dialogue can ensure that communal catechesis involves transformation as well as transmission.

It was shown above that the documents contain an inherent danger, characteristic of an educational enterprise that shapes selves through cultural transmission. They could be accused of promoting domestication or indoctrination. To overcome this danger, theorists need the human sciences. This is not to say that theological and liturgical perspectives should be discarded. They are not sufficient alone. To preserve and promote freedom the catechetical enterprise needs to hone out a new idiom by which it can confidently articulate and communicate the faith in the concrete life of the believing community. It needs theological hermeneutics for the ongoing interpretation of the symbols of the faith. But it also needs the benefit of cultural anthropology and the sociology of religion to establish the dynamics of symbolic transformation in a religious tradition, and to understand the interplay between a religious body and its contemporary cultural setting.

There is a vital question for catechetical theorists that must be answered adequately if freedom is to be concretely attained. Can cultural reality transmitted by the faith community be continually broken open to prevent stagnation and yet maintain continuity with the past? Or, in other words, how does a nurturing community maintain a built-in critical principle? A tentative answer to this question is suggested above. The question will only be fully answered as theorists are prepared to bracket theological-liturgical language and to examine phenomenologically the process of faith communication. They will draw upon humanistic psychology, sociology, and cultural anthropology to aid this enquiry.

However, this phenomenological investigation, important as it is, will be ultimately barren and unproductive unless it turns back again and links up with a theological hermeneutics similar to that employed by "liberation theology." The great liberation themes of the Christian tradition—the Exodus and the Passover—need to be explored again from the horizon of contemporary world problems. Liberation theology has the potential of providing a nexus between the imperative to transmit the Christian tradition and the imperative to act to transform sinful social structures in the world. The community of faith in the act of regenerating itself by catechesis needs to reinterpret the symbols of Christian freedom in a less privatistic and individualistic way.

It is fitting that this study should conclude with an appeal to the methodology of liberation theology. It began with a survey of religious educational and catechetical theory this century. It described the historical tension between the "liberal" and "neo-orthodox" movements. This tension was between the will to transform the status quo and the will to transmit the tradition. While the "liberal" approach stressed social transformation, the "neo-orthodox" approach stressed the handing on of distinctively Christian symbols. Their rapprochement is crucial to the issue of freedom. Liberation theology has the advantage of providing such a rapprochement. It seeks to restore the transformative power of the traditional symbols in the Christian community. The story of Exodus and Passover are retold in a social and political perspective. In this way, catechesis which is rooted in the tradition can become a living word for our time.

NOTES FOR CHAPTER 6

1. The GCD can be found, together with commentary, in Berard Marthaler, *Catechetics in Context: Notes and Commentary on the General Catechetical Directory Issued by the Sacred Concregation for the Clergy* (Huntington, Ind.: Our Sunday Visitor, Inc., 1973); SLF has been published as *Sharing the Light of Faith: National Catechetical Directory for Catholics of the United States* (Washington, D.C.: U.S.C.C., Department of Education, 1979); the MPG is available in *The Living Light* 15 (Spring 1978): 86–97; an English translation of *Catechesi Trandendae*, which has no official English title, can be found in *Origins* 9/21 (November 8, 1979): 329–49, also published as *Catechesi Trandendae* (Washington, D.C.: U.S.C.C. Publications, 1980).

2. The "genesis and genius" of the GCD has been traced by Marthaler; see *Catechetics in Context*, pp. xvi-xxx.

3. The catechetical directory represents a new genre which is to be distinguished from the "catechism" genre. See Marthaler, *Catechetics in Context*, p. 229.

4. At this writing, the official commentary on SLF is still in press. The *Living Light* has offered a special issue with commentaries on theological, liturgical, moral, and catechetical aspects of the directory. See *The Living Light* 16 (Summer 1979); see also Anne Marie Mongoven, *Signs of Catechesis: An Overview of the National Catechetical Directory* (New York: Paulist Press, 1979). See also Mary Charles Bryce, "Sharing the Light of Faith: Catechetical Threshold for the U.S. Church," *Lumen Vitae* 34 (1979): 393–407.

5. Marianne Sawicki has provided an analysis of the purpose, papers, and the

proceedings of the synod in an issue of the *Living Light* entirely devoted to synodal reports and commentaries. See Marianne Sawicki, "The Process of Consensus: Purpose, Papers, and Proceedings of the Synod," *The Living Light* 15 (Spring 1978): 7–31.

6. The English translation was published as *On Evangelization in the Modern World* (Washington, D.C.: U.S.C.C. Publications, 1975); it can be found also in *The Pope Speaks* 21 (Spring 1976): 4–51; *AAS* 68:5–76.

7. A synopsis of the "thirty-four points" appeared in the 17 November 1977 English language edition of *L'Osservatore Romano*. This summary has been published in *The Living Light* 15 (Spring 1978): 74–80.

8. A comparative analysis between *Catechesi Trandendae* and the "thirty-four points" reveals that the Holy Father was faithful to the spirit of the synod. All of the points appear in some way in the papal document.

9. Another example of this interrelationship is the influence exerted by *SLF* upon the synod. The process of developing *SLF* was almost completed when the U.S. delegation went to the synod. Their numerous interventions significantly shaped the course of synodal deliberations. These interventions were of a high quality because they were prepared within the context of concentrated attention in the U.S. upon production of *SLF*. See Wilfrid A. Paradis, "Excerpts from a Personal Journal," *The Living Light* 15 (Spring 1978): 107–27. For the texts of the interventions of the U.S. delegates, see *Synod of Bishops—1977: Fourth General Assembly Rome (September 30–October 29, 1977): Message to the People of God and Interventions of the U.S. Delegates* (Washington, D.C.: U.S.C.C. Publications Office, 1978).

10. Pope Paul VI endorsed *communautés de base* which he observed "spring from the need to live the church's life more intensely, or from the desire and quest for a more human dimension such as larger ecclesial communities can only offer with difficulty . . . ." *Evangelii Nuntiandi,* par. 58. Basic Christian communities have sprung up especially in the Third World. In Latin America they are seen as the church itself in process of renewing and fulfilling its mission. The Medellin Conference of Latin American Bishops (1968) called the Christian base community "the first and fundamental ecclesiastical nucleus, which on its own level must make itself responsible for the richness and expansion of the faith, as well as of the cult which it is an expression." See *Second General Conference of Latin American Bishops: The Church in the Present-Day Transformation of Latin America in the Light of the Council. II. Conclusions* (3d ed.) (Washington, D.C.: National Conference of Catholic Bishops, Secretariat for Latin America, 1979), p. 185. The Pueblo Conference (1979) reinforced the concept of *communidades eclesiales de base* (CEBs), pointing out that

"As a community, the CEB brings together families, adults, and young people, in an intimate interpersonal relationship grounded in faith. As an ecclesial reality, it is a community of faith, hope, and charity. It celebrates the Word of God and takes its nourishment from the Eucharist, the culmination of all the sacraments. It fleshes out the Word of God in life through solidarity and commitment to the new commandment of the Lord; and through the service of approved coordinators, it makes present and operative the mission of the church and its visible communion with the legitimate pastors."

See *Third General Conference of Latin American Bishops: Evangelization at Present and in the Future of Latin America: Conclusions* (Washington, D.C.: National Conference of Catholic Bishops, Secretariat, Committee for the Church in Latin America, 1979), p. 126. The CEBs are envisaged by the Puebla conference as centers for evangelization, instruments for the ongoing renewal of ecclesial structures, motive forces for liberation from oppressive cultural heritage, places where the poor can discover their dignity and work to transform their situation, and communities of service and missionary witness. See Jacques Van Nieuwenhove, "Puebla and the Grass-Roots Communities," *Lumen Vitae* 34 (1979): 311–30. In Africa, basic communities are also considered indispensable to the renewal of the church. See Michael Singleton, "A Changing Church in a Changing Continent," in *Concilium*, vol. 106: *The Churches of Africa: Future Prospects*, ed. Claude Geffré and Bertran Luneau (New York: The Seabury Press, 1977), pp. 15–25; and Marie France Perin-Jassy, *Basic Community in the African Churches*, trans. Jeanne Marie Lyons (Maryknoll, N.Y.: Orbis Books, 1973).

11. Berard Marthaler, who has been influenced by the ecclesial view of the documents, uses this terminology in an article designed to broaden the concept of catechesis from exclusive attachment to schools. He observes:

"It was common for authors to distinguish the *ecclesia discens* and the *ecclesia docens* so sharply that the church seemed to be comprised of two discrete classes, teachers and learners. The result was a distorted ecclesiology that has caused endless problems for religious education. . ." (Marthaler, "Total Religious Education: A Blueprint for a Learning Society," *The Living Light* 11 (1974: 277).

12. *Rite of Christian Initiation of Adults: Provisional Text* (Study Book ed.) (Washington, D.C.: U.S.C.C., 1974). There have been numerous commentaries upon the significance of this document, and upon Christian initiation in general. For an introduction to this literature, see *Made Not Born: New Perspectives in Christian Initiation and the Catechumenate* (Notre Dame, Ind.: University of Notre Dame, 1976); *Becoming a Catholic Christian: A Symposium on Christian Initiation* (New York: Sadlier, 1979); Aidan Kavanagh, *The Shape of Baptism: The Rite of Christian Initiation* (New York: Pueblo Publishing Company, 1978); idem, "The Norm of Baptism: The New Rite of Christian Initiation for Adults," *Worship* 48 (March 1974): 143–52; idem, "Initiation: Baptism and

Confirmation," *Worship* 46 (May 1972): 262–76; idem, "Christian Initiation for Those Baptized as Infants," *The Living Light* 13 (Fall 1976): 387–98; Nathan Mitchell, "Christian Initiation: Decline and Dismemberment," *Worship* 48 (October 1974): 458–79; Ralph A. Keifer, "Christian Initiation: The State of the Question," *Worship* 48 (September 1974): 392–404; Charles W. Gusmer, "The Revised Adult Initiation and Its Challenge to Religious Education," *The Living Light* 13 (Spring 1976): 92–98; Thomas P. Ivory, "The Restoration of the Catechumenate as a Norm for Catechesis," *The Living Light* 13 (Summer 1976): 225–35; and Raymond Kemp, *Journey of Faith* (New York: Sadlier, 1979).

13. "Memory," or *anamnesis*, is to be distinguished from rote memorization. At the synod there was a renewed interest in "memorization." Archbishop Ryan of Dublin intervened on the subject, pointing out that "memorization" has a role in the growth of faith ("Summaries of Selected Interventions," *The Living Light* 15 (Spring 1978): 45–47). *SLF* took up this plea:

> "While catechesis cannot be limited to the repetition of formulas and it is essential that formulas and facts pertaining to faith be understood, memorization has nevertheless had a special place in the handing-on of the faith throughout the ages and should continue to have such a place today, especially in catechetical programs for the young. It should be adapted to the level and ability of the child and introduced in a gradual manner, through a process which, begun early, continues gradually, flexibly, and never slavishly" (*SLF*, 176e).

Pope John Paul, addressing the "unfortunate consequences of disregarding the human faculty of memory," calls for an "attempt to put this faculty back into use in an intelligent and even an original way in catechesis" (*CT*, 55). There is an agreement that "memorization" should never become a slavish, unthinking form of rote learning. The old technique used to memorize questions and answers in catechisms is considered destructive. "Memorization" is given value in the broader context of the *anamnesis* of the community. *Anamnesis* ensures that catechesis does not degenerate to the dull mechanical repetition of past formulas. *Anamnesis* is not a privatistic effort, but a communal remembrance of common shared meaning. See Una O'Neill, "Memorization in Catechesis," *The Living Light* 16 (Summer 1979): 209–16.

14. The documents do not endorse any one type of human science. However, the "interactionist" model suggests compatibility with a broad spectrum of human sciences, including developmental psychology and sociology. The structural developmentalists see knowing as a process of interaction between the structure of the organism and the structures of the environment. Jean Piaget deals with the development of cognitive structures—growth is toward a greater reciprocity between the action of the organism on the perceived object, and of the action of the perceived object on the organism. See Hans G. Furth, *Piaget*

for Teachers (Englewood Cliffs, N.J.: Prentice-Hall, Inc., 1970). While Piaget deals mainly with the physical environment, Robert Selman and Lawrence Kohlberg deal with interaction between the person and the social environment. Selman offers a stage theory of social perspective-taking, or role-taking. The capacity to take the view of another person or group develops through interaction with the given role models within society. See Robert L. Selman, "Social-Cognitive Understanding": A Guide to Educational and Clinical Practice," in *Moral Development and Behavior: Theory, Research and Social Issues,* ed. Thomas Lickona (New York: Holt, Rinehart and Winston, 1976), pp. 299–316. Kohlberg emphasizes that development in the capacity for moral reasoning depends on role-taking opportunities in the environment. He also points out that the general atmosphere of the institution itself, the "justice structure," can impede growth in a person's ability to make moral judgments. Exposure to the moral reasoning of significant others, which differs from one's own, is an occasion to jog one's inner moral reasoning. Furthermore, exposure to dilemma situations within group discussions causes critical disequilibrium in one's own moral reasoning and is an occasion for restructuring of one's perspective. See Lawrence Kohlberg, "Stage and Sequence: The Cognitive-Developmental Approach to Socialization," in *Handbook of Socialization Theory and Research,* ed. David A. Goslin (Chicago: Rand McNally and Company, 1969), pp. 347–480, and idem, "Moral Stages and Moralization: The Cognitive-Developmental Approach," in ibid., pp. 49–53. From the sociology of knowledge the theory of Peter Berger and Thomas Luckmann offers a similar "interactionist" model. Socialization is seen as a dialectic, including world constructions as well as internalization of objectified meanings. See Peter L. Berger and Thomas Luckmann, *The Social Construction of Reality* (New York: Doubleday and Company, Inc., 1966). For further reading in the socialization process, see *Childhood and Socialization,* ed., Hans Peter Dreitzel (New York: Macmillan Publishing Co., Inc., 1973); *Socialization and Society,* ed. John A. Clausen (Boston: Little, Brown and Company, 1968); Orville G. Brim, Jr., and Stanton Wheeler, *Socialization after Childhood: Two Essays* (New York: John Wiley and Sons, Inc., 1966). From a different perspective, Erik Erikson has developed a psycho-social model of lifelong growth. The inner capacities of the individual and the outer exigencies of the society conspire to bring about a series of psycho-social crises which are opportunities for personal growth. See Erik Erikson, *Childhood and Society,* 2d ed. (New York: W. W. Norton and Company, Inc., 1963), pp. 247–74, and idem, *Insight and Responsibility* (New York: W. W. Norton and Company, Inc., 1964), pp. 111–57. From an educational standpoint, Robert J. Havinghurst has shown that society provides a lifelong series of developmental tasks which come both as a challenge and as an enabling force, allowing persons to develop their capacities in distinct steps. See Robert J. Havinghurst, *Developmental Tasks and Education,* 2d ed. (New York:

David McKay, 1952), and idem, *Human Development and Education* (New York: Longmans, Green and Co., Inc., 1953).

15. *Justice in the World* (Washington, D.C.: U.S.C.C. Publications, 1971); the text can also be found in *Catholic Mind* 70 (March 1972): 52–64.

16. This chapter in the papal document refers to the Vatican II *Declaration on Religious Liberty*, which states that "all men should be immune from coercion on the part of individuals, social groups, and every human power so that, within due limits, nobody is forced to act against his convictions in religious matters. . . ." *Dignitatis Humanae*, 2. CT does not apply this principle to freedom within the church, but to the freedom of the church to exercise its catechetical ministry.

17. See *Human Life in Our Day: A Collective Pastoral of the American Hierarchy* (Washington, D.C.: U.S.C.C., 1968), p. 18.

18. However, following Vatican II's *Gaudium et Spes,*, SLF does make a strong affirmation of conscience as the "most secret core and sanctuary" of the person, where one "is alone with God" (*Gaudium et Spes*, 16). SLF goes on to point out that "decisions of conscience must be based upon prayer, study, consultation, and an understanding of the teachings of the church. One must have a rightly formed conscience and follow it" (*SLF*, 103).

19. A suggestion for catechetics to move in this direction has been made by Berard Marthaler, "Handing on Symbols of Faith," *Chicago Studies* (forthcoming).

Index of Names

Index of Subjects

WESTMAR COLLEGE LIBRARY